HISTORY OF NEPAL

HISTORY OF NEPAL

TRANSLATED FROM THE PARBATIYA

BY
MUNSHI SHEW SHUNKER SINGH
AND
PANDIT SHRI GUNANAND:

WITH AN INTRODUCTORY SKETCH
OF THE

COUNTRY AND PEOPLE OF NEPAL

BY THE EDITOR

DANIEL WRIGHT, M.A., M.D.,
LATE SURGEON-MAJOR H. M.'S INDIAN MEDICAL
SERVICE, AND RESIDENCY SURGEON AT KATHMANDU

GYAN

Published by

GYAN

Gyan Publishing House
5, Ansari Road
Daryaganj, New Delhi-110002
Phone: 011-47034999, 9811692060
E-mail: books@gyanbooks.com

Distribution Network
gyanbooks.com
India, USA, Canada, UK, Australia, France

ISBN : 978-81-212-3531-0 (PB)
First Published, 1877

2nd Impression 2020

Printed at: Gyan Press, Delhi.

History of Nepal
Author: Daniel Wright

HISTORY OF NEPĀL,

TRANSLATED FROM THE PARBATIYĀ

BY

MUNSHĪ SHEW SHUNKER SINGH

AND

PANDIT SHRĪ GUNĀNAND:

WITH AN INTRODUCTORY SKETCH

OF THE

COUNTRY AND PEOPLE OF NEPĀL

BY THE EDITOR,

DANIEL WRIGHT, M.A., M.D.,

LATE SURGEON-MAJOR H. M.'S INDIAN MEDICAL SERVICE, AND RESIDENCY SURGEON AT KĀṬHMĀNḌŪ.

Cambridge:
AT THE UNIVERSITY PRESS.

LONDON: CAMBRIDGE WAREHOUSE, 17, PATERNOSTER ROW.
CAMBRIDGE: DEIGHTON, BELL, AND CO.
1877

PREFACE.

THE few following remarks are all that seem necessary, by way of preface, regarding the contents of this small volume.

For the Introductory Sketch I alone am responsible. It is based upon personal observation and inquiry, during a residence of ten years in the country, and I have inserted nothing in it but what, to the best of my belief, is correct as far as it goes. It does not, of course, pretend to be a full account of the country; for such a work is hardly possible while our relations with Nepāl remain as they are at present, and would, moreover, be out of place in a book of this sort.

The translation of the History has been made by Shew Shunker Singh, the Mīr Munshī attached to the British Residency, who has lived in Nepāl for nearly thirty years. He was assisted, when necessary, by Pandit Shrī Gunānand, who is a native of Nepāl, residing at Pātan, and whose ancestors, for many generations, have been the compilers of this History.

I am not myself an Oriental scholar, and have had nothing to do with the translation beyond revising it for publication, and adding a few notes regarding the customs and places mentioned. The work translated is the *Vansāvalī* or Genealogical History of Nepāl, according to the Buddhist recension. The original manuscript, written in Parbatiyā with an admixture of Sanskrit and Newārī, is in the possession of Professor Cowell. There is another redaction, or at all events a similar work, recognised by the Gōrkhas and Hindū races of the country, copies of which are in the British Museum and the University Library of Cambridge.

At the present time the orthography of Oriental proper names is somewhat unsettled. In general, throughout the History, the names have been written as nearly as possible in their original form, the vowels having the Italian sounds. The different sounds of the letters *d*, *t*, *s* and *sh*, in Sanskrit, have not been systematically indicated by points or otherwise. The Munshī often uses *kh* for *sh*, *j* for *y*, and *b* for *v*. In the names of some well-known places, and in such familiar words as *Durbār*, *Jung*, etc., the usual spelling has been retained, more especially in the Introduction. Some names may be found spelled differently in different places, but this is usually not owing to any mistake, but because the words have intentionally been given as written in the original manuscript.

The Illustrations are copies of drawings made for me by a native of Nepāl. Though not of much value as works of art, they convey a very fair idea of the places and objects represented. The Portraits are from photographs taken by a friend.

The Appendix contains, among other things, a short vocabulary, Parbatiyā and Newārī; some Newārī songs, with a literal translation; and a list of the manuscripts which I have procured for the University Library of Cambridge. These, though of slight interest to the general reader, may, I am told, prove interesting to Oriental scholars.

In conclusion, I must acknowledge my obligations to Professor Cowell of Cambridge, and Professor Eggeling of Edinburgh, both of whom have given me much assistance in the correct writing of Sanskrit words. My brother, Professor W. Wright of Cambridge, has greatly helped me in revising the proof-sheets and superintending the publishing of the work, the cost of which has been most liberally undertaken by the Syndics of the University Press at Cambridge.

DANIEL WRIGHT.

CAMBRIDGE,

12th *January*, 1877.

TABLE OF CONTENTS.

SKETCH OF THE PORTION OF THE COUNTRY OF NEPĀL, WHICH IS OPEN TO EUROPEANS.

CHAPTER I.

CHAPTER II.

CHAPTER III.

CHAPTER IV.

CHAPTER V.

HISTORY OF NEPĀL.

CHAPTER I.

CHAPTER II.

CHAPTER III.

CHAPTER IV.

CHAPTER V.

CHAPTER VI.

CHAPTER VII.

CHAPTER VIII.

CHAPTER IX.

CHAPTER X.

CHAPTER XI.

CHAPTER XII.

APPENDIX.

DESCRIPTION OF THE PLATES.

PLATE I. Frontispiece.

Sir Jung Bahādur Ranā, G. C. B., G. C. S. I., etc., etc.

He is dressed in a Chinese robe of silk, lined and trimmed with fur, and wears the insignia of the Bath and other decorations. His jewelled headdress is said to be worth £15,000. His right hand rests on his sword, to which is attached a long handkerchief.

PLATE II., p. 10.

The Square in front of the Palace at Kāṭhmāṇḍū.

In it may be seen various temples and monoliths. The Hanumān gate and the stone with Rājā Pratāpa Malla's prayer are on the left-hand side. The figure of Hanumān has an umbrella over it.

PLATE III., p. 17.

The Temple built by Bhūpatīndra Malla, at Bhātgāoṇ, A.D. 1703.

PLATE IV., p. 23.

View of the Chaitya and other buildings on the summit of the Swayambhū hill.

At the top of the staircase stands the large brazen bajra, mentioned in the Introduction (p. 24). The buildings to the extreme right and left give a good idea of the houses occupied by the lower and middle classes in the towns. In front are groups of worshippers, Newārīs and Bhōtiyās; one of the latter is twirling in his hand a small prayer-cylinder.

PLATE V., p. 28.

A RĀNĪ OR NEPALESE LADY OF RANK.

PLATE VI., p. 43.

THE FIVE BUDDHAS; THE FIVE TĀRĀS, THEIR WIVES; AND THE FIVE BŌDHISATWAS, THEIR SONS.

These images are worshipped by the Nepalese Buddhists.

PLATE VII., p. 78.

THE FOOTSTEPS OF MANJUSRĪ AND OF BUDDHA.

These are carved on stone, and let into the pavement in front of a temple or holy place.

PLATE VIII., p. 80.

VIEW OF THE HILL ON WHICH THE SWAYAMBHŪ CHAITYA STANDS.

The mountain to the right is Nāgārjun. Houses of Newārī agriculturists, shrines, and pātīs, are in the foreground. In the centre of the picture, on the road leading through the wood to the temple, is seen the colossal figure of Sākya Muni (p. 23).

PLATE IX., p. 100.

VIEW OF THE TEMPLE OF BŌDHNĀTH.

In the niches in the outer wall may be seen the prayer-cylinders, which are twirled by worshippers.

PLATE X., p. 116.

MATIRĀJYA CHAITYA, THE ASŌKA CHAITYA ON THE PARADE-GROUND OF PĀTAN.

PLATE XI., p. 174.

SPECIMENS OF SEVERAL FORMS OF CHAITYAS.

The central one is an old, pure Buddhist, mound-temple. That to the left is a more modern Buddhist form. The one to the right is a mixed Hindū and Buddhist shrine, combining the linga and jalharī with Buddhist figures.

PLATE XII., p. 193.

GATEWAY AND WINDOW OF THE DURBĀR BUILT AT BHATGĀOṆ, A.D. 1697, BY RĀJĀ BHŪPATĪNDRA MALLA.

The oval in the centre of the carved window, immediately above the door, contains the piece of glass mentioned in the text.

PLATE XIII., p. 213.

THE PRAYER COMPOSED, AND WRITTEN IN FIFTEEN CHARACTERS, BY RĀJĀ PRATĀPA MALLA, A.D. 1654.

It is inscribed on a stone, built into the wall of the Palace at Kāṭhmāṇḍū, near the Hanumān gate (Plate II.).

PLATE XIV., p. 267.

DHĀRĀ OR FOUNTAIN, BUILT BY GENERAL BHĪMASĒNA IN THE REIGN OF RĀJĀ GĪRBĀN-JUDDHA VIKRAM SĀH.

In the background is a pātī or dharmasālā.

PLATE XV., p. 284.

THE PRESENT KING OF NEPĀL, SRĪ SURĒNDRA VIKRAM SĀH.

PLATE XVI., p. 288.

GENERAL JAGAT JUNG BAHĀDUR, THE ELDEST SON OF SIR JUNG BAHĀDUR, IN MILITARY UNDRESS.

Behind him stands an officer of the Nepalese army, in the ordinary summer-dress of a Gōrkhālī gentleman. He carries a kukhrī in his kamarband or waistband.

CORRECTIONS.

Page 13, line 2. Read "Dharēra."
,, ,, line 21. Here and elsewhere read "Thāpāthalī."
,, 16, line 21. Here, and in a few other places, read "Buddhist."
,, ,, last line but one. "Bhaktapur" is the correct form of the name.
,, 19, line 13. Read "Bogmati."
,, 22, line 12. The more correct form of the name is "Gōkarna."
,, 23, last line. Read "Buddha."
,, 35, no. 3. Read "*Siti.*"
,, 36, line 15. Read "Bauddha-mārgi."
,, 53, last two lines. Read "Rājēndra Bikram."
,, 55, line 14. Read "Māthabar."
,, 77, line 12. The MS. has "Vipashwī," which the Munshī writes "Bipaśwī;" but the correct form is, I believe, "Vipashyi."
,, 78, line 21. Read here, and in some other places, "Manjusrī."
,, 89, line 27. Read "Ling and."
,, 92, line 26. Here, and on pages 97—99, and page 114, note, for "Buddha Nīlkantha" read "Buḍhā-Nīlkantha" or Buṛhā-Nīlkantha."
,, 115, line 18. Read "in possession."
,, 176, line 11. More correctly "Kasāhīs."

SKETCH

OF THE

PORTION OF THE COUNTRY OF NEPĀL,

WHICH IS

OPEN TO EUROPEANS.

CHAPTER I.

Preliminary remarks. Description of the road leading to the Valley of Nepāl. The Valley itself. Hills around it. Rivers. Extent. Kāṭhmāṇḍū. Its buildings, temples, and palaces. Parade-ground. Thāpatali, the residence of Sir Jung Bahādur. British Residency. Willow avenue. Description of Pātan. Description of Bhātgāon, Kīrtīpūr, and other towns. Pashupati and its temples. Gaukarna. Bodhnātha. Bālājī. Swayambhūnātha. Pātīs and Dhārās.

As any one may ascertain by consulting a map of India, the kingdom of Nepāl is a small independent State, situated on the north-eastern frontier of Hindustān. It is a strip of country about five hundred miles long and a hundred and thirty broad, lying between the snowy range of the Himālaya on the north, Sikkhim on the east, and the provinces of British India on the south and west.

The name Nepāl, however, is restricted by the natives of the country to the valley surrounding the capital, and it is of this portion of the country alone that the following history and the present sketch treat. This is the only part of the kingdom which is open to the investigations of Europeans; and it would be a hopeless task to attempt the description of places which cannot be visited, or the collection of accurate information regarding a country where every inquiry made by a European is viewed with the most jealous suspicion, where the collection of statistics is looked on as mere folly, and where, above all, Baron Münchausen himself would have been considered a marvel of accuracy and truthfulness!

After leaving the frontier-station of Segowli, there is little to attract the notice of the traveller till he reaches the sāl forest. The first portion of the road, as far as Ruksowl, is, like most of the roads in Tirhūt and Chumpārun, a very fair driving road, with bridges over the rivers and nullahs. Beyond this there is a mere rough cart-track, as far as Simrabāsa, which is a small village close to the margin of the forest. From this village a narrow sandy road passes almost straight through the forest to Bichiakōri or Bīchakōh, which consists of a few huts and a large powah or traveller's house of rest, and is situated on the bank of a shallow stream.

The road now lies along the bed of this stream, and is very rough, but still passable by bullock-carts during the dry season. After a mile or two, the road runs through the Chiriaghatti range of hills, passing beneath sandy cliffs several hundred feet in height and crowned with firtrees and other timber. After about six miles, the road quits the bed of the river, and again enters a forest of sāl trees, growing on low undulating hills. Here much of the timber used in Kāṭhmāṇḍū is cut during the cold season. The road then crosses a small stream, the Kurrū, by a wooden bridge; and about a mile beyond this it reaches the village of Hetowra.

Here there is a large powah, and, in the cold season, a considerable village; but the place is almost deserted from April to November on account of the *āoul*, or malarious fever, which is deadly to all except the natives of the Terai. During the cold weather almost all the imports for the supply of Nepāl pass through Hetowra, and, in consequence, a Nepalese officer and guard of soldiers are stationed there, who however retire to the hills as soon as the hot weather sets in.

The road now winds along the banks of the Rāpti, and the scenery for some eight or ten miles is as grand as can be found in almost any part of the lower Himālaya. An excellent road has been cut from Hetowra to Bhimphēdi, and bridges have been thrown across the river in several places. This work was executed by the soldiers of the Nepalese army between 1865 and 1870. About eight miles from Hetowra are the village and powah of Nimbūatār, and seven miles farther on stands the village of Bhimphēdi. All along this valley there is a considerable amount of cultivation, wherever the land is level enough to admit of it; and near Bhimphēdi there are several small hamlets.

From Bhimphēdi the road passes up a most rugged and precipitous hill, on which stands the small fort of Sisaghuri or Chisapāni, so named from a spring of very cold water a little above the fort. The fort is about sixteen hundred feet above the level of the village of Bhimphēdi, and it takes a traveller nearly an hour and a half to reach it. Sisaghuri is in the hot weather the quarters of the officer and guard that go to Hetowra in the cold weather, and there is a small village below the fort, where custom duties are levied on all goods and travellers entering the country.

The road now runs upwards to a gap, near the top of the ridge on which the fort stands, at a height of about 2,300 feet above Bhimphēdi. The descent on the northern side is not so steep nor so long as the ascent, but is still rugged and difficult. At the foot of the hill runs a clear rapid stream, up which the road proceeds, crossing it in several places by temporary bridges made of stones and brushwood. In the cold season this stream is small, but in the rains it becomes formidable, and in one place it has been found necessary to throw a lofty bridge across it. The hills on both sides of the bed of this stream are steep and bare. At the extremity of the gorge stand a powah and a small village named Mārkhū, after passing which the road lies over a low, bare, undulating range of hills, called the Ekdunta, till the valley of Chitlong or little Nepāl is entered.

This valley is well cultivated, and contains several small villages. It is on a higher level than the large valley of Nepāl, and in consequence its climate is considerably colder. It is subject, too, to violent storms of wind and hail, which frequently do much injury to the crops. After passing through Chitlong, the road runs over the mountain-range of Chandragiri. This range is steep and rugged but well wooded, and the ascent from Chitlong is by no means equal in these respects to the descent into the Nepāl valley. From the summit of the pass a magnificent view is obtained of both valleys[1].

The Valley of Nepāl, in which stands the capital of the country, and in which are the residence of the court and the head-quarters of the army, is an extensive tract of comparatively level ground, entirely surrounded by lofty mountains. Its length from east to west is about twenty miles, and its breadth from north to south about fifteen. The length and breadth vary greatly, as there are numerous spurs running out from the hills and enclosing narrow valleys, but the above is a fair statement of the average length and breadth. The more prominent mountain-peaks are named as follows: to the east, Mahādeo Pokhri; to the north, Munichūr, Seopūri, Kukani and Kowhilia; to the west, Nāgārjun; to the south, Chandragiri, Champa Devi, Phurphing, and Phūlchowk. The last-mentioned is the highest of the surrounding peaks, measuring 9,720 feet above the level of the sea[2]. The other peaks vary from 6,000 to 7,500 feet. The level of the valley itself is 4,500 feet above the sea.

[1] Route from Segowli to Kāṭhmāṇḍū.

Stages.	Miles.	Rivers crossed.
Segowli to Ruksowl	16	Sikrāna, Ruksowl, Tilaway.
Ruksowl to Simrabāsa......	14	Ruksowl and Tilaway.
Simrabāsa to Bīchakōh	10	Small stream.
Bīchakōh to Hetowrah......	12	Kurrū.
Hetowra to Nimbūatār ...	7	Sāmri and Rāpti.
Nimbūatār to Sisaghuri ...	8	Small stream.
Sisaghuri to Mārkhū	7	Mārkhū.
Mārkhū to Thānkōt	8	Small stream.
Thānkōt to Kāṭhmāṇḍū ...	7	Kālimati and Vishnumati.

[2] The height is so given in maps, but with the aneroid I did not find it to be more than 9,300. Possibly, however, my instrument was not correct.

The surface of the valley consists of ground on two levels, constituting a series of table-lands (tārs), and valleys (kholas), through each of which latter a small stream usually flows, though many of these are dried up in the hot season. The difference in level between the tārs and kholas varies greatly. Near the base of the hills it is not great, but it rapidly increases towards the centre of the valley, and in some places the precipitous edges of the tārs are from 30 to 100 feet in height.

The country is well watered, but none of the streams are of great size, as they all rise from the neighbouring hills. Some of them are mere mountain-torrents, and are quite dried-up in the hot weather; but others, which rise from springs at the foot of the hills, always contain a fair amount of water. The principal streams are the Bāgmati and Vishnumati. The former rises from the northern side of the Seopūri peak, and enters the valley through a narrow gorge, about the middle of the northern side. It flows south and south-west to its junction with the Vishnumati. The latter rises from the southern side of Seopūri and Kukani, towards the north-west corner of the valley, and flows south and south-east. Both streams receive numerous small tributaries, so that when they unite, just to the south of Kāṭhmāndū, they form a considerable river. The united stream flows south-east, passing through a rocky ridge, which crosses the valley, by means of a deep narrow cleft, which is spanned by an iron suspension bridge, the only one of the kind in the country. The river makes its exit through the hills at the south-east corner of the valley, and its banks are there steep and in many places impassable.

Both the above-mentioned rivers, and also several of the smaller streams, are crossed by well-built bridges, which, with few exceptions, have been erected during the present reign, or, more properly speaking, while the present minister, Sir Jung Bahādur, has been in power. These bridges are all built upon massive sāl piles and cross beams, also of sāl, on which is laid a strong road of brickwork, with a parapet of about two or three feet in height.

The valley is almost entirely under cultivation, and, as irrigation is much employed, its surface is almost never destitute of a crop of some sort. From the eastern extremity of the valley a road passes through a rocky defile leading to a long narrow valley called Banēpa; and from this another road leads southwards across the hills to the town and valley of Panowti, which can also be reached by a path from the main valley across the northern shoulder of Phūlchowk. Both these valleys are fertile and well-cultivated. The streams which water them run to the east and join the Kūsi.

At the western end of the valley are two deep valleys, the Dhūni and Ḳolpū Biyāsi. The former is the more southerly of the two, and is on a much lower level than Kāṭhmāṇḍū. The streams from these valleys run to join the Gunduk.

From the north-east corner of the valley a rugged path runs across Kukani. This is the main road leading to Gorkha and to Tibet. From the summit of the pass a magnificent view of the Himālaya snowy range is obtained, the foreground being occupied by numerous minor ranges, some of which too are always snow-capped, and between which lie several large, fertile, well-watered valleys.

The principal peaks of the snowy range seen from Kukani are: Mount Everest, 29,000 feet; Gosāin Thān, 26,000 feet; Yāsa and Mutsipūtra, 24,000 feet; and the so-called Diwalgiri, 26,800 feet. There are many intermediate peaks, and on a favourable day the snow may be seen from Kinchinjunga on the east to Diwalgiri on the west, stretching over at least 120 degrees of the horizon.

The principal valleys seen from the pass are the Liku and Taddi Kholas and the valley of Noākōt. Through the latter runs the Trisūl Gunga, a large and rapid stream, afterwards known as the Gunduk. All these valleys are fertile and well cultivated, and being much lower than the valley of Nepāl are of course warmer, and produce in abundance all the fruits found in the plains of Hindustān.

No Europeans are allowed to cross the Trisūl Gunga, though there is an excellent bridge about four miles from the town of Noākōt.

On reaching the top of the Chandragiri pass, a stranger is at once impressed with an idea of the denseness of the population of the valley. Besides three large towns, which are conspicuous objects in the view, there are many smaller towns and innumerable hamlets, studded all over the higher grounds and slopes of the hills; and in addition to these, in almost every field there appears to be a cottage. The natives themselves estimate the population of the valley at about half a million, and probably this is not far from the truth.

The names of most of the towns and villages will be mentioned in the history, so it is only necessary here to give a short description of the present condition of a few of the most important.

Kāṭhmāṇḍū, the capital of Nepāl, stands near the centre of the valley, in Lat. 27°42′N., and Long. 85°36′E. It is situated at the junction of the Bāgmati and Vishnumati rivers, but lies closer to the latter, extending along its eastern bank for about a mile. When seen from above, its shape is very irregular, but it is said by the natives to resemble the Khoṛa or sword of Devi. It is known by several names, such as Yindōsi, Kāntipūr, and Kāṭhmāḍū or Kāṭhmāṇḍū. It is said to have been founded by Rājā Gunakāmadeva, in the Kaligat year 3824 (A.D. 723).

The town is built on no regular plan; but the main street may be said to run nearly north and south, and it is crossed at various angles by several others, while between these is a network of narrow dark lanes. The population, including that of the suburbs, is stated at 50,000, but probably 30,000 would be nearer the truth. The houses are from two to four stories high, and are all built of brick and tiled, except in the suburbs, where the roofs are of thatch. The better class of buildings is elaborately ornamented with plaster and paintings, and the houses in general possess large projecting wooden windows or balconies, which are richly carved. Some of the windows represent a peacock with outspread tail; others contain groups of figures of gods, men, griffins, horses, birds, lizards, etc., and are surrounded by garlands of flowers. The carving, as a rule, is bold and well-executed, but the best specimens are to be found on the older buildings, as the taste for it seems to be dying out. In several parts of the town there are small open spaces, paved like the streets with brick and stone. In these the markets are held, and in the mornings they are quite gay with the flowers, fruit and vegetables exposed for sale.

In the centre of the town stands the Mahārājā's palace, which is a huge, rambling, ungainly building. Part of it is very old, built in pagoda fashion and covered with elaborate and grotesque carvings. Other parts of it, such as the Durbār-room, have been built within the last ten years and possess glass windows, which are rare in Nepāl, being found only in the houses of the wealthiest. In the square in front of the palace are numerous handsome temples. Many of these are like pagodas, of several stories in height, and profusely ornamented with carvings[1], painting, and gilding. The roofs of many of them are entirely of brass or copper gilt, and along the eaves of the different stories are hung numerous little bells, which tinkle in the breeze. At some of the doorways are placed a couple of large stone lions or griffins, with well-curled manes, which remind one strongly of the figures found at Nineveh. Another description of temple is built of stone with pillars and a dome. Though less ornamented and less picturesque, this style is far more graceful than the other. Close to the palace, on the north, is the temple of Talēju, one of the largest of the pagoda type. It is said to have been built by Rājā Mahīndra Malla, about A. D. 1549. It is devoted entirely to the use of the royal family. In front of several of the temples are tall monoliths, some surmounted by figures of old Rājās, who founded the temples, others by the winged

[1] It is unfortunate that the carving on many temples and powahs, and sometimes even on private houses, contains most obscene groups of figures. I have never been able to get any reason assigned for this filthy custom, except that such figures are supposed to protect the buildings from being struck by lightning.

Maclure & Macdonald Lith.rs London

(Plate II) SQUARE IN FRONT OF THE PALACE AT KAṬHMĀṆḌU (p. 10)

figure of Garūṛ. The figures are often in a kneeling posture, facing a temple, and are generally overhung by a brazen snake, on whose head is perched a little bird. Not far from the palace, and close to one of the temples, is an enormous bell, suspended to stone pillars; and in another building are two huge drums, about eight feet in diameter. The bell is sounded by pulling the tongue, but the peal is by no means what might be expected from its size. Here too are several huge and hideous figures of Hindū gods and goddesses[1], which on festival days are dressed up and ornamented in the usual way.

About two hundred yards from the palace stands a large semi-European building, called the Kōt, which is famous as being the place where, in 1846, the massacre took place of almost all the leading men of the country, by which event the present prime minister was established in power.

Besides the temples already noticed, many others are to be found in every street and lane. In fact, at a first glance, the town seems to consist of almost nothing but temples. They vary in size from the gigantic pagoda of Talēju to a diminutive shrine cut out of a single stone, with an image a few inches high in the centre. Many of them present a most repulsive appearance, being dabbled over with the blood of cocks, ducks, goats, and buffaloes, which are sacrificed before them.

The streets of Kāṭhmāṇḍū are very narrow, mere lanes in fact; and the whole town is very dirty. In every lane

[1] During my residence in Nepāl I have twice heard of people having committed suicide on the steps in front of one of these images. The suicide always takes place at night, and the body is found in the morning, with its throat cut from ear to ear, and its limbs decorously arranged, lying on one of the steps!

there is a stagnant ditch, full of putrid mud, and no attempt is ever made to clean these thoroughly. The streets, it is true, are swept in the centre, and part of the filth is carried off by the sellers of manure; but to clean the drains would now be impossible without knocking down the entire city, as the whole ground is saturated with filth. The houses are generally built in the form of hollow squares, opening off the streets by low doorways; and these central courtyards are too often only receptacles for rubbish of every sort. In short, from a sanitary point of view, Kāṭhmāṇḍū may be said to be built on a dunghill in the middle of latrines!

On leaving the town by the north-east gateway, and turning to the south, the first object one sees is a large tank, the Rānipokhri. It is surrounded by a wall, and in the centre is a temple, united to the western bank by a long narrow brick bridge. On the south side is a large figure of an elephant, cut out of, or rather built of, stone, bearing the image of Rājā Pratāpa Malla, the maker of the tank, and of his Rāni. A little farther south the road passes through an avenue of bukāyun trees, which runs between the city and the great parade-ground or Tudikhel. This ground is a large open space, covered with a fine green sward, and here the troops are daily drilled and exercised. In the centre is a square stone building about thirty feet high, which was erected by Sir Jung Bahādur after his return from England in 1851. On the top, till lately, stood a figure of Sir Jung Bahādur, holding a sword in one hand and a scroll in the other, and at the four corners were hideous brazen griffins or dragons. All these have however been removed to a new temple built by Sir Jung Bahādur on the bank of the Bāgmati. To the west of the parade-ground is a more graceful object, namely the Darōra or column erected by a former prime minister, General Bhīmasena Thāpā. This column is beautifully proportioned, standing on a base of stone, and rising to a height of 250 feet. This is the second column of the kind that was built by Bhīmasena, the first having been thrown down by a violent earthquake in 1833. The column now standing was struck by lightning in 1856, and a large rent was made all down one side. It was repaired, however, in 1869, and now looks as well as ever. There is a good winding staircase inside, and from the windows at the top a fine bird's-eye view of the town and its environs may be obtained.

A little farther south stands the arsenal, and to the east of the parade-ground are store-houses for ammunition, cannon, etc., and a manufactory where these are cast and bored. A new workshop on a larger scale has lately been built about four miles south of the city, on a small stream, the Nukkū, near Chaubahāl.

The road now turns to the east, and at about a mile south-east of Kāṭhmāṇḍū it reaches Thāpatali, the residence of Sir Jung Bahādur. This is an immense building, or rather range of buildings, situated close to the northern bank of the Bāgmati, just where it is crossed by a bridge leading to Pātan.

Thāpatali consists of a succession of squares of gigantic houses, four or five stories in height, which are occupied by Sir Jung Bahādur, his sons, and their numerous families. The buildings and grounds are kept in good order, and the place is well worth visiting, especially as the owner most obligingly allows strangers to inspect the public rooms, and the grounds, with all the curiosities contained in them. The four public rooms are large, lofty, and ornamented with pictures and carvings. They are full of curiosities of Nepalese, Chinese and English manufacture. Of the last it is difficult to say what there is not. From a baby's frock to a reflecting telescope or an Erard's piano, there seems to be a specimen of everything, all jumbled together. The Durbār-room is beautifully furnished with satin sofas, mahogany and ivory chairs, pianos, etc. The walls are graced with pictures of Her Majesty Queen Victoria and Prince Albert, which were given as presents to the King, besides full-length portraits of Sir Jung Bahādur, his brothers and other relatives, which were painted in England and France. In the centre of the hall stands a crystal chandelier some thirty feet in height, which was also brought from London, and cost, it is said, £500. After inspecting the public rooms, the stranger is shown the trophies of Sir Jung Bahādur's hunting expeditions. These consist of skulls of elephants, tigers, rhinoceroses, wild buffaloes, and gayal; stacks of deer-horns of all sorts; skins of the above-mentioned animals, crocodiles, and snakes, with many other curiosities. In the Elephant court are generally to be found some fine males, used for hunting wild elephants, and also frequently one or two comical little young ones, born after their mothers have been caught in the annual hunting expedition. The stables, cowhouses and kennels are likewise open for inspection, and are well worth looking at.

Before crossing the Bāgmati to Pātan, it may be as well to return by the road just described and proceed northwards. The road skirts the suburbs of Kāṭhmāṇḍū and then passes a series of large houses, built like Thāpatali, but on a smaller scale, which belong to three of Sir Jung Bahādur's brothers. Just beyond these houses, a road strikes off straight north, leading to the British Residency, which lies about a mile to the north of Kāṭhmāṇḍū[1]. It is pleasantly situated on a high table-land, and is well sheltered by lofty pinetrees. A little to the north-east stand the lines of the Resident's escort, which consists of one company of sepoys.

The road that is now being described turns to the west, and leads, through a splendid avenue of willow-trees, across the Vishnumati, to a place called Bālājī, where the King has a pleasure-house and gardens. Here the main road ends, and a footpath proceeds across the hills to the north-west.

From Thāpatali a road runs across a bridge over the Bāgmati and leads to Pātan. From the centre of the bridge a good view is obtained of the numerous temples lining the northern bank, and also of the houses and grounds of Thāpatali. At the northern end of the bridge stands a curious stone pillar, supported on the back of a gigantic tortoise, and surmounted by a grotesque figure of a lion. This was erected by General Bhīmasena Thāpā, the builder of the bridge.

The town of Pātan stands on a rising ground, a short distance from the southern bank of the Bāgmati, and about two miles south-east of Kāṭhmāṇḍū. It is an older town than Kāṭhmāṇḍū, having been built in the reign of Rājā Bīr Deva in the Kaligat year 3400, A.D. 299. The tradition connected with its building is given in the History. It is known by the names of Yellon-

[1] This spot was assigned for the British Residency because, owing to a deficient supply of water, it was a barren patch, supposed to be very unhealthy and to be the abode of demons! Now the place is one of the best wooded and most beautiful spots in the valley.

dēsi and Lalita Pātan. The latter name is derived from Lalit, the founder of the city. Its general aspect is much the same as that of the capital. The streets are as narrow and dirty, the gutters as offensive, and the temples even more numerous; but it appears much more dilapidated than Kāṭhmānḍū, many of the houses and temples being in ruins. The main square, however, in the centre of the town, is very handsome. On one side is the old Durbār, with a fine brazen gateway, guardian lions, and endless carvings. In front of this are monoliths, with the usual figures on them, and behind these is a row of very handsome old temples of every description.

One of Sir Jung Bahādur's brothers sometimes resides at the Durbār, being in command of the division of the army which is quartered at Pātan. The parade-ground lies to the south-east of the town, the road to it passing through a suburb abounding in pigs. The parade-ground is extensive, and there are several large tanks to the west, while on the northern side stands a huge Budhist temple of the most primitive description. This temple is merely a mound or dome of brick-work, covered with earth. There is a small shrine at each of the cardinal points, and on the top what looks like a wooden ladder. Many similar mound-temples, or Chaityas, exist in and around Pātan. The population of the town is said to be about 30,000.

From Kāṭhmānḍū a wide road leads nearly due east to the third large town or city of the valley, Bhātgāon, which is about nine miles from the capital. This town was founded by Rājā Anand Malla, A.D. 865, and was at first named Bhagtāpūr, but was also known as Dharma Pātan and Khopodēsi. Its shape is said to

TEMPLE BUILT BY BHŪPATĪNDRA MALLA
(Plate III) AT BHĀTGĀON. (pp 17, 195.)

be that of the *Dambrū*[1] of Mahādeo. It is built on high ground, stretching from east to west, and most of the side streets run down a steep incline towards the bank of a small stream on the southern side, which afterwards joins the Bāgmati. Bhātgāon has much wider, better paved, and cleaner streets than either of the other towns. Its houses too seem in better repair, and it strikes a stranger as being altogether in a more flourishing condition. The population is estimated at about 30,000.

The main square, as usual, contains an immense number of temples, conspicuous among which is the central one, called by the Newārs Nyātpōla Dēwal, or the five-storied temple. None but the priests are allowed to enter it, so that the common people do not even know to what god it is dedicated. This five-storied temple is pagoda-shaped, and stands on a base consisting of five platforms. The staircase leading to the entrance is guarded on each platform by two colossal figures. The lowest are statues of Jayamalla and Phatta, two champions of a Bhātgāon Rājā, each of whom is said to have had the strength of ten men. The next are elephants, ten times as strong as the men. The third are lions, ten times as strong as the elephants. The fourth are sārdūls or griffins, ten times as strong as the lions. And the fifth are Byāghrinī and Singhrinī, two goddesses of supernatural power. The same design is seen in many of the smaller temples in Bhātgāon, the rhinoceros, horse, and camel, however, sometimes taking a place in the series. Some of the finest carvings are to be found in the square in front of the old Durbār, which is famous

[1] A *dambrū* or *damrū* is a small drum shaped like an hour-glass.

for a magnificently designed brazen gateway. At the Durbār is the residence of the youngest brother of the minister, General Dēr Shamshēr, who commands the Bhātgāon division of the army.

To the west and south of the town are several large tanks. One of these, which stands close to the western gate, and between it and the parade-ground, is above the level of the ground, and is surrounded by a wall with four gates in the middle of the sides. This tank is full of gold and silver fish, which were originally brought from China in the time of General Bhīmasena. These fish are now common in many of the small tanks in the valley. Close to this tank, on the north, is a small house, built by the Bhātgāon general for the use of the British resident.

Besides these three large towns, there are about sixty smaller ones scattered over the valley, to give a description of which would only lead to tiresome repetition. The names of the principal ones only will therefore be given, and a few words said about them.

At the foot of the Chandragiri pass is a small town called Thānkōt; and eastward of this, on a rocky ridge that runs across the valley, are several villages. The chief of these, Kīrtīpūr, consists of several long narrow streets, built along the top of the ridge. This town is famous among the Nepalese for religious reasons, and also for the resistance it offered to the Gorkha conquerors. It sustained several sieges, and the brother of Prithwi Nārāyan, the Gorkha king, was killed before it. At last it was entered by treachery, and the savage conqueror ordered the noses of all the men, women and children to be cut off. There is no doubt of the truth of this, as it was recorded by Father Giuseppe[1], who was then present in the country; and thirty years afterwards, when Colonel Kirkpatrick visited Nepāl, he saw many of the unfortunate victims. The population of Kīrtīpūr is said to be about 4000. East of Kīrtīpūr, and about two miles south of Kāṭhmāṇḍū, stands Chowbahāl, which is a small town of about 1000 inhabitants. It is built on a conical eminence, rising out of the ridge already mentioned; and to the east of the town is the narrow gorge through which the Bāgmati passes.

About three miles south-east of Chowbahāl, on the eastern bank of the Bāgmati, stands the village of Bhōgmati, famous in Nepalese traditions, in connection with Machchhindranātha. Across the river, embedded in jungle on the mountain-side, stood a shooting-box belonging to Sir Jung Bahādur. Unfortunately this was burned down a year or two ago.

Some miles farther south, on the southern side of the river, but placed high on the hill-side, is the small town of Phurphing. A road passes Phurphing across the mountain to Chitlong, but it is so rugged and steep that it is scarcely ever used.

From Pātan two roads pass out. One of these runs south, through the villages of Sonagutti and Thecho, and leads to the small town of Chāpagāon or, as it is more usually pronounced, Champagāon. This town stands on a small eminence, and close to it is a sacred grove, containing an old temple and many fine old trees.

The other road runs out from Pātan to the south-east, and passing through the small towns of Harsiddhi,

[1] A description of the country, with a full account of the invasion of the Gorkhas, written by Father Giuseppe, is to be found in the second volume of the *Asiatic Researches*.

Thyba and Bauragāon, terminates at Godāvari. Godāvari is one of the holiest places in Nepāl, and once every twelve years a great mēlā is held there for a whole month, to which thousands of people come from all parts of Nepāl. The spring, according to tradition, is in direct communication with the river Godāvari in Madras. There are several little temples and tanks picturesquely situated at the foot of the hills, and Sir Jung Bahādur and his brothers have built large country houses here, which however are seldom occupied.

Large cardamom gardens have been constructed at Godāvari and yield a profitable crop.

A narrow footpath leads up from one of the temples to the summit of Phūlchowk. This mountain is said to be 9,720 feet high, and the ascent is long and tiresome, though by no means difficult. It is thickly wooded, and at the top very fine tree-rhododendrons are found, of every hue, from pure white to dark crimson. Among the jungle, the wild rose, yellow jessamine, arbutus, iris, etc., grow in profusion. At the very top is a small shrine, often visited by pilgrims from the valley, and close to this are two heaps, one consisting of weavers' shuttles, and the other of small iron tridents, which are deposited here by the pilgrims.

On the road from Kāṭhmāṇḍū to Bhātgāon, there are three towns, Nadi, Budi and Themi, the last of which is famous for the manufacture of earthenware of all sorts.

Another narrow road, paved with stone, leads from the capital in a north-easterly direction to the sacred shrines of Pashupati. This road passes by the villages of Navasāgar, Nandigāon, Harigāon, Chabāhil, and Devapātan, all of which are famous in tradition.

Pashupati stands on the western bank of the Bāgmati, about three miles north-east of Kāṭhmāṇḍū. The town itself is rather dilapidated, and consists of one main street, running east and west, and a few side streets, which are horribly dirty and abound with pigs. Close to the bank of the river stands the holiest temple of Nepāl, the shrine of Pashupatinātha. It is a handsome building in the pagoda style, with a brazen gilt roof, and large richly carved silver gates. A good view of it is obtained from the high bank on the opposite side of the river, but no European is ever allowed to approach even the outer wall of the temple. The banks of the river are paved for several hundred yards, and there are stone steps and places for burning the dead here and there. The river is crossed by two handsome bridges, from which a good view of the buildings is obtained. The stream is here narrow, and runs between precipitous banks of 80 or 100 feet in height. The banks are wooded above the temples, and amongst the trees on the face of the banks are some curious fakīrs' caves. On the eastern side of the river is a hill, covered with lofty trees (chiefly oak and champā) and jungle, which is alive with monkeys, who are as familiar and impudent as in most other holy places. This wood is the Mrigasthali of Nepalese tradition. In the centre of the wood are numerous small shrines and temples, including a large one lately built by Sir Jung Bahādur.

To Pashupati almost all the dying are brought when their end approaches, and at the last moment they are hurried to the edge of the stream, and their lower extremities are immersed in the water. Here too the bodies of the dead are burned, and there is a spot close by where Satīs are immolated.

Every year, in the month of February, from 10,000 to 20,000 pilgrims from the plains of Hindustān come to visit Pashupati and bathe in the Bāgmati. The minor festivals held at the place are innumerable, and hardly a day passes that it is not visited by crowds for religious purposes.

About four miles east of Pashupati is a small town, Chāngū Nārāyan, and two miles north-east of this stands Sānkhu, which was once a place of some importance, but is now only noted for the religious ceremonies performed there.

About four miles west of Sānkhu is Gaukarna, a small and very holy village, frequently mentioned in Nepalese traditions. It stands on the banks of the Bāgmati, about two miles above and north-east of Pashupati. Close to Gaukarna is a large jungle, which has been enclosed as a deer park by Sir Jung Bahādur.

Between Gaukarna and Pashupati, about a mile north of the latter, and about three and a half miles from Kāṭhmāṇḍū, is a peculiar village called Bodhnāth. This village is built in a circle round an immense Budhist temple. The temple consists of a circular platform of brickwork, on which is raised a solid dome of brickwork, surmounted by a brazen minaret of peculiar shape. Around the platform are niches, in each of which are painted cylinders, about 15 inches high and 6 inches in diameter, fitted into an iron frame. Each of these is filled with a roll of the usual Budhist prayers, and the pious twirl the cylinders as they walk round the temple performing their devotions. The mound is about 100 yards in diameter, and has the usual four shrines at the cardinal points. This place is a favourite resort of the Bhotiyas and Tibetans, who visit the valley in the cold season, and many of the houses are occupied as jewellers' shops, wherein are manufactured peculiar amulets, armlets, necklaces, etc., which the Bhotiyas wear in great profusion.

At the foot of the Seopūri mountain is a small village containing the tank and shrine of Nīlakantha, which is also famous in Nepalese history.

At the extremity of the willow avenue, already mentioned, stands a small village named Bālājī. This is situated at the foot of the Nāgārjun mountain, which is often mentioned in the History. The mountain has within the last six years been inclosed by a wall, and it is now made a deer park and game preserve for Sir Jung Bahādur. There are several caves and fakīrs' huts along the northern side of the hill, and some small temples on the crest of the hill and at the very summit. At the foot of the hill are springs, in one of which lies a huge recumbent figure of Mahādeo. The king has a pleasure-house and garden here, and in the grounds are several large tanks, full of big fish, which are very tame and come to be fed.

To the west of the capital, at a distance of about a mile and a half, stand the village and temple of Simbhūnāth or more properly Swayambhūnātha. As this is fully described in the History, and as a very correct picture of it is given in this work, it is needless to say more about it here. There are two roads leading to it from Kāṭhmāndū, which cross the Vishnumati by narrow bridges. These roads are paved with stone, and the top of the hill, where the temples stand, is reached by a staircase of about 400 stone steps. The height is about 250 feet above the level of the valley.

At the foot of the staircase is a colossal statue of Sākya Sinha, an incarnation of Budha. At the top of the staircase is a circular erection about three feet high, covered with brass, and bearing a large gilt Bajra or thunderbolt of Indra, which resembles a double-headed sceptre. Around the large central dome-shaped temple or mound are numerous small temples, shrines, bells, etc.

Simbhūnāth is much frequented by the Newārs and Bhotiyas, but is not held in great respect by the Hindū part of the population.

South-east of Simbhūnāth, between it and Kāṭhmānḍū, lies the artillery parade-ground, on which stands a large house, used as an arsenal and museum of old weapons of all sorts.

As regards the buildings of the country one point remains to be noticed, and that is the number of Powahs, Pātīs, and Sātals scattered all along the roads and paths. These are resting-places for travellers and pilgrims. Some are large square two-storied buildings, frequently attached to temples and shrines. Others are mere sheds, consisting of a wall with a tiled verandah supported on wooden pillars. All of them are erected by private persons, and supported by the descendants of the builders. Many of them therefore are falling into ruins, but new ones are as constantly erected to replace them. The building of these resting-places, and of Dhārās or watering-places, is considered a highly meritorious act by the Nepalese.

(Plate IV.) CHAITYA AND OTHER BUILDINGS ON THE TOP OF SWAYAMBHŪ HILL. (pp. 28, 84, 215, 229)

CHAPTER II.

Population of the country. Various races. Gorkhas, Newārs, Magars, Gurungs, Limbūs, Kirātis, Bhotiyas, and Lepchas. Their appearance, languages, dress, and ornaments. Food. Drinks. Education. Religions. Marriage. Satîs. Adultery and its punishment. Divorce. Eras in use in Nepāl. Religious festivals.

FOR the size of the country Nepāl possesses a great variety of races in its population. The principal of these are the Gorkhas, Newārs, Magars, Gurungs, Limbūs, Kirātis, Bhotiyas and Lepchas.

The Gorkhas, or Gorkhālis, so named from the former capital of their country, are the dominant race. They formerly occupied the district around the town of Gorkha, which is about forty miles west of Kāṭhmānḍū. They are said to be of Rājpūt descent, and to have been driven out of Rājputāna on the occasion of an invasion by Musulmāns[1]. They first settled near Pālpa, having passed through the Kumāon hills, and gradually extended their dominions to Gorkha. A little more than a hundred years[2] ago they invaded Nepāl, and the country to the eastward, and they have remained the ruling race ever since.

The Gorkhas are in general rather fine-looking men. Some of the higher castes, such as are found in some regiments of the army, are tall and slim in figure, but

[1] The royal family claims to be descended from that of Udaipūr.

[2] The centenary of the conquest was in 1868.

muscular and wiry, and have high features like the natives of Hindustān. However, owing to intermarriage, etc., the various races have become much mixed. They are essentially a military race, and form the bulk of the army. They are temperate and hardy, and make good soldiers, but they are by no means industrious, and take but a small share in the agricultural or mechanical labours of the country. They live chiefly in Kāṭhmānḍū, but many are scattered about in the other towns and throughout the country.

The Newārs constitute the largest section of the inhabitants of the valley, but are not numerous beyond its limits. They were the occupiers of the country prior to the invasion of the Gorkhas, and they still form the bulk of the population of Pātan, Bhātgāon, and most of the smaller towns. They are in general a shorter set of men than the Gorkhas, and their features are more of the Mongolian type. They perform almost all the agricultural and mechanical work of the country, and many of them are skilful carpenters, masons, workers in metal, painters and embroiderers[1]. Most of the trade of the country too is in the hands of Newārs, and a few of them are very wealthy.

The Magars and Gurungs inhabit chiefly the country to the west of the Nepāl valley. They are short powerful men, of Mongolian cast of features. These are the men mostly to be found in what are called the British Gorkha regiments.

[1] They are industrious enough when working for themselves in the fields or elsewhere, but when employed by Europeans they are the most idle, exasperating workers that it is possible to conceive. The only way to get them to work is to have a sepoy to watch them. Most of them too are Bānras or Budhist priests, and on an average they take four holidays in a week!

The Limbūs and Kirātis occupy the hilly country to the eastward of the valley. The Limbūs are much employed in the army, and both they and the Kirātis are famous as hunters. They are both short flatfaced people, powerfully built, and decidedly Mongolian in appearance.

The Lepchas occupy the hills near Sikkhim, and in general characteristics closely resemble the Bhotiyas.

The Bhotiyas are the hillmen living around the valley, and between it and Tibet. They are powerful, muscular, but ugly people. Much of the carrying of burdens is performed by them, and the load they can bear is surprising. It is by no means uncommon for them to carry two maunds, though one maund (80 lbs.) is the regular load, and this too has to be carried over hills several thousand feet in height, where the paths are of the most primitive construction. The Bhotiyas always carry loads on their backs, supported by a strap across the forehead, whereas the Newārs invariably carry theirs in baskets with a pole across the shoulder.

In addition to these regular inhabitants of the valley, a number of natives of Bhotān and Tibet visit it in the cold season, generally living around Bodhnāth and Simbhūnāth.

A few Musulmāns, consisting of Kashmīrī and Irāḳī merchants, live in Kāṭhmānḍū. The former have been established there for several generations. Altogether they do not number more than about one thousand.

These various races differ greatly from each other in many respects. The language used by the Gorkhas is Parbatiyā, which is a modern dialect of the Sanskrit, and is written in the same character. The Newāri language is quite distinct, and the written character also is somewhat different. The other races have each a language, or at least a dialect, of their own; and some of them, such as the Limbūs and northern Bhotiyas, use the Tibetan language.

The Gorkhas are decidedly the best-dressed part of the population. In summer they wear pāejāmas and a jacket, or long tunic, of white or blue cotton, with a kamarband, in which is invariably fastened a kukhrī, or large heavy crooked knife. In winter they wear similar clothes padded with cotton, or, if they are able to afford it, lined with fur. The headdress is generally a small closely-rolled turban of dark cloth, but they often wear a loosely folded pagrī, or a gaudy little skull-cap, ornamented with tinsel and braid.

The poorer classes of the Newārs wear in general little but a waist-cloth and a jacket of coarse cotton or woollen cloth, according to the season. Some of the wealthier, particularly merchants who have visited Tibet, wear a handsome dress, consisting of very full short trousers, a long tunic, and a fur-edged cap. Some of the men, especially the inhabitants of Harsiddhi, wear a long robe like a woman's gown, reaching to the ankles, and gathered into numerous plaits at the waist. The head-dress of the Newārs is a small skull-cap of black or white cloth, thinly wadded with cotton, and generally turned up for an inch or so at the border. The dress of the other races varies little from those already described.

The women of all the races dress much alike, wearing a cloth[1] by way of petticoat, gathered into a mass of plaits in front and almost touching the ground, but short behind, barely reaching the knee. Besides this, they

[1] The ladies of the higher classes like their muslin to be sixty or eighty yards in length. Of course they cannot walk much with such a bundle round them.

(Plate V) A RANI OR NEPALESE LADY OF HIGH RANK (pp. 28 29)

wear a jacket, and a sārī (shawl or sheet), which is either worn as in the plains of India, or wrapped round the body like a broad kamarband. Headdress they have none. The Newār women may be distinguished from those of the other races by having their hair gathered into a short thick club on the crown of the head, whereas the others have it plaited into a long tail, ornamented at the end with a tassel of red cotton or silk.

All the women wear a profusion of ornaments, such as golden or brass plates with jewels on the top of their heads, necklaces of beads (coral or gold), rings, earrings of peculiar shapes, nose-rings, etc. The handsomest, or at any rate the most peculiar, ornaments are worn by the Bhotiya women, and consist of necklaces of agate, coral, and other stones, massive chains, silver amulets of great size, bracelets of shells, and the like.

All classes are very fond of flowers and use them greatly for ornamenting their hair, especially on festival days. Both men and women generally have flowers stuck in their hair or behind their ears.

The next subject to be noticed is the food of the people.

The Brāhmans of course live in the same way as their brethren in the plains of India, but the bulk of the population consumes a great deal more flesh than is customary in Hindustān. The Gorkhas eat chiefly the flesh of khasīs, or gelding goats, which are imported in great numbers both from the Terai and the northern hills. The higher classes also consume large quantities of game, such as deer, wild boar, pheasants, etc. The wild pigs are caught when young, and kept and fed like domestic pigs in England. They become very tame, and may often be seen on the roads, following their owners from distant villages just like dogs. The Newārs are great consumers of buffaloes, and also of goats, sheep, ducks and fowls. The sheep they eat are all imported from the hills to the north and west, as they will not use the sheep from the plains of India, because they have long tails! The Magars and Gurungs are Hindūs, but of low caste. The former eat pork but not buffaloes' flesh; while the latter eat the buffalo but not the pig. The Limbūs, Kirātis and Lepchas are Budhists, and live in the same way as the Newārs. It is not very often, however, that the poorer classes can indulge in flesh, and the greater part of their food consists of rice and vegetables, which are generally plentiful throughout the year. They are especially fond of garlic, both raw and cooked, and of radishes. The latter they use in a semi-fermented or rotten state called Sinkī, the smell of which is something unutterably abominable. Hence it is anything but pleasant for a European to find himself in a crowd of Newārs, or even to follow a string of them along a narrow path.

The Newārs, and most of the lower castes, consume a considerable quantity of a coarse spirit called Rakshī, which is distilled from rice and wheat[1]. It is prepared by families in their own houses, and there is no tax on it when made merely for home consumption, but a license is required if it is to be sold. Amongst the Newārs the consumption of this is habitual, but drunkenness is after all not very common among them, except on the mēlā days and during the season of transplanting the rice.

[1] The higher classes are supposed not to touch spirits, as they would lose caste by so doing. Strange to say, however, no trade is so profitable in Nepāl as that of importing brandy or champagne!

The higher classes, and the lower too when they can afford it, consume a large quantity of tea[1]. This is imported from Tibet. It is prepared in two ways; either boiled with spices, when it tastes like weak negus; or made with ghee and milk, when it more resembles weak chocolate.

The subject of schools and colleges in Nepāl may be treated as briefly as that of snakes in Ireland. There are none. Sir Jung Bahādur and some of the wealthier class have tutors, either Europeans or Bengāli Bābūs, to teach their children English; but there is no public provision for education of any sort. Every man teaches his own children, or employs the family priest or Pandit for the purpose. The lower classes are simply without education of any kind whatever.

As might be expected among so many races, there are several religions. The Kashmīris and Irāḳis are Musulmāns. The Gorkhas, Magars, and Gurungs, are Hindus. Their religion and customs are very much the same as those of the inhabitants of Hindustān, and they are divided into the same castes, and observe the same rules as regards food and water.

Polygamy is generally practised, and some of the wealthy men have numerous wives. The marriage of widows is forbidden, and Satī was formerly of common occurrence. Of late years, however, that is, since Sir Jung Bahādur's visit to England, this custom has been discouraged, and various restrictions have been placed upon it. Thus women having young children are not allowed to immolate themselves; nor are intending Satīs

[1] The tea preferred by the Nepalese is the brick-tea. Ordinary tea, such as the English use, is not prized, and is only kept and drunk by a few of the higher classes who have visited Calcutta.

prevented from altering their intention even in presence of the fatal pile. Formerly a woman having once declared her intention was forced to adhere to it, and if she attempted to escape, she was stoned to death. These improvements, as well as many to be hereafter noticed, are entirely due to the personal influence of Sir Jung Bahādur, and have been carried out in spite of the greatest opposition from the priests and Brāhmans. The Gorkhas punish breaches of conjugal fidelity most severely. An erring wife is imprisoned for life[1], and the dishonoured husband was expected to cut down the seducer with his kukhrī the first time he encountered him. Sir Jung Bahādur has however placed restrictions on this custom, as he found it open to much abuse. The culprit is now arrested, and after his guilt is proved, the injured husband is allowed to cut him down in public, the victim being allowed a chance of escaping by running away, for which purpose he is given a start of a few yards[2]. Practically however his chance of escaping is very small, as he is generally tripped by some of the bystanders. The old laws against adultery, and also against breaches of caste, were most severe and brutal, but as these revolting punishments are now things of the past, it is of no use dwelling upon them.

The Newārs, Limbūs, Kirātis, and Bhotiyas are all Budhists. Their religion has become singularly mixed up with Hinduism, and there are several castes or

[1] Besides the imprisonment she is generally in the first place subjected to very severe domestic discipline, in the shape of a most cruel flogging.

[2] The man can save his life, with the loss of caste, if he passes under the lifted leg of the husband, but this is so ignominious that death is usually preferred. The woman can save her paramour if she persists in saying that he is not the first man with whom she has gone astray. Massacres of this sort frequently take place, and I have known of several instances wherein young men highly connected have fallen victims.

divisions among them, but their customs are in the main much alike.

In their worship they make great use of offerings of flowers and fruit, and some sects sacrifice buffaloes, goats, cocks, and drakes at their shrines. The blood alone is sprinkled on the shrines, and the flesh is consumed by the worshippers. Formerly much barbarity was practised in the performance of these sacrifices, but of late years, thanks to Sir Jung Bahādur, the ceremony is restricted to the decapitation of the victim and the sprinkling of the blood.

The marriage-tie is by no means so binding among the Newārs as among the Gorkhas. Every Newār girl, while a child, is married to a bēl-fruit, which after the ceremony is thrown into some sacred river. When she arrives at puberty, a husband is selected for her, but, should the marriage prove unpleasant, she can divorce herself by the simple process of placing a betel-nut under her husband's pillow and walking off. Of late years, however, this license has been somewhat restricted, and a divorce cannot now be effected in so simple a manner. Widows are allowed to remarry. In fact, a Newārin is never a widow, as the bēl-fruit to which she was first married is presumed to be always in existence. Adultery is but lightly punished among the Newārs. The woman is divorced, and her partner in guilt has to make good the money expended by the husband on the marriage, or, failing this, he is imprisoned.

The Newārs burn their dead, and widows may, if they please, immolate themselves as Satīs, but it is very seldom that they avail themselves of this privilege.

The laws of inheritance are the same in Nepāl as throughout Hindustān. The eldest son obtains the largest portion of the property of his deceased father; but provision is made for the younger children and widow or widows.

There are three principal eras in use in Nepāl. The introduction of these and the traditions connected with them are given in the History.

The Sambat of Vikramāditya commences 57 years before the Christian era; the Sākā era of Sālibāhana begins 78 years after the Christian era; and the Nepalese era dates from October, A.D. 880. The Kaligat era is also sometimes used; it begins B.C. 3101.

The Sambat and Sākā years in Nepāl begin on the 1st of Baisākh Badi, instead of the 1st of Chait Sudi as in Hindustān. The Nepalese year begins on the 1st of Kārtik Badi.

As the shrines in Nepāl are estimated at the modest number of 2,733, it may naturally be supposed that the religious festivals are somewhat numerous. To a stranger indeed they seem never ending, and the marvel is when the people find time to earn their livelihood.

The origin of most of these festivals is fully noticed in the History, so that it is unnecessary to repeat the traditions here. To give a complete list of them would be a prodigious task. Only a few of the principal will therefore be mentioned.

I. *The Machchhīndra Jātra.*

This festival is in honour of Machchhīndranātha, the guardian deity of Nepāl. The traditions connected with it are fully given in the History. Machchhīndra's temple and image are at the village of Bōgmati. The ceremonies commence on the 1st of Baisākh, when the idol is bathed with holy water and the sword of the king is presented to it. The image is then taken to Pātan, mounted on a large rath or car, on which is placed a shrine ornamented with carvings, evergreens, flowers, etc. This progress lasts for several days, generally a week, as there are regular stages, at each of which the image halts for a day, and its attendants are fed at the expense of the neighbourhood. The image remains at Pātan for a month, and then on an auspicious day it is taken back to Bōgmati. This day is called Gudri-jhār, because the blanket of Machchhīndra is shaken before the people to show that he carries nothing away from them, and that, though in poverty, he is contented.

2. *Bajra Joginī Jātra, on the 3rd of Baisākh.*

Bajra Joginī was originally a goddess of the Budhists only, but is now worshipped by Hindus as well. Her temple is on the Manichūr mountain near Sānkhū. Not far from her temple is that of Kharg Joginī, where fire is always kept burning, and near which is the image of a human head. The traditions connected with these are given in the History. The Jātra of Bajra Joginī is held at Sānkhū, and lasts for a week. The image of the goddess is placed in a khat, or wooden shrine, and carried through the town on men's shoulders.

3. *Sithī Jātra.*

This takes place on the 21st of Jeth, on the banks of the Vishnumati, between Kāṭhmāṇḍū and Simbhū-nāth. After feasting, the people divide into two parties and have a match at stone-throwing. Formerly this used to be a serious matter, and any one who was knocked down, and fell into the hands of the opposite party, was sacrificed to the goddess Kankeshwarī, who has a temple near the place. Nowadays, however, the stone-throwing is confined to children.

4. *Gathiā Mogal or Ghantā Karn.*

This is the name of a Rākshasa or demon, and the festival is to celebrate his expulsion from the country. The Newār boys make a straw figure, which they beat and drag about in the streets, and they beg for a dām from everybody they meet while so doing. The figures are burned in the evening. This festival takes place on the 14th of Sāwan.

5. *Bānra Jātra.*

This festival takes place twice a year, on the 8th of Sāwan and 13th of Bhādon. The Bānras, or priests of the Baudha-mārgī Newārs, go about from house to house, and receive a handful of rice or grain at each. This is done in commemoration of their ancestors having been Bhikshus, or mendicant priests, who lived on alms and followed no trade. The Newārs on these occasions decorate their shops and houses with pictures, flowers, etc., and the women sit in front with large baskets of rice and grain, which they dispense in handfuls to the Bānras as they pass. A wealthy Newār may get up a private Bānra Jātra at any time, if he pleases; but it is an expensive amusement, as he has to make large presents to the first Bānra who gets his foot over the threshold of the house. If the king is invited to this Jātra, he must be presented with a silver throne, umbrella, and cooking utensils.

6. *Rākhi Pūrnimā.*

This festival takes place on the last day of Sāwan. It is observed both by Budhists and Hindus, but with different rites. The Budhists bathe in sacred streams and visit their temples. The Brāhman priests tie an ornamental thread on the wrists of all their followers, and in return receive presents. Many persons on this occasion go on pilgrimage to Gosāīn Thān and bathe in the sacred lake there.

7. *Nāg Panchamī.*

This festival takes place on the 5th of Sāwan. This is the anniversary of a great struggle between a famous Nāg and Garūr. The stone image of Garūr at Chāngū Nārāyan is said to perspire on this occasion, as a result of the struggles of Garūr. The priests wipe off the perspiration with a handkerchief, which is sent to the king. Water, in which a thread of this handkerchief has been steeped, is said to be a sovereign remedy for snake-bites. Fortunately, poisonous snakes are almost unknown in Nepāl!

8. *Janm Ashtamī.*

This festival takes place on the 8th of Bhādon, and is in memory of the birthday of Krishna. The shops and houses in the towns are ornamented with pictures, etc.

9. *Gāī Jātra.*

This is purely a Newār festival. It takes place on the first day of Bhādon. All Newārs who have lost members of their family during the year ought to disguise themselves as cows and dance round the palace of the king. The ceremony nowadays is performed vicariously, and consists merely of a masked dance with singing of songs.

10. *Bāgh Jātra.*

This takes place on the 2nd of Bhādon. The dancers on this occasion ought to be disguised as tigers, but it is now merely a repetition of the Gāī Jātra.

11. *Indra Jātra.*

This festival lasts for eight days, beginning on the 26th of Bhādon. On the first day a high wooden post is erected before the king's palace, and all the professional dancers of the country assemble, disguised with all sorts of hideous and ludicrous masks, and dance around the palace. If an earthquake happens during the festival, it is considered a very bad omen, and the festival must be begun anew, reckoning the day on which the earthquake took place as the first. On the third day a number of young virgins are brought before the king and worshipped as Kumārī devīs, after which they are mounted on cars and carried through the city. When the cars arrive at the palace, the gaddī is brought out, and the king's sword (sometimes the king himself) is placed on it, and presents are given by all the officials. This day is called Anant Chaudas. It was on this occasion that Prithwī Nārāyan, the Gorkha conqueror of Nepāl, entered Kāṭhmāṇḍū with a few followers, and when the gaddī was brought out, he seated himself on it. Most of the Newārs being drunk, he met with little opposition, and the Newār Rājā fled from the city.

12. *Dasahra or Durga Pūjā.*

This festival takes place on the 26th of Kūār, and is observed in the same way as in Hindustān. The festival lasts for ten days, and many buffaloes, goats, etc. are sacrificed. In Nepāl, however, the clay image of Durga is not made as in Bengāl. On the first day of the festival the Brāhmans sow barley at the spot where they worship, and sprinkle it with sacred water daily. On the tenth day they pull it up and present small bunches of it to their followers, in return for the presents which they receive from them.

13. *Dewālī.*

This takes place on the 15th of Kārtik. The people worship Lakshmī, the goddess of wealth, illuminate their houses, and gamble all night long. In Nepāl gambling in public (which is illegal at other times) is permitted for three days and nights, and during these the streets in the towns are almost impassable, on account of the groups of gamblers squatted all over them. The Nepalese are inveterate gamblers, and stake heavily on the dice. Many curious tales are told of them, such as staking their wives, etc. One man is said to have cut off his left hand and put it down under a cloth as his stake. On winning the game, he insisted on his opponent cutting off his hand, or else restoring all the money which he had previously won.

14. *Khichā Pūjā.*

This is a Newār festival, which takes place on the 16th of Kārtik. It consists in doing pūjā to dogs, and on this occasion all the dogs in the country may be seen with garlands of flowers round their necks.

There are also days for doing pūjā to bullocks, crows, and even frogs.

15. *Bhāī Pūjā.*

On the 17th of Kārtik every woman visits her brother's house, puts a ṭīkā or mark on his forehead, and a garland round his neck, and then washes his feet, and gives him sweetmeats to eat. In return she receives a present of money, clothes and ornaments.

16. *Bālā chaturdasī or Satbyū.*

This takes place on the 14th of Āghan. People on this day go to the forest of Mrigasthalī (i.e., the small wood opposite the temple of Pashupati), and scatter about rice, vegetables, and sweetmeats—much to the delight of the monkeys who dwell there.

17. *Kārtik Pūrnimā.*

On the first day of this month many women go to the temple of Pashupati, and remain there the whole month, fasting and drinking only the water with which the image is bathed. Credat Judaeus. It is said that occasionally some die, but in general they survive their month's fasting. On the pūrnimā, or last day of the month, there are great rejoicings and an illumination of the temple of Pashupati, and the night is spent in singing and dancing. On the next morning the Brāhmans (as usual) are fed on the Kailās hill, at the base of which the temple of Pashupati stands; and then the women who have been starving return home amid the congratulations of their friends and relatives.

18. *Ganēsh Chauth.*

This festival, which is held on the 4th of Māgh, is in honour of Ganēsh, the god of wisdom. Fasting and worship are the order of the day,—with feasting as a sequence at night.

19. *Basant or Srīpanchamī.*

This takes place on the 20th of Māgh, and is in honour of Saraswati, the goddess of learning.

20. *Holī.*

This festival takes place on the last day of Phāgun. In Nepāl a wooden post or *chīr*, adorned with flags, is erected in front of the palace, and this is burned at night, representing the burning of the body of the old year.

21. *Māghī Pūrnimā.*

Some of the young Newārs bathe in the Bāgmati every morning during Māgh, and on the last day of the month some of the bathers are carried in procession from the bathing-places to the temples. They are carried in ornamented ḍolīs, lying on their backs, with lighted chirāgs (lamps) on their chests, arms and legs. As most of them wear green spectacles, to protect their eyes from the sparks, the sight is rather mirth-provoking. Behind the ḍolīs follow the other bathers, bearing on their heads earthen water-pots, perforated with innumerable straws, through which the water escapes. Passers-by catch a few drops and sprinkle them on their foreheads.

22. *Ghorā Jātra.*

On the 15th of Chait, all horses and ponies belonging to government servants are assembled on the grand parade-ground, and raced past the king and officials, who are stationed on the monument in the centre of the ground.

On the anniversary of the completion of the monument just mentioned, which bore Sir Jung Bahādur's statue, a mēlā is held on the parade-ground, all government officials have to pitch their tents, and gambling is allowed for two days and nights. The festival winds up with an illumination of the monument.

As Sir Jung Bahādur's statue and the four dragons have been transferred to a new temple built by him, the locale of this festival has been changed this year (1875).

(Plate VI.) I. The Five Buddhas. II. The Five Tārās, their wives. III. The Five Bōdhisatwas, their sons (p. 43.)

CHAPTER III.

Occupations of the people. Brāhmans. Priests. Astrologers. Baids. Clerks. Laws and punishments. Castes. Slavery. Trade and manufactures. Agriculture. Live stock. The army. The revenue. The roads.

As this sketch is not intended for a Gazetteer, it is unnecessary to enter at great length into the subject of the occupations of the people.

Priests and Brāhmans of course are very numerous, and have much influence in a country where there are so many temples, and at least half the time of the people seems to be spent in pūjās and religious holidays. The Rāj Gurū is a wealthy and influential person in the state, and has a large income from government lands, and also from the fines inflicted for offences against the rules of caste. Many other priests, Gurus and Purōhits, have lands assigned to them, and many of the temples have been richly endowed by their founders. Still, a great many of the priests depend for their support on the offerings of their jajmāns (clients), who pay them fees for the ceremonies performed at births, marriages and deaths. Every family has a special priest, whose office is hereditary. Immense sums are wasted in feeding Brāhmans on all sorts of occasions. As an instance, it may be mentioned, that, when Sir Jung Bahādur met with an accident at Bombay in 1875, fifteen thousand rupees were spent in feeding Brāhmans at Kāṭhmāṇḍū.

Astrologers form another large class of the learned community. Some of them are also priests, but in general the professions are distinct. In Nepāl astrology must be a profitable pursuit, as no great man thinks of setting out on a journey, or undertaking any business whatever, without having an auspicious moment selected. Indeed the time for everything, from the taking of a dose of physic to the declaration of a war, is determined by the astrologers.

Baids, or medical men, are also numerous in Nepāl, and all families of any pretension have at least one permanently attached to their service. There are, however, no public hospitals or dispensaries, nor any means provided for the relief of indigent sick people.

The duties of clerks and accountants are performed by a special class of people, chiefly Newārs.

Lawyers are not held in much estimation in Nepāl. The chief justice gets a salary of some two hundred rupees a month, so that the inducements for bribery and corruption are great.

As an appeal can always be made to the Council (which practically means Sir Jung Bahādur), justice is on the whole pretty fairly administered.

The old savage code of punishments, involving mutilations, stripes, etc., etc., was abolished by Sir Jung Bahādur on his return from England. Treason, rebellion, desertion in time of war, and other offences against the state, are punished by death or imprisonment for life; bribery and peculation by government servants, by fines, imprisonment, and dismissal from office.

Killing cows and murder are punished by death; maiming cows and manslaughter, by imprisonment for life; and other acts of violence by imprisonment or fines.

If a low caste person pretends to belong to a higher caste, and induces a high caste person to partake of food or water from his hands, he renders himself liable to a heavy fine, or imprisonment, or the confiscation of all his property; or he may even be sold into slavery. The victim of his deception is re-admitted to his caste on payment of certain fees to the priests, and the performance of certain fasts and ceremonies (prayaschit).

Brāhmans and women are never capitally punished. The severest punishment for women publicly is imprisonment for life with hard labour, and for Brāhmans the same with degradation from caste.

Slavery is one of the institutions of Nepāl. Every person of any means has several slaves in his household, and the wealthy have generally a great number of both sexes. It is said that there are from twenty to thirty thousand slaves in the country. Most of these have been born slaves; but free men and women, with all their families, may be sold into slavery as a punishment for certain crimes, such as incest and some offences against caste. In a few of the wealthier households the female slaves are not allowed to leave the house; but in general they enjoy a great deal of freedom in this respect, and the morals of the female slaves are very loose in consequence. They are generally employed in domestic work, wood-cutting, grass-cutting, and similar labour. The price of slaves ranges for females from 150 to 200 rupees, and for males from 100 to 150 rupees. They are usually well treated, and on the whole seem quite contented and happy. Should a slave have a child by her master, she can claim her freedom.

All the trade and manufactures of the country may be said to be in the hands of the Newārs and a few foreigners. A few families of Kashmīrīs have been settled at Kāṭhmāṇḍū for generations, and they, and some Irākīs, are the principal traders in articles of European manufacture. There is a community of about 3,000 Nepalese established at Lhāsā, where there is a Nepalese *vakīl* (consul or resident), and these, who are chiefly Newārs, carry on the trade between Nepāl and Tibet. Most of the traders in corn, oil, salt, tobacco, confectionery, and other articles of domestic consumption, are Newārs.

The manufactures of the country are few, consisting chiefly of cotton and coarse woollen cloth, a peculiar kind of paper (made from the inner bark of several species of Daphne), bells, brass and iron pots, ornaments of silver and gold, and coarse earthenware. All the mechanics of the country are Newārs, except a few workmen from the plains of India, employed by the government in the public workshops and arsenals.

The great bulk of the population is employed in agriculture, as almost every family holds a small piece of ground. The soil of the valley cannot be said to be very fine, but the inhabitants certainly make the most of it. Every available scrap of ground is cultivated, the hill-sides being terraced wherever water can be obtained for irrigation. Indian corn and rice are the chief crops in the hot weather, and in the cold weather wheat, garlic, radishes, red pepper, ginger, potatoes, etc. are grown. Most lands yield two crops every year, and from some even three crops are obtained. The work of cultivation is done almost entirely by hand, though of late years the plough is being more extensively used.

There are few cattle in the valley, as there is no grazing ground except at the foot of the hills. Buffaloes, sheep, and goats for food are all imported. What few there are in the valley are small and of inferior breeds. Ducks and fowls are plentiful and of good quality. Much pains are bestowed on the rearing of ducks, as their eggs are greatly prized as an article of food. They are carried out daily to the rice fields in large baskets and allowed to feed there, and in the evening they are collected and carried home again.

The military art of course has great attention bestowed on it by the Gorkhas. In fact, most of the revenue of the country is wasted in playing at soldiering, and in manufacturing very useless rifles and cannon. The actual standing army consists of about 16,000 men. These are divided into twenty-six regiments of from 500 to 600 men each. Besides these, however, there is a large force consisting of men who have served for several years and taken their discharge. These men, after staying a few years at home, may again enter the ranks, and take the place of others, who in turn lie by for a year or two. Thus the Nepalese could with little trouble raise a force of 60,000 or 70,000 men, who have been trained to arms.

The regiments are formed on the British model, and are drilled with English words of command, or at least what are supposed to be so. The army is officered much in the same way as the English army. There is, however, no regular system of promotion, all appointments being renewed annually, and greyhaired lieutenants are often to be seen in the same regiment with beardless colonels. In fact, all the higher ranks are filled up by the sons and relatives of Sir Jung Bahādur and his brothers.

Practically speaking, Sir Jung Bahādur is the head

of the army, as well as of every other department; but the post of Commander-in-Chief is held by his eldest surviving brother, General Ranadīp Singh, K.S.I. Of the two younger brothers, Generals Jagat Shamshēr and Dēr Shamshēr, each commands a division of the army, at Pātan and Bhātgāon respectively. Besides these, there are numerous generals and major-generals, varying from thirty down to five years of age, who are either sons or nephews or grandsons of Sir Jung Bahādur.

The usual undress of the army is a blue cotton tunic, with pāejāmas of the same colour; and for full dress most regiments have red cloth tunics and dark trousers with a red stripe. The artillery uniform is blue. The headdress consists of a small tightly-rolled turban, on which each soldier, as a distinctive mark of his regiment, wears a badge of silver, the property of government. Some of these are crescent-shaped, others oval, and so on. The non-commissioned officers wear chains on their turbans in addition to the badge, and the badges of the officers are jewelled and plumed in various ways, according to their rank. The value of the headdress of the officers is very great. Sir Jung's own is said to be worth £15,000.

The arms of the troops are very heterogeneous. Some regiments have still old flint muskets, others the percussion "brown Bess," and others Enfield rifles, either given to the Nepalese by the British after the campaign of 1858, or else manufactured at Kāṭhmāṇḍū[1]. Every soldier in addition to his bayonet carries the national weapon, the kukhrī.

[1] Many of the rifles said to be manufactured in Nepāl, especially the breech-loaders of recent date, are *undoubtedly smuggled into the country through Bombay* by the aid of some Pārsī merchants there.

The cavalry of the Nepāl army is on a very limited scale, consisting of about 100 men. Indeed the country is not adapted for the manœuvring of horse.

The artillery is on a larger scale; and there is an attempt at horse artillery too. There are also four mountain batteries drawn by mules. These have been added to the armament of Nepāl of late years, since it has pleased the British Commander-in-Chief to patronise General Babar Jung and carry him about as an A.D.C. to the camps of exercise and other places. There is a large number of cannon in store, and more are being cast and bored daily. Percussion-caps are also manufactured in the arsenal, with machinery imported from England, but they are by no means of first-rate quality. Powder of an inferior kind is likewise made and stored in great quantities.

As regards the efficiency of the army, there is no doubt that the material is good, and for defensive purposes, in their own hills and forests, the soldiers would fight well, and be formidable foes; but for purposes of aggression it is doubtful if they would be of any use against Europeans. The officers are in general uneducated and ignorant young men, and the troops, though daily drilled, so as to be tolerably perfect in their regimental exercises, have had no practical experience of war for many years. Their weapons are very poor; a commissariat department can hardly be said to exist; they are badly clothed, and their accoutrements are of the most miserable and dirty description[1].

[1] Their rifles are rusty and dirty-looking outside. As for the inside, I have often seen a soldier sitting by the side of a ditch, busied in scouring his *rifle* with a wisp of grass and a handful of sand!

To give an idea of the force which can be assembled, I may mention that the troops employed in the last war with Tibet, in 1854, amounted to 27,000 men, with 29,000 partially armed coolies and camp-followers, and 390,000 unarmed baggage-coolies ; leaving about 7,000 fighting men at home. The utmost efforts, however, were made in this war, and the country was reduced to the greatest distress, the sole result being that the Tibetans agreed to pay an annual tribute of 10,000 rupees (£1000).

The revenue of Nepāl is about 96 lakhs of rupees (say £96,000). It is chiefly derived from land-tax, custom-duties, the produce of the sāl forests in the Terai, and various Government monopolies.

Of the roads in Nepāl there is little to be said. The only route by which Europeans are allowed to enter the country has been fully described already. As far as Hetowra there is a rough cart-track. From Hetowra to Bhimphēdi the road is good, and the streams have been bridged. Beyond Bhimphēdi the road is a mere pag-dandī or footpath over the hills, impassable for laden beasts of burden. Within the valley there are only two good roads. One of these extends from Tānkot, at the foot of the Chandragiri pass, to Bhātgāon. The other runs from Thāpatali to Bālājī, and is only about three miles in length. On these roads the streams are all substantially bridged. The other roads in the valley are rough footpaths, quite unfit for vehicles or even for laden beasts of burden. The two roads to Tibet are mere rugged paths over the hills.

CHAPTER IV.

Brief sketch of the recent history of the country, and of the intercourse with the British. Colonel Kirkpatrick's mission. War with the British in 1814. Appointment of a Resident. Domestic intrigues and struggles for power. Death of General Bhīmasena Thāpā. General Mātabar Singh. First appearance of Jung Bahādur. His rise to power. The Kōt massacre. Sir Jung's visit to England. War with Tibet in 1854. Troops sent to assist the British in 1857. The Nānā Sāhib. Sir Jung's proposed visit to England in 1875.

ALTHOUGH the native history of the country will be given in full, it may not be amiss to insert here a short account of the principal events in the intercourse of the British with Nepāl.

The two governments first came into collision as early as the time of the Gorkha invasion. The former Rājās applied to the British for assistance, and Captain Kinloch with a few companies of Sepoys advanced into the Terai in 1765, but was repulsed by the Gorkha troops.

In 1791 the Gorkhas had entered into a commercial treaty with the British, and hence, when in difficulties with the Chinese in that year, they applied for assistance to Lord Cornwallis. In consequence of this, a mission under Colonel Kirkpatrick was despatched to Nepāl, and reached Noākōt in the early part of 1792. By this time, however, the Gorkhas had submitted to the Chinese, and British interference was unnecessary. This was the first occasion on which a British officer entered the country. One result of the mission was the signing of another commercial treaty on the 1st of March 1792.

In October 1801 a new treaty was signed by the British and Nepalese authorities, and Captain W. D. Knox was appointed British Resident at the Nepalese court. Many obstacles were thrown in the way of this officer's entering the country, but at last he succeeded in reaching the capital, in April 1802. Little benefit, however, arose from his presence in Nepāl. He soon found that nothing could be done with a people "amongst whom no engagements, however solemnly contracted, are considered binding, when deviation from them can be committed with any prospect of impunity;" and in consequence of their failing to adhere to their engagements, he was withdrawn from the country in April 1803.

In January 1804 the treaty with Nepāl was formally dissolved by Lord Wellesley; and though an attempt was made at negotiation in May 1810, the relations between the countries gradually became worse, till at length the encroachments of the Nepalese on British territory could no longer be endured, and on the 1st of November 1814 war was proclaimed by the British.

Of the progress of the war under Generals Marley, Wood, Gillespie, and Ochterlony, it is unnecessary here to give details. At first, from ignorance of the country and the enemy to be encountered, the British met with several disasters, under Generals Wood and Marley; and General Gillespie fell during the assault on a small fort named Kalunga. General Ochterlony was more successful, and the Gorkhas retired beyond the Kālī river, and began to negotiate for peace. Inflated, however, by their temporary successes, the Nepalese would not listen to reason, and again took up arms. General Ochterlony was now put at the head of the expedition, and under him the British troops soon made their way to Makwānpūr, a town and fort in the Terai, to the south of the valley of Nepāl, distant only thirty-five miles from the capital. The Gorkhas, finding themselves worsted, now submitted; and after much delay, and a threat on the part of General Ochterlony of again resuming hostilities, a treaty was at length signed in March 1816. By this treaty the Nepalese relinquished large portions of their newly acquired territory to the British. Some of these were assigned to chiefs who had aided in the war, others were retained by the British, and a large part of the Terai was not long afterwards restored to the Nepalese.

In fulfilment of the terms of the treaty, a British Resident was appointed, and Mr Gardiner was the person selected to fill the post. As there was some delay, however, in his taking up the duty, Lieutenant Boileau was appointed to officiate for him, and this officer reached Kāṭhmāṇḍū in April 1816.

The king of Nepāl was at this time still a youth, and the reins of government were held by General Bhīmasena Thāpā.

Soon after the British arrived in the country, smallpox broke out, and committed great ravages among the people. Amongst other victims, the king died on the 20th of November 1816. One of his Rānīs and six female slaves immolated themselves as Satīs along with him. On the 8th of December, the young Prince, Rāj Indra Bikram Sāh Bahādur Shamshēr Jung, was placed on the throne. As the new monarch was only three years old, the government was still carried on by General Bhīmasena Thāpā.

In the meanwhile, the Nepalese were intriguing with China for assistance to expel the British Resident and renew the war, but they failed in their designs.

Towards the end of 1817, Dr Wallich visited Nepāl, and carried on his botanical researches for a year.

From this time onwards the records of Nepāl furnish little of interest, except a history of intestinal struggles for power between the Thāpā and Pānṛe factions, and futile attempts at forming combinations with other states in Hindustān against the British. In 1824 the young king was married, and on the 5th of October 1829 a son and heir was born.

In 1833, the king, instigated by one of the Rānīs, who was of an ambitious disposition, attempted to free himself from the rule of Bhīmasena, but without success. The attempt, however, was renewed in 1836, and in 1837 Bhīmasena was removed from office, and imprisoned on the charge of having poisoned an infant son of the king. He was, however, released and pardoned after a few months' confinement, but he never regained his former position; and in May 1839 he was again put in irons, on the old charge, and kept closely confined. His wife and female relatives were threatened with exposure and shameful ill-treatment in public; and preferring to die rather than be a witness of such disgrace, Bhīmasena committed suicide in prison. At least so the government reported, though there were grave doubts at the time as to whether it was not a case of assassination. His corpse was dragged through the streets of Kāṭhmāṇḍū, and flung upon a heap of rubbish, on the other side of the bridge leading from the town across the Vishnumati to the west. So ended the life of a gallant old chief, who had ruled Nepāl for five-and-twenty years.

From this time on to 1843, the enemies of Bhīmasena, the Kālā Pānṛe faction, continued in power, though sometimes ousted from office for a time by other factions. Intrigues both within the country, and in Hindustān, were being constantly carried on; and there were frequent disputes with the British Government, which sometimes threatened to terminate in open hostilities. Fortunately, however, by the skilful management of the Resident, Mr Hodgson, war was averted.

In 1843 the nephew of Bhīmasena, a dashing soldier named Mātabar Singh, returned from exile[1]. He soon obtained favour with the Court and army, and the first exertion of his power was to effect the destruction of his enemies, the Kālā Pānṛes, who were seized and executed in May 1843.

About this time mention is often made, in the reports of official proceedings, of a rising young soldier named Jung Bahādur. He was one of a band of seven brothers, the sons of a Kājī, or Nepalese official. He had, as usual, entered the military service when young, and for a time had been the personal attendant of the young prince. By this time, however, he had risen to the rank of Colonel, and in 1844 his uncle, Mātabar Singh, expressed some alarm at the increase of his influence at Court and with the army.

The Resident, Sir Henry (then Major) Lawrence, mentions him as an intelligent young man, particularly

[1] He had been sent on an embassy to Calcutta in 1836, and subsequently to Ranjīt Singh. His conduct having been suspicious on the latter occasion, he had been detained by the British under surveillance, receiving, however, an allowance of 1000 rupees a month.

expert in all military matters, but, though young in years, profoundly versed in intrigue.

He continued to ingratiate himself with one of the Rānīs, who held the chief power in the Court, and at last, finding himself in a firmer position, he began to develope his ambitious projects. On the 18th of May 1845, Mātabar Singh, who, though prime minister, had become unpopular at Court, was summoned to an audience with the king at the palace. On entering the room where he expected to find the king, he was killed by a rifle-shot, fired from the Zenāna gallery at the end of the room. His body was then thrown out of the window, and dragged away by an elephant to the banks of the Bāgmati at Pashupati. Next morning Jung Bahādur reported the circumstance officially to the Resident, but for the time the king was said to have been the slayer of the prime minister, and the deed was acknowledged, and even boasted of, by the king. Subsequently, however, it appeared that Mātabar Singh was killed by Jung Bahādur, at the instigation of the queen; and the king, who was little better than an imbecile, was made to take the credit of the deed.

Jung Bahādur now took a prominent part in the government, though not actually included in the ministry, which consisted of a sort of coalition of various factions, the prime minister being Gagan Singh.

In 1846 Sir Henry Lawrence left Nepāl, and was succeeded by Mr Colvin, who, however, was soon obliged to quit the country on account of ill-health, leaving Major Ottley in charge. On the 15th of September 1846, the Resident was surprised by a visit at midnight from the king, who in much agitation informed him that a fearful tragedy was being enacted in the city.

This is what is known as the Kōt massacre, and as it is an important event in the history of Nepāl, it may be as well to give a detailed account of it.

The king at this time was a mere tool in the hands of the Rānī, who, after the murder of Mātabar Singh, may be said to have been the actual ruler of the country. In the coalition ministry she had one especial friend named Gagan Singh. This noble, on the night of the 14th of September, was shot in his own house, while he was in the act of performing his devotions in a private room. Who instigated this deed has never been satisfactorily determined, although afterwards a person named Alī Jāh, said to have been the murderer, was executed. The Rānī, however, at once blamed her enemies in the ministry, and insisted on the king assembling all the ministers and nobles in council to find out the assassin. Fatḥ Jang and his colleagues, surprised at the untimely summons, hurried to the place of meeting at the Kōt, a large building, somewhat in European style, near the palace. Here, in the meantime, were assembled the Rānī, Jung Bahādur, his band of brothers, and his faithful body-guard, armed with rifles. The queen's party was carefully arranged and heavily armed, whereas the members of council came as they were summoned, in a hurry, each from his own house, and with no weapons but their swords. There is no doubt that the whole affair was arranged beforehand, and that written orders were given by the Rānī to Jung Bahādur. A stormy discussion ensued, insults were freely exchanged, and when Fatḥ Jung laid his hand on the hilt of his sword[1], it seemed to be the signal for an attack by

[1] According to another story, an attempt was made to arrest Fatḥ Jung, and his son attacked and wounded some of Jung Bahādur's brothers and party with his sword. Jung Bahādur shot Fatḥ Jung with his own rifle, as he was going to draw his sword to cut down one of his brothers.

Jung Bahādur and his faithful soldiers, who in the meantime had guarded the entrance of the building. In a few minutes thirty-two of the nobles of the country, and upwards of a hundred of the lower ranks, were shot down. The poor king, alarmed by the noise of the struggle, mounted his horse and rode off to the Residency. On his return, within an hour, he found the gutters around the Kōt filled with the blood of his ministers, and what little power he possessed in the state was gone for ever.

Jung Bahādur, backed by his band of brothers and the army, was now the most powerful man in Nepāl. A few of the old Sardārs, however, still tried to make head against him, but without success. On the 2nd of November thirteen more of the Sardārs were put to death, and in December the king fled from the country to Benāres.

The Rānī, who had hoped by means of Jung Bahādur to establish her own power, and to secure the succession to her own children, found herself bitterly disappointed, and was soon obliged to leave the country, and take refuge at Benāres.

In 1847 the king made an attempt to regain his power, and advanced as far as Segowli. Several plots were formed to assassinate Jung Bahādur, but without success; and the only result of them was that the agents were put to death, and the king declared by his conduct to have forfeited his right to the throne. Accordingly, on the 12th of May he was deposed, and the heir-apparent placed on the throne. The king now determined to make one struggle more, and entered the Terai with a small force, but he was attacked and easily taken prisoner.

From this time Jung Bahādur has been the undisputed ruler of the country. The old king is a prisoner in the palace. The present king is kept under the strictest surveillance, and not allowed to exercise any power whatever. The heir-apparent is also kept in a state of obscurity, being never permitted to take a part in any public business, or even to appear at the Durbārs, to which the British Resident is invited. In fact, one may live for years in Nepāl without either seeing or hearing of the king.

The present heir-apparent was born on the 1st of December 1847.

In 1848 an offer was made to the British Resident of eight regiments of Nepalese troops to assist in the war against the Sikhs. This however was declined.

In April 1849 the Rānī of Lahore, the mother of Dhuleep Sing, took refuge in Nepāl.

Jung Bahādur, having got rid of every possible opponent, and having strengthened his position by connecting his family by marriage with every person who had any influence in the country, considered that he was perfectly secure. He therefore, in 1850, proposed to visit England, and started for this purpose with a large retinue on the 15th of January. One of his brothers was left to act as prime minister in his absence. This visit had a most beneficial effect, as Jung Bahādur was accompanied by two of his brothers and several of the influential men of the country, who thus had an opportunity of becoming acquainted with the power and resources of the British. The whole party were much delighted with the welcome they received in England, and they still talk in the warmest terms of admiration of all the wonders they beheld.

On the 6th of February 1851, Jung Bahādur returned to Nepāl, and one of his first proceedings was to revise the criminal code of the country. Mutilation, which used to be inflicted as a punishment for many crimes, was abolished, and capital punishment was restricted to cases of murder and high treason. Regulations and restrictions were made for Satī, and many other reforms introduced. In short, whatever may be said of the way in which Jung Bahādur obtained power, there is no doubt that he has always exercised it for the good of the country, and he is undoubtedly the greatest benefactor that Nepāl has ever possessed.

Shortly after his return, his enemies once more began to conspire against Jung Bahādur, and they were supported by some of the most orthodox and conservative of the nobles, who wished to make out that by his visit to England he had lost caste, and was unfit to hold the post of prime minister. Among the conspirators were the king's brother, one of Jung Bahādur's own brothers, and his cousin. These were arrested, and only saved from decapitation or mutilation by the British Government consenting to retain them as prisoners at Allahabad, where they were confined for several years. On some of the minor conspirators public degradation from caste was inflicted, a most disgusting ceremony.

From this time till 1854, all went on quietly in the country, with the exception of two more attempts to get rid of Jung Bahādur, in November 1852 and June 1853.

In 1853 a treaty for the extradition of criminals was proposed by the British Government, but it was not ratified till the 23rd of February 1855.

In 1853 the conspirators imprisoned at Allahabad were released, at the request of the Nepalese Government, and allowed to return to their country, where, however, they were kept under surveillance. Jung's brother was made governor of Pālpa and Butwal, a district of the Terai, to the westward; he died in 1873. The king's brother, who seems to be tainted with hereditary insanity, became a fakīr, and may still (1875) be seen wandering about and bathing at the various holy places, in all the odour (and filth) of sanctity.

In March 1855 proposals were made for the admission of a scientific expedition into Nepāl, under the Schlagintweits, but Jung Bahādur steadily refused to hear of such a thing.

In 1854 the Nepalese began to have disputes with the Tibetans, originating in the ill-treatment experienced by the embassy to China, which used to take tribute and presents every fifth year to the emperor. On the last occasion of the embassy passing through Tibet, it was plundered of merchandise and presents, and some of the officials were insulted. Great preparations were made by the Nepalese for this war for a whole year. Stores were collected, and coolies employed in carrying guns, ammunition, and food, to the frontier, and large bodies of troops were raised.

The war was carried on with varying success for nearly two years. The Nepalese experienced great difficulty in conveying their guns and stores over the mountains, and the troops suffered greatly from the severe cold and scarcity of food. To alleviate the latter, Jung Bahādur is said to have discovered, and got the Rāj Gurū officially to corroborate the fact, that Yāks were not *oxen* but *deer*, and hence that they could be used as food by the orthodox Hindus!

Indeed, the obstacles met with were so great, that, though the Bhotias and Tibetans could not resist them in the open field, still the Nepalese were unable to penetrate beyond Jūnga, and the Kerong and Kutti passes. The difficulties to be encountered, had they advanced farther, would have increased at every footstep, and it may be doubted if they would ever have succeeded in entering Tibet.

In November 1855, news reached Kāṭhmānḍū that Kuttī had been surprised and retaken by the Bhotiyas, and that Jūnga and Kerong were also surrounded by large bodies of troops. Reinforcements were at once hurried up; Kuttī was retaken, and after some severe fighting Jūnga and Kerong were relieved. The relieving force at Jūnga, however, was besieged for twenty-nine days, and the troops suffered greatly from cold and want of food.

The Tibetans now began to find that they could not contend successfully with the Nepalese, and proposals for peace were made. The negotiations, however, lasted for months, as frequent references had to be made to the Chinese authorities at Lhāsā. In the meantime six fresh regiments were being raised at Kāṭhmānḍū, a war-tax was about to be levied on all officials, above the rank of Jamadār, of one-third of the produce of their land, and every preparation was made for pushing on the war in the next season. Fortunately, however, terms were agreed on, and a treaty of peace was signed on the 25th of March 1856. The main points of it were, that Tibet should pay 10,000 rupees (£1000) annually, on condition of the Nepalese evacuating the Tibetan territory which they had occupied; that the import duties on goods from Nepāl should be remitted; and that a Gorkha official should be allowed to reside at Lhāsā, to protect the interests of Nepalese traders. Several other minor points, such as exchange of prisoners, pardon for Tibetan subjects who had assisted the Nepalese, etc., were provided for. Thus ended the war with Tibet, much to the satisfaction of the Nepalese, upon whose resources the supporting of such a huge expedition was a burden that could not much longer have been endured.

On the 1st of August 1856, Jung Bahādur resigned the post of prime minister in favour of his brother Bam Bahādur, and he himself was created Mahārāja, with sovereignty over the two provinces of Kāskī and Lamjung, and with power to act as adviser to the king and prime minister.

At the end of this year Mr Schlagintweit was permitted to visit the country, and to take a few observations, such as could be taken within the narrow limits assigned to Europeans.

In the beginning of 1857 there was an uneasy feeling in the Nepalese army, which at one time threatened to produce serious consequences, but fortunately the disturbances were put down without bloodshed.

In June intelligence was received of the mutiny of the native army in Hindustān, and the Durbār at once offered to send troops to the assistance of the British. On the 15th of June two regiments started, and three more were to follow at once. Unfortunately, however, the measures adopted by the Resident, General G. Ramsay, were not approved of by the Governor-general, and the troops were recalled. Had they gone on, it is probable that the massacre at Cawnpore would never have occurred.

On the 26th of June, however, a telegram was received by the Resident, instructing him to accept the offer of troops, and 3000 men started on the 2nd of July, while 1000 more followed on the 13th and 14th of August.

At the end of June Jung Bahādur resumed the offices of prime minister and commander-in-chief, and shortly afterwards offers were made of more troops to assist the British; but it was not till the 10th of December that Jung Bahādur set out himself with an army of 8000 men. This force was joined by Colonel MacGregor, as military commissioner, and assisted in the campaign of 1857 and 1858 against the rebels.

Early in 1858 numbers of fugitive rebels took refuge in the Nepalese Terai; and as there were but few troops in that part of the country, they remained there almost unmolested. Amongst those who came subsequently, were the Begum of Lucknow and her son, Brijis Kadr, the infamous Nānā Sāhib, Bālā Rāo, Mammū Khān, Benī Mādho, and about fifty more of the principal leaders of the rebellion. The rebels suffered greatly in the Terai from sickness and want of provisions; and in September the Nānā himself was said to have fallen a victim to malarious fever. This, however, is doubtful. The fact seems to have been, that the Nepalese temporised with the rebels till they had got all the jewels and money they could out of them, in the meantime throwing every possible obstacle in the way of attempts on the part of the British to arrest them. At last, at the end of 1859, the Nepalese organized an expedition, and, in concert with the British troops, swept the remainder of the mutineers out of the Terai.

In February 1860, the Nānā's wives took refuge in Nepāl, where they still reside in a house close to Thāpatālī. There are not wanting those who say that the Nānā himself is still living in the interior of Nepāl; and as far as the British Resident's power of obtaining intelligence goes, he might be within twenty miles of the capital any day, without his ever being heard of. The Begam of Lucknow and her son also took refuge in the country, and still (1875) reside there in a house not far from Thāpatalī.

The strength of the auxiliary force supplied by the Nepalese in the campaign of 1857-58 was upwards of 8000 fighting men, with more than 500 artillerymen, and 24 guns, and of course a number of followers. All these, as well as the 4000 men of the earlier expedition, were fed and paid by the British from the day of their leaving Kāṭhmāṇḍū.

In addition to the outlay thus incurred, all the troops employed received batta, and a large portion of the Terai was made over to Nepāl. This ground contains valuable sāl forests, and yields a revenue of several lakhs of rupees yearly. Besides this, General Jung Bahādur was created a G. C. B., an honour of which he is not a little proud.

There is no doubt that it was entirely owing to the personal influence of Sir Jung Bahādur that troops were sent to assist at all; and had it not been for his representations of the power and resources of the British, it may be doubted whether the Nepalese would not have held aloof from the struggle, or, more probably, have been induced to side with the rebels. Now, however, all parties see the wisdom of the course adopted, and Sir Jung Bahādur's position has no doubt been rendered more secure by the benefits which the country has derived from his policy.

From the conclusion of the expedition against the remnants of the mutineers up to the present time, there is but little that is worth chronicling.

Some alterations have been made in the treaties for the extradition of criminals; but all efforts to induce the

Nepalese to relax their jealous rules regarding the exclusion of foreigners have proved fruitless, and the country, except for fifteen miles around the capital, is as much a *terra incognita* as it was when Colonel Kirkpatrick visited it nearly a hundred years ago.

In 1873-74 there were some disputes with Tibet, which it was at one time feared might lead to another war. For the present, however, all danger of this seems to have passed away.

In 1873 Sir Jung Bahādur was created a G.C.S.I.; and at the same time received from the Emperor of China the title and insignia of Thong-lin-pim-ma-ko-kāng-vāng-syān.

In 1874 he proposed to revisit England with several of his brothers, sons, and nephews, and he had got as far on the way as Bombay, when he met with an accident, which put a stop to the intended journey.

On 8th of August 1875, a son was born to the Crown Prince, the mother being one of Sir Jung's daughters. A son had been born four years before this, but he was a sickly child and died within a month of his birth.

CHAPTER V.

Remarks on the aspect of political matters in Nepāl at the present time. Sir Jung Bahādur's influence. His numerous relatives. Prospect of the country being thrown open to Europeans. Trade. Character of the Nepalese. Position of the Resident and other Europeans in Nepāl. Means of obtaining information regarding the country. Amusements and employments of young men of the upper classes. Concluding general remarks on the country and its climate.

HAVING now described the Valley of Nepāl, and given a brief sketch of its people and its history, it only remains for me to add a few remarks on the probable future of the country, the general condition of the people, the prospects of trade, and the social intercourse existing between the Nepalese and Europeans. To treat of all these subjects fully would increase the bulk of this introduction to an unreasonable extent; I shall therefore be as succinct as possible.

As long as Sir Jung Bahādur retains his present influence in the country, it is extremely unlikely that there will be any change in the relations existing between the British and Nepalese. He has obtained a most astonishing hold upon the country. His word is law, and his power seems unlimited. Owing to the intermarriages between his numerous relatives and all ranks of the upper classes, his family interests are interwoven with those of almost every other family, from that of the king down to the lowest officials.

5—2

The Heir Apparent to the throne is married to three of his daughters; the second son of the king to a daughter and niece; his eldest son married a daughter of the king, and has a boy of ten years of age; the nephew of the king has married a daughter; and so on through all grades of the higher classes. As Sir Jung Bahādur has had upwards of a hundred children, the opportunities for increasing his connexions have been tolerably extensive. Besides his own children merely, the immense nùmber of his nephews and nieces must also be remembered.

Great though his power is, there are still some matters in which Sir Jung Bahādur dares not interfere with the customs and prejudices of the people. Thus, though he has restricted Satī, still he seems unable to abolish the custom entirely, as the priests, who are a most influential body, are of course strongly opposed to such a course. And as regards throwing open the country to Europeans, I believe that he himself would not be unwilling to do so; but the measure would be so unpopular among all grades of the inhabitants, that to attempt it might endanger his position, if not his life. Bhīmasena's unfortunate fate is often ascribed to the fact of his having been a party to the admission of a European Resident into the country; and the Nepalese have a proverb somewhat to the effect that "with the merchant comes the musket, and with the Bible comes the bayonet!" Sir Jung Bahādur is now advanced in years, being about sixty. What may happen in the event of his becoming frail, or dying suddenly, it is difficult to anticipate. Most probably there will be a succession of struggles for power, accompanied with much bloodshed, amongst his relatives; such in fact as usually occurs when "an Amurath an Amurath succeeds." Some of the officials, who have grown gray in the service of the State without obtaining any promotion, and who have seen themselves passed over by children and favourites, are by no means well pleased or contented; and some of these might be prepared to follow any influential leader; but it is difficult to conceive where such a one is to be found outside of Sir Jung Bahādur's own family.

As regards trade, I am aware that it is very generally believed that there is a great field for European enterprise in Nepāl, and through it with Tibet. I suspect, however, that this is an erroneous idea. The people are poor, and have few wants that are not supplied by their own country. The export trade from Nepāl is very small, and it is difficult to imagine that it could be much increased, as the country is a poor, rugged, mountainous land, just producing enough for the support of its population. The imports consist chiefly of cloth, and a few European articles used by the highest classes. The lower orders infinitely prefer their home-made cloth, both cotton and woollen, which is far more lasting than that which is imported.

One or two Europeans, who have been employed as tutors by Sir Jung Bahādur, have tried to develope trade; but beyond exporting musk, and dealing in a few muslins, etc. for the families of the higher classes, they were quite unsuccessful.

The Nepalese, too, are a most penurious and avaricious people. They take every possible advantage of a foreign trader, and unhesitatingly break any bargain, if they think they can profit by so doing. They must not be judged by the wasteful extravagance that is displayed by the few officials who visit Calcutta and the plains of India. These make a great display for a few months, out of a mere spirit of ostentation; and these very people, when they return to their own country, are the most penurious and miserly in their habits.

As long as the roads between British India and Nepāl, and between Nepāl and Tibet, remain as they are at present, any trade with the last-named country I conceive to be impracticable; and no change will be made, as long as Nepāl is held by the Gorkhas. If the British are prepared to force a commercial intercourse with Nepāl and Tibet, they must first annex Nepāl. Of course this could be easily done, if a few millions of money, and the lives of some thousands of soldiers, were ready to be expended; but I doubt if the game would be worth the candle.

The population of Nepāl, as I have already said, is but a poor one. Some parts of the country, such as the valley around the capital, are densely, too densely, peopled; but most of the country, so far as we are aware, consists of rocky ranges of hills, and narrow, unhealthy valleys, where the people can barely earn enough to feed and clothe themselves in the poorest manner. The Terai is the most valuable part of the country, and that, in case of hostilities, the British could seize and hold with the greatest ease, thereby utterly ruining Nepāl. Though poor, the people in general are contented. They have few taxes to pay, and their customs and prejudices are not interfered with. Justice is fairly administered, and the "law's delays" are by no means so great as in more civilized regions. There are no legal harpies to foment litigation, no municipal corporations, no road-funds, no educational taxes, nor any of the thousand and one innovations that so exasperate the subjects of the British in India. "Dastūr," the mighty deity of the East, reigns paramount. Each family has a scrap of ground, for which they usually pay the good old established rent of half the produce. They cultivate this, and earn enough to feed themselves, to provide their simple clothing, and to leave a trifle for expenditure on the numerous high-days and holidays, which take up, perhaps, a third of their time. Beyond these they have no wants, and are contented, and enjoy life in their own way. "Such are natural philosophers," we may say with Touchstone. Foolish ones, perhaps; and no doubt their successors might be raised in the scale of humanity,—at the cost of infinite suffering to the present generation. Whether we have a right to force our commerce and civilization upon people who do not want them; whether the people would really be benefited by them; and whether the means we should adopt for the purpose are the most likely to be successful; are questions that I leave for political economists to decide.

The position of the Resident in Nepāl is a somewhat peculiar one. It differs from similarly named appointments in the protected States of India in this, that in Nepāl the Resident has nothing whatever to do with the government of the country. In fact, he merely acts as consul, in the same way as the British Consul at any European court. The Nepalese are particularly proud of their independence, and most jealous of any interference with their domestic policy.

Social intercourse there is none. The Prime Minister visits the Residency ceremonially, twice a year, and the Resident returns the visits in like manner. Besides these visits, the Resident and Minister may meet a few times in the year, when any especially important business occurs; or on the occasion of a marriage in the royal family the Resident may be invited to look on at the procession; but this is all the intercourse that takes place.

There is a guard of Nepalese soldiers on the road leading to the Residency, and no Gorkha can enter the limits of the Residency without permission from Sir Jung Bahādur, and without being accompanied by the Vakīl.

Whenever a European goes out walking, he is followed by a Nepalese soldier from the guard; and I believe a daily report is made of everything that occurs at the Residency.

Such being the state of affairs, it can be easily understood how difficult it is for the Resident, or any European, to obtain information on any subject beyond what actually comes under his own observation. Long ago it used to be the custom to employ and pay what may be called spies,—"secret intelligence department" was the polite phrase,—and much money was expended in this way. It turned out, however, that when the Resident gave fifty rupees, the Durbār gave a hundred; and of course the information obtained was most valuable! One unfortunate man, who was employed to explore the country, disappeared; and long afterwards, when a change of ministry had taken place, it was ascertained that the poor fellow had been suspected, and in consequence murdered. In extradition cases, unless the Nepalese are utterly indifferent in the matter, it is almost impossible to obtain the arrest of a criminal. In short, Nepāl is the Alsatia of Northern India, and the Nepalese pride themselves on never surrendering a fugitive, provided, that is, that he is a Brāhman, or likely to be useful to them in any way.

Personally, the higher classes are overpoweringly polite and affable to European officials, or to any one who is likely to be able to benefit them. Otherwise their bearing is rude and insolent in the highest degree. In fact, they seem to think rudeness a proof of manly independence. They are always ready to ask for favours, either public or private; but when any return is expected, the less that is looked for from them the better. A royal Duke, or a Governor-general, or even a Resident, will meet with a great show of friendliness when he goes on a hunting expedition in the Terai; but in the valley of Nepāl a sportsman generally finds infinite pains taken to spoil his sport.

Owing to our mistaken policy of always giving way to their demands, and lavishly bestowing honours and titles, I believe that the younger and more foolish portion of the community firmly believe that the British are afraid of them, and that their army is quite a match for any force that could be brought against it. It is strange that such should be the case, as many of these young men have lived for years at Calcutta, and have been present at various camps of exercise; but the Gorkhas are so arrogant and self-conceited, that I believe nothing will ever convince them of their inferiority, till they meet with some severe disaster. It is most unfortunate that Sir Jung Bahādur's project of visiting England in 1875 was not carried out, as it would have been highly beneficial to the conceited young gentlemen who would have accompanied him.

How the Gorkhas occupy and amuse themselves is as yet an unfathomed mystery to me. They have no business, except playing at soldiering; they have no out-of-door games; they never shoot, except when they go to the Terai; and they have no literature to occupy them in their houses. In short, they seem to have nothing to fill up their leisure hours, which must be numerous; and in consequence they are given up to gossipping, gambling, and debauchery of all sorts. Attempts have been made at various times by their tutors to get the young men to play at cricket and other games, but such amusements are thought degrading. Even to walk is beneath their dignity, and when moving about in their own houses and grounds, they are generally carried pick-a-back by a slave or attendant. I have often seen boys of from eight to fifteen years of age thus riding to their tutor's house of a morning, a distance of, perhaps, two hundred yards.

I may be thought harsh in my statements regarding the Nepalese. All I can say is, they are true; and I see no good purpose to be served by praising and saying fine things of people who do not deserve it. Of course I do not say that there are no exceptions. Sir Jung Bahādur himself is always most kind and courteous in his demeanour, and whatever may be his failings, he always bears himself as a gentleman. He is undoubtedly also a most acute and talented man, and it would be well for Nepāl, if there were a few more amongst the rising generation fit to be compared to him. Some of the young men also are pleasant and gentlemanly in their manners, but I am afraid that what I have previously stated is true with regard to most of them.

As for the country of Nepāl, it would take the pen of a Ruskin and the pencil of a Turner or a Claude to do justice to its beauties. The road through the Terai, and the Noākot valley, are most lovely; and the views of the snowy range obtainable in the cold season from the Valley, and from the hills on the northern side, are, I believe, unrivalled for extent and magnificence. The climate is delicious. In winter the air is clear and bracing, and there are frequently hoar-frost and ice in the mornings. I have seen the thermometer as low as 20^{0}, when exposed in the open air at night. The summer is not very hot, and the thermometer indoors, with all the windows open, seldom ranges above 80^{0}. The average mean temperature for the year is 60^{0}, and the average rainfall 60 inches. What a magnificent sanatorium the Valley would be for the inhabitants of Calcutta!

HISTORY OF NEPĀL.

CHAPTER I.

Mythological period of the history, extending through the Satya, Trētā, and Dwāpar Yugas or ages. It contains numerous curious legends regarding the temples, towns and holy places of the country.

THE valley on the southern side of the snowy range, which is within Sumēru (the Himālaya), which was created by Īshwar (who emanated from the great Īshwar, the first Buddh, who in his turn sprang from Sachchit Buddh, who was the first of all), was formerly known as Nāg Hrad, *i.e.*, the tank of the serpent.

In Satya Yuga, Bipaswī Buddh came from a city known by the name of Bandhumatī; and, having taken up his abode on the mountain to the west of Nāg Hrad, sowed a lotus-seed in the tank, on the day of the full moon in the month of Chait. Having named the mountain on which he dwelt, Jāt Mātrochcha[1], he returned to his former abode, leaving on the spot his disciples, to whom he foretold future events. In honour of this circumstance, a Mēlā (or fair) is held on the mountain on the day of the full moon in the month of Chait.

In the same Yuga, the lotus-seed that had been

[1] Now called Nāgārjun.

sown brought forth a lotus-flower, in the middle of which Swayambhū (who had come from Aknisht Bhuban) appeared in the form of light, on the day of the full moon in Āswin. Having heard of this, Sikhi Buddh came from Arunpurī, and after much meditation and observation of the Swayambhū-light from a mountain, he uttered prophecies, and then incorporated himself with the light on the Mēsh Sankrānti day[1]. From this time the mountain was called Dhyānochcha[2], and a Mēlā is held there on the anniversary of that day.

After this, in the Trētā Yuga, Biswa-bhū-buddh came from a country called Anūpam, and having seen the Swayambhū Buddh from a mountain, and made an offering of a lākh of flowers, which had fallen from the trees on the mountain, to Swayambhū, he declared that the mountain should in future be called Phūlochcha[3]. Then, having shown to his disciples the place through which the water of the Nāg Hrad should be made to run out, he returned to his former abode.

After this, in the same Trētā Yuga, Bōdhisatwa Manjūsrī came from Mahāchīn (China), and stayed on Mahāmandap[4] for three nights, and saw the Swayambhū-light. He then thought of cutting a passage through the mountains to drain the Nāg Hrad. For this purpose he went to the low hills on the southern side, and placed his two goddesses, named Bardā and Mokshadā, one on Phūlochcha and the other on Dhyānochcha, himself remaining in the middle. He then cut through the mountain, which he called Kotwāl[5], and let the

[1] The day on which the Sun enters Aries.

[2] Now called Champadēvī, east of Chandragiri and south of Kaṭhmāṇḍū.

[3] Now called Phūlchōk, above Godavari, 9720 feet high.

[4] A small hill one mile east of Bhātgāon, also called Manjūsrī Thān, because there is a chaitya there dedicated to Manjūsrī.

[5] Or Kotwāldār, the place where the Bāgmatī passes out of the valley.

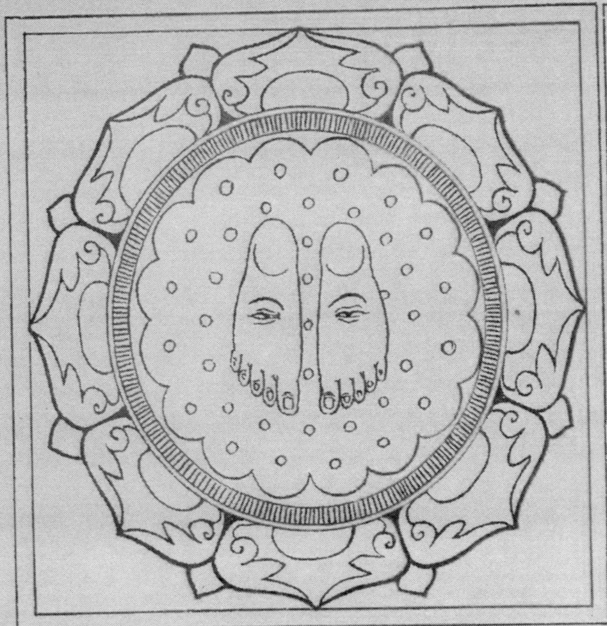

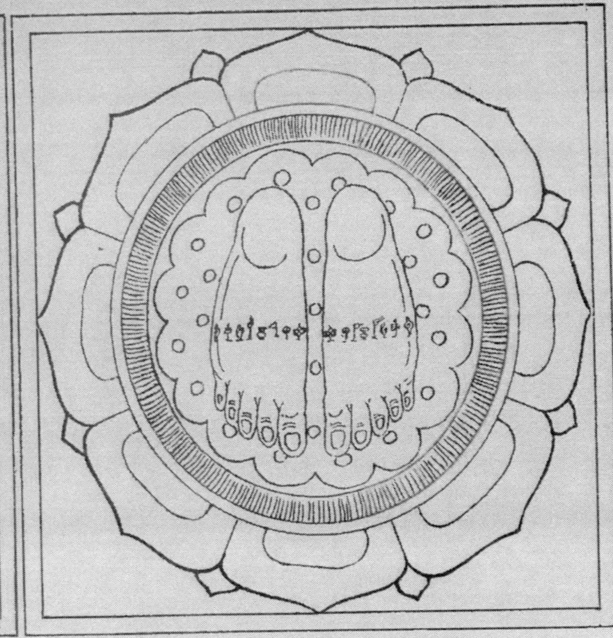

(Plate VII) MANJUSRĪ PĀDUKĀ BAUDDHA PĀDUKĀ. (p. 78.)

water run out. As the water escaped, several Nāgs and other animals living in it went out, but he persuaded Karkōtak, king of the Nāgs, to remain; and on the Mēsh Sankrānti day, having pointed out to him a large tank to live in[1], he gave him power over all the wealth of the valley.

He then saw Swayambhū, in the form of Biswarūpa, on the day of the full moon in Kārtik. He also discovered Guhjēswarī, and saw her in the form of Biswarūpa, on the night of the 9th of Pūs Krishn. He then became absorbed in meditation, and worshipped Swayambhū in the centre of the lotus-flower, whose root was at Guhjēswarī[2]. He next made the hill Padma[3], from which place to Guhjēswarī he built a town called Manju Pattan. He planted trees near Guhjēswarī, and peopled the town with those of his disciples who wished to live as Grihasths, or householders. To those of them who wished to live as Bhikshūs, or religious mendicants, he allotted a bihār[4]. He then installed a king, by name Dharmākar, and himself returned to China.

Sometime after this, some disciples of Manjūsrī built the Manjūsrī Chaitya, or Buddhist mound, near Swayambhū[5], to worship Manjūsrī in connection with Swayambhū. This took place on the 5th of Māgh Sudi. Therefore[6], from that time, the tank appointed as the dwelling-place of the Nāg was called Tau-dahān (or

[1] The tank called Taudāh, of which more hereafter.

[2] About a quarter of a mile above Pashupati temple, on the left bank of the Bāgmatī, and on the north of the Pashupati wood.

[3] The same as Swayambhū hill.

[4] A square of houses, with a shrine inside, used in former times as a monastery, but nowadays occupied by Bānras and their families.

[5] This temple is on the western peak of Swayambhū hill.

[6] There seems to be some confusion here in the MS.

Taudāh), *i.e.*, the large tank, and people bathe there on the Mēsh Sankrānti, and worship Swayambhū Chaitya[1] on the day of the full moon in Kārtik, when also a Mēlā is held. A great ceremony also takes place at Guhjēswarī on the 9th of Aghan, on which day the goddess revealed herself; and likewise at Manjūsrī Chaitya on Srī-panchamī, or the 5th of Māgh Sudi, the anniversary of its building.

After this, in the same Trētā Yuga, Krakuchhand Buddh came from Kshēmāvatī, and saw Guhjēswarī in the form of the Swayambhū-light, which led him to think of consecrating a mountain, after the example of the other Buddhs, who had formerly visited the place. With this intention he ascended the high mountain to the north, and fixed his abode there. He then explained the merits of Swayambhū and Guhjēswarī to his followers, and instructed them in the ways and doctrines of Grihasths and Bhikshūs. He then permitted seven hundred of his disciples, of the Brāhman caste of Gundhwaj and the Chhētrī caste of Abhayandad, to live as Bhikshūs; but finding no water on the mountain, with which to perform the Abhishēk[2] on them, he called on Swayambhū and Guhjēswarī, and said, "Let water run out of this mountain." At the same time he thrust his thumb into the mountain, and made a hole, through which Gangā Dēvī appeared in corporeal form, and offered Argh[3] to the Buddh; and then, changing

[1] A *chaitya* is a Buddhist temple; in its primitive form, a mere mound of earth, like a barrow; afterwards built of brick or stone in various shapes, with images, etc., as shown in the plate.

[2] A person is bathed; then mantras are recited, and holy-water (from the Ganges, or from different *tīrthas* mixed) is sprinkled upon him.

[3] Water is taken in the sacrificial vessel called *arghā*, and rice, flour and powdered sandalwood are put into the water, which is then poured at the feet of an image or on a shrine.

Maclure & Macdonald Lith^rs London

(Plate VIII) SWAYAMBHU HILL (p. 80)

her form into water, ran out of the mountain on the Mōsh Sankrānti day, and became known as Bāgmatī. With this water Krakuchhand performed Abhishēk. Half the hair cut from his disciples' heads on the mountain he buried under a mound, and the other half he threw up into the air. Wherever the hair fell, a stream was formed, which was called Kēsāvatī, from *kēs* (hair)[1]. Hence, on the Mēsh Sankrānti day, people go to this mountain to bathe in the river, because of its sanctity in having been brought forth by the command of Krakuchhand; whence also the place was named Bāgdwār. People also visit the hair-chaitya, and bathe at the source of the Kēsāvatī river on the same day. After this, Krakuchhand taught the four castes (*i.e.* Hindūs) the way of living as Grihasths and Bhikshus, worshipping Swayambhū and Guhjēswarī. Then naming the mountain Phūlochcha, he went to Guhjēswarī, and saw in the wood planted by Manjusrī the three gods Brahmā, Vishnu, and Mahēswara (Siva), in the form of deer. He pointed these out to his disciples as worshippers of Swayambhū and Guhjēswarī and protectors of the people. He said also that they had come as prophesied by Padma-pāni-Bōdhisatwa-Lokēswara, to whom they had given their promise to that effect, and had foretold that, in Kali Yuga, Umēswar Pashupati would be a very celebrated name. He then called the place Mrigasthalī, after the three deities who appeared in the form of deer[2]. He then permitted those of his disciples who wished to live as Grihasths to inhabit Manju Pattan; and to those who wished to live as Bhikshus he allotted bihārs and

[1] Kēsāvatī is another name for the Vishnumatī, which is formed by the junction of several streams at the N.W. corner of the valley.

[2] The wood on the left bank of the Bāgmatī, opposite Pashupati temples.

temples. Having done all this, he returned to his former abode.

After this, Mahēswara, in the shape of a deer, disclosed himself in the form of light, which pervaded the seven firmaments above Bhūlōk (the earth) and also the seven firmaments below Rasātal (Hades). On seeing this, Brahmā went upwards to see how far the light extended, and Vishnu went downwards for the same purpose. The place whence Vishnu departed is called Vishnu-Gupt, and the Mahādēva was called Pashupati. From there being many Slēshmāntak (*Lapsi*) trees, the forest was called Slēshmāntak-ban. Some inspired devotees say that this *ban* was called Slēshmāntak because Mahādēva, having come from Badrī Kedār, showed himself in it, at the time when three hundred years of the Trētā Yuga remained to be completed. Brahmā and Vishnu, having returned from their journeys to see how far the light of Mahādēva extended, met at the place where Sēsh Nārāyana[1] is; and on comparing notes, Vishnu said that he was not able to find the limit to which the light extended, whilst Brahmā declared that he had gone beyond it. Vishnu then called for witnesses, and Brahmā produced Kāmdhēnu (the celestial cow), who, on being asked to declare the truth, corroborated Brahmā's assertion with her mouth, whilst she shook her tail by way of denying it. Vishnu then, seeing what was the truth, uttered a curse on Brahmā, to the effect that his image should nowhere be worshipped, and on Kāmdhēnu, that her mouth should be impure, but her tail sacred. Having done this, he remained in that place with the Sēsh and cow, but Brahmā disappeared.

Dharmākar Rājā, who was made king by Manjusrī,

[1] A place near Phurphing, a village on the hill south of Kāṭhmāṇḍū.

having no issue, appointed as his successor Dharmapāl, who had come with Krakuchhand and resided in Manju Pattan. He then died, having obtained salvation through the worship of Swayambhū. In the same manner many other persons came, and having gone through a course of austerities discovered holy places and deities.

In the reign of Rājā Sudhanwā, a descendant of Rājā Dharmapāl, the Trōtā Yuga ended, one-fourth part of sin having thus displaced the same quantity of virtue. He was displeased with his palace in Manju Pattan, and therefore changed his residence to a new one, built in a town which he founded on the banks of the river Ikshumatī[1], and named Sānkāsyā-nagarī. From this place he went to Janakpūr, where feats of strength were to be performed by Rājās for the hand of Sītā, the daughter of Rājā Janak. Janak, for some reason which is not known, put Sudhanwā to death, and sent his own brother Kusdhwaj to reign in his stead at Sānkāsyā. Kusdhwaj's descendants ruled the country for some years, after which the dynasty became extinct.

In the Dwāpar Yuga, Kanak Muni Buddh came from the city of Sobhāvatī, and, after visiting the shrines of Swayambhū and Guhjēswarī, ascended into heaven, where he caused Indra, the king of the gods, to practise virtue (*dharm*), and then returned to his bihār. After him Kāsyapa Buddh came from Benāres, and, after visiting the shrines of Swayambhū and Guhjēswarī, preached to the people. Then he proceeded to the Gaur country (Bengāl), the king of which, by name Prachand Dēva, gave him a Pindpātra (sacrificial vessel). The Buddh then directed Prachand Dēva to go to Swayambhū

[1] Now called Tukhucha, a small stream to the east of the British Residency. It runs into the Bāgmatī between Thāpatali and Kāṭhmāṇḍū.

Chhētra (Nepāl), and become the disciple of Gunākar Bhikshu, a follower of Manjusrī. There he was to live a life of celibacy and beggary, till he had read all the Shāstras, on the completion of which task he was to forsake that mode of life, become a teacher, and live for ever. Having given these directions, the Buddh returned to his abode, and Prachand Dēva Rājā obeyed his instructions, abdicated in favour of his son Shakti Dēva, went to Nepāl, and lived as a beggar, under the name of Sāntikar. In due course he became an Āchārya (teacher), and changed his name to Sānt-srī. He then thought that the Kali Yuga, in which mankind would be utterly sinful, was approaching. He therefore covered the Swayambhū light with a stone, and built a chaitya and temple over it. He then built five rooms named Basupūr, Agnipūr, Bāyupūr, Nāgpūr, and Sāntipūr[1], in the last of which he lived, absorbed in devout meditation.

Once upon a time a certain Pandit, of Vikram Sīl Bihār in Benāres, named Dharma Srī Mitra, was reciting some moral traditions from a book, when he came to the mantra of twelve letters, which he could not explain. Ascribing this inability to his not having visited Manjusrī, he determined to go to see him, and for this purpose went to Swayambhū. Manjusrī, having become aware of this through meditation, also went to Nepāl, and began to plough a field, having yoked for that purpose a lion and a sārdūl (*griffin*). Seeing this strange sight, Dharma Srī Mitra went up to Manjusrī, and asked the way to China. Manjusrī replied that it was too late that day to commence his journey, and took him

[1] These rooms are said still to exist round the Swayambhū temple, and a bhikshu lives in one of them. In Sāntipūr it is said that there is a passage leading to a subterranean room under the mound, in which Sāntikar died.

to his house, where he instantly caused a good bihār to spring up, in which he lodged his guest. During the night Dharma Srī Mitra overheard some conversation between Manjusrī and his wife, which made known to him the disguised Manjusrī, and he slept at the threshold of his room. In the morning Manjusrī made him his disciple, and told him the meaning of the mantra. The bihār, in which he lodged, he called Vikram Sīl Bihār, and the field which he was ploughing, when met by Dharma Srī Mitra, he called Sāwā Bhūmī; and to this day this is the field in which rice is planted before all the other fields in the valley[1].

Hearing that there was no Rājā in this country, a descendant of Rājā Sakti Dēva came from Gaur. One of his descendants, Gunkāmdēva, having committed incest, the gods were displeased, and sent a drought and famine on the country. He then, having been initiated in the mysteries by Sāntikar Āchārya, who lived concealed in the Sāntipūr of Swayambhū, brought the nine Nāgs under his control, and caused them to give a plentiful rain. When he was performing the ceremonies to summon the Nāgs, Karkōtak, who lived in the Nāg-dāh, did not come, but the other eight did. Upon this Sāntikar Āchārya gave Gunkāmdēva some *dūb*-grass and *kund*-flowers, through the virtue of which he jumped into the tank, and catching hold of Karkōtak, made him a prisoner. On his way home he became tired, and sat down to rest at the foot of the Swayambhū mount. This place is still marked by an image of Karkōtak, at the south-east corner of the mount,

[1] Vikram Sīl Bihār is now Thambāhil (vulgarly Thamēl), a suburb on the north side of Kāṭhmāṇḍū. Sāwā Bhūmī is now called Bhagwān's Khēt, a field about a quarter of a mile south-west of the Residency. It belongs to the priests of Thamel and is the first spot planted with rice every year.

called Nāgsilā[1]. The road by which he brought the Nāg was called Nāgbātā. When Gunkāmdēva brought Karkōtak before Sāntikar Āchārya, his spiritual guide, all the Nāgs worshipped him, and they each gave him a likeness of themselves, drawn with their own blood, and declared that, whenever there was a drought hereafter, plentiful rain would fall as soon as these pictures were worshipped[2].

During the reign of Sinha Kētu, a descendant of Gunkāmdēva, there was a virtuous merchant by name Sinhal. On a certain occasion he took five hundred Baniyas and proceeded northwards[3] to Sinhal Dwīp (Ceylon). On the way they saw a golden chaitya, and, in spite of Sinhal's warning, the Baniyas took away gold from it. After crossing with great difficulty the arm of the ocean, in the passage of which the power of Sinhal alone saved them, they were met by five hundred and one Rākshasīs (ogresses), who, in the form of lovely damsels, enchanted them, and each took one as a companion. The Lokēswara Āryāvalokitēswara, taking pity on Sinhal, appeared in the wick of his lamp, and told him what these damsels were, and that some day they would devour his followers. He added that, if he doubted him, he should go to Āshaya Kōt, and, if he wanted to be saved, he should go to the sea-shore, where on the fourth day he would meet a horse, which, after making obeisance, he should mount and cross the sea. Sinhal went to Āshaya (or Āyasa) Kōt in the morning, where he saw all sorts of persons who had lost their limbs, which convinced him of the truth of what he

[1] Still known by this name.

[2] These pictures of the Nāgs are still worshipped when there is a drought, and small ones are pasted on the walls of houses.

[3] It ought to be *southwards*.

had been told. He then collected his five hundred companions, and went to the sea-shore, where they mounted the horse Bālāh, which took them across the ocean. Their mistresses the Rākshasīs pursued them, calling them by name. The Baniyas, in spite of the warning of Āryāvalokitōswara, looked back, fell from the horse, and were devoured by their mistresses. Sinhal was the only one who arrived safely at home, followed by his Rākshasī, who remained outside his house, without any notice being taken of her by Sinhal. A rumour regarding a beautiful damsel having reached the ears of the Rājā of Sānkāsyā-nagarī, he sent for her, and kept her in his palace. One day the Rākshasī flew away to the sky, and summoned her sister Rākshasīs, who came and destroyed the Rājā and all his family. Sinhal, having heard of this, went to the Rājā's durbār, and, reciting the mantras of Āryāvalokitēswara, flourished his sword and drove away the Rākshasīs. The people then elected him to be their king, and he ruled for a long time. He pulled down his own house, and built a bihār, and consecrated an image of Bōdhisatwa. In consideration of the Rākshasī, who followed him from Ceylon, having been his mistress, he raised a temple for her worship, and assigned land for its support. He having no issue, the dynasty became extinct on his death. To the bihār which he built he gave the same name that Manjusrī gave to the one which he caused to spring up for Dharma Srī Mitra, viz. Vikram Sīl Bihār.

In the Satya Yuga there was a city named Dīpāvatī (from Dīpankar Buddh, who had an image there), in which lived a virtuous Rājā, whose name was Sarbānand, who was considered to be an incarnation (of Buddh). When visiting Guhjēswarī, he was pleased with the place, and built a durbār and fixed his abode there. This Rājā, being very virtuous, built a bihār adjacent to his palace, and gave it as a residence for bhikshus. He also built a chaitya in front of his palace, and appointed a day for fasting in honour of it. Once upon a time he wished to give presents and alms to beggars, and fixed days for that purpose on the anniversaries of the beginning of the Yugas[1]. At this time there was an old woman who also gave alms, and Dīpankar Buddh appeared in corporeal form and took her alms before those of the Rājā. The Rājā upon this asked him why he preferred to take the old woman's alms first, and he answered that the grain given by her had been collected with much greater labour than the Rājā's gold. This set the Rājā thinking, and seeing a blacksmith working hard with his hammer, so that he was all covered with sweat, he went to work along with him. He remained working here for two months, and brought good luck to his host. The money which he earned he spent in purchasing gifts for the beggars, and fixed the 8th of Sāwan Sukla as the day for distributing them. Dīpankar Buddh again appeared, and, after taking his alms, blessed him, and said that the fame of this meritorious act would last to the end of the world, and that in Kali Yuga salvation would be obtained only through Buddh. The Rājā then placed an image of Dīpankar in his durbār. The bihār which he had built previously to this, in front of which he had made a chaitya, became known by the name of Dīpāvatī; and people celebrate the anniversary of the 8th of Sāwan Sukla by worshipping Buddh[2].

[1] Namely, Dwāpar Yuga on the 3rd of Baisākh sudi; Satya Yuga on the 9th of Kārtik sudi; Trētā Yuga on the full moon of Māgh; and Kali Yuga on the 13th of Bhādon badi.

[2] There is a bihār at Pātan called Dīpāvatī Bihār, where this festival is still celebrated.

After this, many Rājās, such as Manichūr, and many Rishis (ascetics), and many gods and goddesses, such as Mahādōva and Pārvatī, came to practise austerities here. Some discovered holy places; some returned to their former abodes; and some remained and took up their residence here.

The great Rishi, however, from whom Nepāl derives its name, was a devotee named Nē. He performed his devotions at the junction of the Bāgmatī and Kēsāvatī, and, by the blessing of Swayambhū and Bajra Jōginī, he instructed the people in the true path of religion. He also ruled over the country.

Once upon a time, when sixteen thousand years of the Dwāpar Yuga remained, there being no Rājā to rule over the country, the Kirātīs, who dwelt originally to the eastward, but had removed to the city of Suprabhā[1], west of Nepāl, came here and ruled over the country. After a thousand years of their dynasty had elapsed, in the reign of Sankū, a prince named Dharma Datta was born in Kānchī[2]. One day he met a devotee in Kāsī (Benāres), who spoke much about the holiness of this place, saying "that Swayambhū and Guhjēswarī had appeared here in the form of light; that Brahmā and other gods had come to protect and maintain the followers of Manjusrī. Mahādēva appeared in this holy place in the form of a deer. (Everything is contained within him, for the sky is his Lingand the earth his Bīthikā.) By the direction of Buddh he changed his form, and settled down in the form of light called Pashupati. Karkōtak Nāg lived there, and had control over all the wealth of the country. There there were the Bāgmatī, Kēsāvatī, and Rudramatī[3]

[1] Now Thānkōt. [2] Kānchīpūr, or Conjeveram, near Madras.

[3] The Rudramatī is a tributary of the Bāgmatī, between Pashupati and Kāṭhmāṇḍū, now called Dhobiyakhola.

rivers. There also was the Manmatī[1], which was brought forth by Bandēvī, to whom Rājā Manichūr gave the jewel from his head, for cleansing the blood from which the river was produced. There there were the four Kholas (small streams in narrow valleys), Prabhāvatī, Hanumatī, Dānāvatī, and Ikshumatī[2]. There there were the following holy places on the banks of the Bāgmatī, where people obtain salvation; viz., Punya, Sānt, Sankara, Rāja, Manōratha, Nirmala, Nidhi, Gyāna, Chintāmani, Pramōda, Sulakshan, Jaya, and others[3]. There there were Mani Lingēswara, Gokarnēswara, Kīlēswara, Sarbēswara, Gandhēswara, Phanikēswara, Gartēswara, and Vikramēswara[4]. There there were the four Jōginīs; Mani Jōginī, who appeared for Rājā Manichūr; Bajra Jōginī, who appeared for Āryāchārya; Bidyādharī Jōginī, who appeared for Apjasī Pandit; and lastly Hīngū Jōginī[5]. There there were sixty-four lingas, consecrated

[1] Now called Manoharakhola, a tributary of the Bāgmatī, west of Pashupati.

[2] The Prabhāvatī or Nakkukhola runs from Phūlchok south of Pātan and falls into the Bāgmatī above Chaubahāl. The Hanumatī is a rivulet between the Ikshumatī and the Rudramatī. The Dānāvatī is a small western tributary of the Bāgmatī, below the junction of the Vishnumatī. The Ikshumatī is a small stream to the east of the Residency, on the bank of which is a mound with an image of Saraswatī, said to be the only remnant of Sānkāsyā Nagarī.

[3] Punya is near Gokarna, at the junction of a small stream with the Bāgmatī. Sānt lies where a nullah joins the Bāgmatī near Guhjēswarī. Sankara is now called Sankhamūla, north of Pātan on the left bank of the Bāgmatī. Rāja lies on the right bank of the Bāgmatī at the junction of the Rudramatī. Manōratha is on the Vishnumatī near Manāmaijū. Nirmala is on the Vishnumatī near the burning-ghāt opposite Swayambhū. Nidhi is just below the junction of the Vishnumatī with the Bāgmatī. Gyāna is at the junction of the Dānāvatī and Bāgmatī. Chintāmani is a little below Nidhi; Pramōda a little lower down, where the Balkū joins the Bāgmatī from the west. Sulakshan is still lower down, at the junction of another western affluent; and Jaya still lower, at the junction of the Nakkū with the Bāgmatī.

[4] The shrine of Mani Lingēswara is on Manichūr mountain, on the north of the valley. Gokarnēswara is about two miles N.E. of Pashupati, on the Bāgmatī. Kīlēswara is at a place called Chāngūnārāyana. Sarbēswara is in Pātan. Gandhēswara is at Chaubahāl. Phanikēswara is at Phurphing. Gartēswara and Vikramēswara are not known to the translators.

[5] Mani Jōginī's shrine is at Sānkhū; Bajra Jōginī's at Sānkhū and at Phurphing;

by different gods. From this day that place was made as Mahāpītha, because it contains the four most sacred shrines in the world; viz., Swayambhū Chaitya, Guhjōswarī Pītha, Siva Ling Pashupati, and Karbī Smashān[1]. Many years after Nē Muni, a sinner named Birūpāksha went there. Some say that he was a Daitya (demon), some that he was a Brāhman, others that he was a Chhētrī Rājā. The following is his history. Birūpāksha, when twelve years of age, saw it written in his horoscope that he would commit incest with his mother. He was so disgusted at this that he left his home and became a devotee. His mother, however, did the same, and after several years they met, without knowing each other, and the incest was committed. Afterwards Birūpāksha, becoming aware of his sin, went to Siva to enquire how he was to purify himself. Siva told him to drink twelve loads of melted copper. Seeing that he would lose his life by following this advice, he next went to a bhikshū, who gave him a rosary, and told him to recite certain holy names while counting it, and that when the thread of it was worn out he would be pure. Birūpāksha for a time followed this advice, but, finding the occupation very tiresome, he gave it up and went to travel. During his journey, he saw a man cutting down a tree with a needle, and on asking why he did not cut it with a hatchet, the man replied that that would be too laborious a work. This brought him to his senses, and he returned to his rosary, but soon left it again. Then he saw a bird taking water with its bill from a tank full of water, and dropping it into an empty one to fill it. This again brought him

Bidyādharī Jōginī's below Swayambhū; and Hīngū Jōginī's south of Thāpatali and also west of Pātan.

[1] Karbī or Karbīr Smashān is on the Vishnumati, S.W. of Kāṭhmāṇḍū.

to his senses, and he returned to his rosary. Once more, however, he forsook it, but on seeing a man attempting to make a mountain and a plain level with a few handfuls of dust, he returned to his rosary and completed his task. After this he saw an emblem of Siva (the Linga), and saying, 'It was you who advised me to lose my life,' he began to break every emblem of Siva he met with. At last he came to Pashupati, who prayed to Buddh to save him, and through his blessing, and being provided with a head-dress of Buddh, Birūpāksha, instead of breaking, worshipped him[1]. For this reason every emblem of Siva is a little bent to one side, except the one at Pashupati. Then, as Buddhists do not eat when the sun is gone down[2], he requested the sun, whom he caught hold of with one hand, not to set until he had taken his meal; and in this posture he died at Pashupati."

Having heard all these praises of the country from the devotee, Rājā Dharma Datta made over the charge of his city Kānchī to Balkētu, one of his ten sons, and went to the country of Pashupati, with the rest of his sons, and his minister Buddhikshēm. He then prayed to Bāgmatī at the Sundara Tīrtha, who gave him a blessing, by virtue of which he subdued the Kirātī Rājā Sankū, and took possession of the country. He then built a town, extending from Buddha Nīlkantha to Kotwāl, which he named Bisālnagara, and peopled with the four castes (*i.e.* Hindūs). He reigned a thousand years, and with great rites and ceremonies he built the

[1] In commemoration of this, once a year, on the 8th of Kārtik sudi, the image of Pashupati is decorated with a head-dress like that of the images of Buddha, and worshipped.

[2] This is not now the custom in Nepāl, where the Bauddhamārgīs always eat after sunset.

temple of Pashupati, and presented much wealth and many valuable articles to the shrine. He also made a chaitya at the north-west corner of Pashupati, which he named after himself, Dharma Datta Chaitya. He lived a virtuous life, and was blessed with a numerous family and many subjects.

One thousand years after the death of Dharma Datta, an Asur (demon) named Dānāsur, coming to the city of Suprabhā, reigned there a thousand years. Notwithstanding his wife's advice to the contrary, he began to practise austerities on the banks of the Bāgmatī river, with the object of getting possession of the wealth of Indra, the king of the gods. He continued doing this for twelve years, and then Bhakti Basag Tīrtha informed him that for thirty-four years he would have possession of the one-hundredth part of the wealth of Indra. Dānāsur thus, like a thief, stole Indra's wealth; and with the intention of increasing it, he spent none of it in charity, nor did he feed any poor people, but he hoarded it up and buried it in the ground. When Indra sat in his Sudharmā council, and came to know the fate of his wealth, he ordered Karkōtak Nāg to take back his riches, keeping one-fourth for himself, and floating the remaining three-fourths down a river. Karkōtak kept one-fourth in his tank (Taudāh), and floated the other three-fourths down a river, which he created for the purpose, and named Ratnāvatī[1]. By this means the riches were brought into the Bāgmatī. The place where Dānāsur buried his wealth is named Dānāgār[2], and the junction of the Ratnāvatī with the Bāgmatī is

[1] Another name for the Balkū, a right-hand tributary of the Bāgmatī.
[2] The name of Dānāgār is also given to a tributary of the Bāgmatī, which runs past Kīrtīpūr.

named Pramōda Tīrtha, because Dānāsur observed austerities there and gained his object, and Indra prayed there for the restoration of his wealth and also had his desires fulfilled.

One day the wife of Dānāsur, having quarrelled with her husband, bathed in the Bāgmatī, and prayed to Basundharā Dēvī, who, being pleased, caused a daughter to be born to her, who was named Prabhāvatī, and who appeared in the form of a river, springing from a mountain near Phūlchauk, and came to join the Bāgmatī at the place where the wife of the Asur had bathed[1]. The spot is named Jaya Tīrtha, from the wife of Dānāsur having obtained victory (*jaya*) there. Dānāsur, in order to make a pond for his daughter Prabhāvatī to play in, filled up the passage for the water out of the valley at Chaubahār, and the valley became a vast expanse of water. The Gosring[2] and Manichūr mountains were not submerged, on account of their being Swayambhū chaityas.

Formerly, when the valley was a lake, the abode of Nāgs, Manjusrī let out the water, and every animal went out, including Kulik Nāg. This Nāg, seeing the valley now full again, came to live in it. Āryāvalokitēswara-padma-pāni-bōdhisatwa, seeing that this Kulik Nāg was spoiling the memorial of Manjusrī, sent Samantbhadra-bōdhisatwa to make him immovable. He went and sat on the Nāg's back, and became a mountain, called Kīlēswara[3], on which he left a portion of his spirit and then disappeared.

After this, Takshak Nāg, who was also formerly com-

[1] Prabhāvatī is another name for the Nakkū.

[2] Gosring is another name for the hill of Swayambhū.

[3] The hill on which Chāngū Nārāyan stands.

pelled by Manjusrī to leave the valley, became angry, when it was again under water, and began to bite people without any provocation. This sin produced leprosy in his body, and, to expiate his offence against Manjusrī, he came to Nepāl, and began to practise austerities at Gokarn, where the prince Gokarn had obtained salvation. Garuḍ, seeing him, came to catch him, but he, being more powerful than Garuḍ, on account of the austerities he had practised, caught hold of Garuḍ, and kept his head under water. Garuḍ invoked the aid of his master Vishnu, who came, and was going to strike Takshak with his chakra; but in the meantime Āryāvalokitēswara-padma-pāni-bōdhisatwa, seeing that a Nāg observing austerities was being killed, came from Sukhāvatī Bhuvan (heaven) to protect him. Vishnu then took him on his shoulders, and the Lokēswara caused friendship to be established between Garuḍ and Takshak, and put the latter round Garuḍ's neck. Then Garuḍ lifted up Vishnu; and the lion, which had been ridden by the Lokēswara, lifted up Garuḍ, and, flying up into the air, alighted on a mountain, which was named Hari Hari Bāhan[1], where the Lokēswara disappeared. This mountain was in consequence named Chārū, but since then it has been corrupted into Chāngū. This mountain also was not submerged, when the valley was flooded by Dānāsur. Phūlchauk, Dakshin Kālī, and Kachhapāl mountains were also above water; and the light named Pashupati was also not extinguished[2].

Nāgārjunpād had made a cave on the Jāt Mātrochcha

[1] Another name for the hill of Chāngū Nārāyan, five miles east of Kaṭhmāṇḍū. Here there is a composite image, representing Lokēswara upon Vishnu, upon Garuḍ, upon a lion. The Munshī supposes that the object of this is to degrade the Hindū religion in the eyes of Buddhists.

[2] Dakshin Kālī is the hill on which Phurphing stands; and Kachhapāl is another name for the hill of Chaubahār or Chaubahāl.

mountain, where he had placed an image of Akshōbhya Buddh, to worship Swayambhū[1]. As the water filled the valley, it rose up to the navel of this image, whereupon Nāgārjun caught the Nāg that was playing in the water and making it rise, and confined him in the cave. Whatever water is required in this cave is supplied by this Nāg to the present day, and for this reason the Nāg is called Jalpūrit[2]. This Nāgārjunpād Āchārya made an earthen chaitya, and composed or compiled many tantrashāstras, and discovered many gods. He died in the cave. The mountain then became known as Nāgārjun, and it is considered very sacred. People who are anxious to obtain salvation leave orders with their relatives to send their skull-bone (the "frontal bone") to this mountain, where it is thrown high into the air, then buried, and a chaitya built over it.

The valley continuing to be a lake, some say that Bhīmsen (one of the Pāndavas of the Mahābhāratha) came from Dolkhā and used to amuse himself on it in a stone boat. The daughter of Dānāsur, seeing Bhīmsen, ran away. After this Vishnu came, and, having killed Dānāsur, opened a passage for the water through the Chaubahār or Kachhapāl mountain, and carried off Prabhāvatī.

After Vishnu returned to his Baikunth (paradise), and the other gods to their respective abodes, this valley of Nepāl again became inaccessible. When the valley was changed into a lake by Dānāsur, some inhabitants of Manju-pattan, Sānkāsya-nagara, and Bisāl-nagara, saved their lives by fleeing to other places, and some

[1] This hill is now called Nāgārjun, and on its northern side are numerous caves, some of which contain images. One of these is said to be the identical cave mentioned in the text.

[2] Literally, *making full of water*.

were drowned. Some bhikshus saved themselves by going to Swayambhū mount. After the waters ran out and the valley remained inaccessible, the city of Suprabhā was depopulated.

One thousand years having elapsed after this, Brahmā, Vishnu and Mahēswara came here, and took the forms of Bhāt-bhatyānī. They appeared as father, mother and child[1]. They founded a city extending from Sankha-mūla[2] to Jalasayana Nārāyana (*i.e.* Nārāyana sleeping on the water) or Buddha Nīl-kantha, and put it under the charge of a Chhētrī Rājā named Swayambrata, a son of a Rishi or devotee. This Rājā used to propitiate the goddess Mani Jōginī, and obtaining much riches from her, distributed them daily to beggars and poor people. At this time a hero was born in Hindustān, who, having received directions in a dream, came and entered the Rājā's service. When asked his name, and what work he could do, he replied that his name was Bīr Vikramājit, and that he could do anything the Rājā ordered. The Rājā always kept him in his own company, and thus he at last became aware of the way in which the Rājā daily procured the riches which he gave away in charity. Having found this out, one night Vikramājit anointed his body with spices and fried himself in the pan (used by the Rājā)[3]. The Jōginī then devoured him, and being much pleased with the spiced meat, restored him to life and gave him the tree of riches. He then overturned the pan and returned to his home. The Rājā, when he next

[1] The temple of Bhāt-bhatyānī is to the east of the British Residency, and contains the images of a man and a woman with a child between them. Persons afflicted with paralysis are supposed to have incurred the displeasure of these deities.

[2] I.e., Sānkhū.

[3] This pan is still exhibited to the credulous!

went to the place, finding the pan overturned, began to lament; and the Jōginī told him that his servant Vikramājit had got the tree of riches. The Rājā returned to his palace, and after praising the heroism of Vikramājit, abdicated in his favour. Thus Vikramājit became the Rājā of Bisāl-nagara.

In his reign, Basundharā Dēvī of Phūlochcha mountain discovered Godāvarī on the Sinha Sankrānti (*i. e.* on the day when the sun enters Leo), and at that time the planet Guru (Jupiter) was also in Leo. For this reason (*i. e.* because she discovered Godāvarī) any one who digs a well, or builds a *dhārā* or *hithī*[1], first worships Basundharā Dēvī.

After this, considering Nepāl to be a place of great sanctity, the Trisūl Gangā river discovered itself at the foot of the Jāt Mātrochcha mountain[2], on the day of the full moon in Chait.

There are two places which face each other diagonally, one being at the south-east, the other at the north-west corner of the valley. At the time when Rājā Dharmadatta founded the city of Bisāl-nagara, an inspired devotee had built, at a spot at the foot of the Satarudra mountain[3], the shrine of Jalasayana Nārāyana, or Buddha Nīl-kantha. The Rājā Vikramājit visited this shrine every day, and, having obtained the permission of the deity, he made a stone image of the Nārāyana, with four arms, and two dhārās to feed the tank. One of these fountains brings forth a *kund*-flower every year,

[1] A *dhārā* is a fountain with a spout carved as a dragon's head or the like. A *hithī* is a small well or spring, built round with masonry, as a resting-place for travellers.

[2] Another name for Nāgārjun. These springs, at the place now called Bālāji, are said to be in connection with the Trisūl Gangā.

[3] Now called Sivapūrī (or Shupūrī), on the north of the valley.

and he who is fortunate enough to get possession of this becomes wealthy and prosperous.

After this, Vikramājit caused a great temple to be built, to the south of which he erected a summer-house over the spot where he had buried a Sinhāsana (throne), named Dōvī-datta-sinhāsana, which possessed the thirty-two attributes. He used to sit there daily and administer justice to his subjects. He ruled one thousand years, and his glory and fame were great. Having installed his son Vikrama-Kōsarī on the throne, he died at Mani Jōginī.

This Rājā was also very punctual in observing, and much devoted to, the rules and ceremonies of his religion. He built a durbār nine stories high, and surrounded the city with gardens and a wide ditch. He also appointed a day for his subjects to observe the Dewālī Pūjā. Some time after this, he was much grieved at seeing the memorial of his forefathers, the Nārāyana fountain, become dry; and he therefore went to Buddha Nīl-kantha for advice. The deity told him to consult the astrologers. He did so, and after some deliberation they said that it required a sacrifice of a human being possessed of the thirty-two attributes. The Rājā resolved to obey these directions; but, thinking that to sacrifice a subject would be a sin, and to kill his own son, who possessed all the requisite attributes, would be cruel, he determined to be himself the victim. He therefore called his son Bhūp-Kēsarī, and ordered him to kill, without looking at his face, a certain man, whom, on the fourth day after that, he should find lying covered over on the fountain. The prince, going there on the appointed day, in accordance with his father's commands, and not knowing who the person was, cut off his head. Blood rushed out of the dhārā, and the crocodile on the fountain turned back his head that he might not see a parricide. The son then went to wash his hands in the Ikshumatī river, and was surprised to see swarms of worms floating in the water. On returning to his house, he heard a great noise of people shouting out that the prince had killed his father. The prince then silently performed his father's funeral ceremonies, and making over charge of the government to his mother, he went to Mani Jōginī to expiate the sin of parricide. Seeing him very forlorn, the Jōginī informed him that he could expiate his crime by building a large Buddhist temple, two miles in circumference, and having four circles of gods. The spot for the temple would be indicated by the perching of a *kulang* (crane), which would take its flight from that mountain. The bird accordingly alighted, the spot for the temple was marked out, and the work was begun.

Another version of the story is, that it was Rājā Vikmāntī who was sacrificed, and that his son Māndēva was the parricide. The parricide, not being able to disengage his hand, to which the severed head attached itself, went to Mani Jōginī, by whose advice he built the Buddhist temple, and then the head became detached; which head (*i. e.* an image of it) is seen to the present day at Mani Jōginī.

When Māndēva began the work of building the temple, there was a great drought, so that the workmen making the bricks could only get water by soaking cloths (in the beds of the streams) and wringing out the moisture. When the bricks were being made, Bārāhī Dēvī, to test their strength, came in the shape of a sow and trod on them. This visit being repeated, the Rājā inquired who she was, and the Dēvī, acceding

Maclure & Macdonald Lith[rs] London

(Plate IX.) TEMPLE OF BŌDHNĀTH. (pp 22. 100)

to his prayer, disclosed herself in her true form. The Rājā, to show his gratitude, placed her image at the entrance of the Buddhist temple which contained all the deities. The prince Māndēva on this occasion composed a special prayer, which is repeated by every Buddhist when performing pūjā in holy places.

The Prayer.

Reverence to Ratna trayāya.
I bow to thy lotus-like feet, O Lord!
Thou art Buddh—thine asylum I seek.
There are countless merits in worshipping Buddh.
Thou art the master of religion, etc.[1]

According to Bhotiya (*i.e.* Tibetan) tradition, the Lāmā of Bhōt, having died, became incarnate, and lived again as the Rājā of Nepāl, who built the Buddhist temple; and for this reason the Bhotiyas hold it in great veneration[2].

After finishing the temple, the Prince presented himself before Mani Jōginī. She was well pleased with him for having punctually carried out the directions which she had given for building the temple, and said: "You have been cleansed from sin, and your grandfather, who got the tree of riches and expended them in charity, will again appear in the world, when three thousand years of the Kali Yuga have passed away, and he will change the era, which will then be known as Vikram Sambat, or the era of Vikramāditya." Having heard these words, the prince returned to his palace. His mother had meanwhile ruled the people with great justice,

[1] The whole of the prayer is given in the original manuscript.

[2] This temple still exists, and is now called Bodhnāth. It is only 300 yards in circumference, but of course it is the identical temple built by Māndēva!

so that they were full of her praises. She built many monuments, and at last consecrated an image of Nava-Sāgara Bhagavatī. This image, that of Bhagavatī of Palānchauk, and that of Sobhā Bhagavatī, were all made by the same artist[1].

After her death, there came to Bisāl-nagara, as its Rājā, a certain Rājā Bhōj. Being told of the fame of Vikramājit, he boasted that he would also achieve as great exploits, and said that he intended to sit on his throne. As he was about to seat himself on it, each of the thirty-two attributes of the throne assumed the form of an image, and after reciting the great deeds of Vikramājit, they disappeared. Bhōj still persisted in mounting the throne, whereupon it arose and flew away.

This Rājā being haughty, Nava-Sāgara Bhagavatī took offence, and sending forth fire from a well in front of her temple, consumed the city and its inhabitants. Thus Bisāl-nagara was destroyed, and only small hamlets now occupy its place. The people who were spared scattered themselves in different directions. Some of these, people of the four castes (Hindūs), went and fixed their abode beyond the Manōharā. Others went south, across the Bāgmatī, and founding a city called Matrājya, resided there. Others, being jealous of the founders of Matrājya, went elsewhere, and founded another city called Īrkhārājya. Some bhikshus went to live in the Swayambhū mountain, where Gunākar formerly resided; and others went to live at Kachhapāgiri[2].

Long ago, when Ōdiyāchārya invited all the gods on

[1] Palānchauk is a village east of Banēpa, which is in another valley to the east of the valley of Kāṭhmāṇḍū. The image of Sobha Bhagavatī is still shown at the burning-ghāt on the Bāgmatī. Witches are said to worship these deities.

[2] Another name for Kachhapāl or Chaubahāl.

the mountain, except Ganēsha, the latter took offence at this slight and began to molest him. Lokēswara-padmapāni then sent Kshiti-garbha Bōdhisatwa, who created the god Bighnāntaka to protect him from Ganēsha's attacks. Ganēsha, being foiled in his attempts, submitted to Bighnāntaka, who in return said, that from that day any one commencing a work should first worship Ganēsha, in order to prevent any interruption. For this reason Ganēsha is first propitiated before any work is undertaken. After this, Kshiti-garbha went away, leaving his spirit in the chhatra established by Ōdiyāchārya, and this chhatra became known as Gandhēswara. The people who went to live there erected an image of Lokēswara, naming it Anandadilokēswara, or the Giver of happiness to the people of the world[1]. Some bhikshus went to live there as beggars, in accordance with their customs, and those who lived as householders paid their recluse brethren money for performing the Lokēswara jātrā.

There was a chaitya in Bisāl-nagara, which was not destroyed by the flood caused by Dānāsur. Its votaries, not being able to support themselves when Bisāl-nagara was destroyed, thought of removing. One night they were told in a vision that they were to remove to a place which would be indicated by a bird flying from the chaitya. In the morning they saw a kite perched on the top of the chaitya, which on their approach flew away, and alighted again at a spot where they raised another chaitya, and named it Imādo, from *Imā*, "a kite" (in Newārī)[2].

Some bhikshus went to live at Manichūr, where Rājā Manichūr, formerly the king of Sākēta-nagara,

[1] This image is shown at Chaubahāl.

[2] A mound-chaitya about half a mile to the east of Pātan.

performed penance and the ceremony of Nirguna[1] yagya; and where, on account of his giving away as alms the Mani (jewel) on his forehead, ten things sprang up, viz., Manichūragiri, Manilinga, Manirohinī, Manitalāva, Manijōginī, Manichaitya, Manidhārā, Maniganēsha, Manimahākāla, and Manōharā. Some Bauddhamārgī householders followed them, and lived as votaries of Manijōginī. Some four-caste people (Hindūs) also accompanied them, and settled at Padmakāshthagiri[2], at the south-west corner of the valley. They first peopled the spot with cowherds. Of Bisāl-nagara not a vestige remained. Small hamlets sprang up on its ruins.

A city was founded where the Rudramatī flows, between Sāntēswarī and Gyānēswara. This town also was destroyed. A thief, having heard that there was the Sparsa Mani (philosopher's stone) in Gyānēswara, began to cleave the linga there with a hatchet; whereupon the Mani fled, and took refuge in the Prabhāvatī. A certain Rājā, having heard that the Sparsa Mani was in the Prabhāvatī, went to search for it, and tried to discover it by bringing metal in contact with the pebbles in the bed of the river. He failed however in his attempt, although the metal all became gold.

One thousand years after this, a certain Rānī of the Mārwāra country, by name Pingalā, having been disgraced by her husband, came to Guhjēswarī, to which she was directed in a vision. Here she performed penance by fasting, and the goddess, being propitiated, told her to build a house and live there, and to apply to her eyes a certain anjana (black ointment), which would enchant the Rājā her husband. The Rānī did

[1] In the original apparently *Nirargaḍa*.
[2] The Kīrtipūr hill, so-called because many *padma* or cherry-trees grow there.

as she was told, and placed images of gods and goddesses in the Bahāla Kōt, which she built and named Pingalā Bahāla[1]. Through the effects of her great penance, the mind of Sudatta, Rājā of Mārwāra, became uneasy, and he came here in search of his wife. While he was paying a visit to Guhjēswarī, the Rānī was also there, and some of the gods tried to catch hold of her. She in terror called out to the goddess that she was Pingalā. The Rājā, hearing this, looked at her attentively, and recognised some traces of his former love, although she was now changed to a perfect beauty. He accordingly claimed her, whereupon a quarrel ensued, which was terminated by the intercession of the goddess, who reconciled the Rājā and Rānī, and persuaded the gods not to interfere. The royal couple, having appointed Bauddhamārgī priests to take care of the Pingalā Bahāla Kōt, returned to their own country.

After this, knowing that the influence of the gods was great in Nepāl, the four Bhairavas, Nuwākot, Bhaktpūr, Sāngā and Panchlinga, came here; and finding that they could not get blood to drink, as there were no Rājās, they determined to appoint them. Then Indrānī also came and settled here, taking as her name Manā Maijū[2]. Next came the Kumārīs, viz., Bāl Kumārī of Thēmī, in the east; Kwātha Kshē Bāl Kumārī in the south; Maiti Dēvī Kumārī in the west, near Gyānōswara; Mangalapūr Kumārī in the north, formerly in Bisāl-nagara, near Bhasmēswara. These deities had power during the Dwāpar Yuga.

[1] Only ruins of this building remain, at a place south of Pashupati, where a new temple and house have been built by Colonel Sanaksingh, a brother-in-law of Sir Jung Bahādur.

[2] A place on the Vishnumatī, about four miles above Kāṭhmāṇḍū.

Satya Yuga lasted 1,728,000 years. In this Yuga men lived 10,000 years, and practised virtue. Prān Vāyu, or the principle of life, existed in the spinal marrow. The abode of men was white.

Trētā Yuga lasted 1,296,000 years. Men lived in this Yuga for 5,000 years. Prān Vāyu existed in the bone.

Dwāpar Yuga lasted 834,000 years. Men in this Yuga lived for 1,000 years. Prān Vāyu existed in the blood, flesh, and skin.

Kali Yuga will last for 432,000 years. In its first quarter, Prān Vāyu exists in food. In the second quarter, great eaters will live for 50 years. In the third quarter, men will live 16 years, feeding on vegetables, fruit, and flowers. In the middle of Kali Yuga, a Rājā, by name Vijayābhinandana, will bring all kings under his rule, and he will live 1,000 years. At the end of Kali Yuga the incarnation of Vishnu as Kalakī will take place.

The Kirātīs came into Nepāl at the 15,000th year of the Dwāpar Yuga, and they ruled over the country for 10,000 years. The gods came into the country after the Kirātīs. Dharmadatta Rājā reigned 1,000 years. After this the country remained without a king for one thousand years. Bisāl-nagara existed for 2,000 years. Pingalā's adventures extended over fifty years. When 950 years of the Dwāpar Yuga still remained, the gods came to the decision that it was necessary to appoint a Rājā. After this the Kali Yuga commenced.

CHAPTER II.

Founding of the Gupta dynasty by Nē Muni. Discovery of Pashupati in Bhuktamāna's reign. Ahīr dynasty from Hindustān. Kirātī dynasty. Commencement of Kali Yuga. Sākya Sinha Buddha comes to Nepāl. Asōka visits Nepāl. Somabansī Rājpūts invade the country and seize the throne. Sūryabansī Rājpūt dynasty. Sunayasrī Misra. Introduction of cultivation into Nepāl. Shankarāchārya visits Nepāl and overthrows the Buddhist religion. Religious persecutions. Vikramāditya visits Nepāl and introduces his era.

THE ancient temple of Pashupati having fallen down, the light was buried under the ruins. Some cowherds came into the country in the train of Srī Krishna, who came from Dwārikā to help his grandson in letting out the water from the valley through a passage, which he made at Chaubahāl, and in carrying off the daughter of Ḍānāsur, who had stopped the outflow of the water. These men settled down at Padmakāshthagiri, and built cowsheds. One of their cows, by name Nē, was a milch cow, but gave no milk. Every day at a certain time she went running to a certain place. One day the chief cowherd followed her, and saw milk issuing from her udder, and saturating the spot on which she stood. His curiosity was excited to know what was under the spot, and on removing some earth he discovered the light, which however consumed him.

Nē Muni, from whom Nepāl derives its name, then came, and having persuaded the people that there would be no Chhētrī Rājās in the Kali Yuga, he installed as king the son of the cowherd who had been consumed by the light.

1. This Rajā, by name Bhuktamāna, reigned 88 years, and Pashupati was discovered in his reign. He used to play at a game called Kilātarī[1] in the Slēshmāntakban.

2. His son Jaya Gupta reigned 72 years.
3. His son Parama Gupta reigned 80 years.
4. His son Bhīm Gupta reigned 93 years.
5. His son Bhīm Gupta reigned 38 years.
6. His son Mani Gupta reigned 37 years.
7. His son Vishnu Gupta reigned 42 years.
8. His son Yaksha Gupta reigned 71 years.

These Rājās had their residence near Mātā Tīrtha[2], and used to tend Brāhmans' cows. These eight Rājās were descended from the cowherd, who was installed as king by Nē Muni.

The origin of Mātā Tīrtha is thus described. In the time of Nē Muni, one of his cowherds, being much distressed by the death of his mother, went into the jungle near his house on the 15th day of Baisākh, and offered a ball of boiled rice to her in the tank, into which water was collected from the mountain. His mother's face and hand appeared in the tank, and the hand accepted the offering. For this reason, Nē Muni called the place Mātā Tīrtha, and to the present day people resort there, on that date, to offer balls of boiled rice to their deceased mothers.

The cowherds reigned through eight generations, extending over 521 years. Yaksha Gupta, having no issue,

[1] A military game, a sort of sham fight.
[2] At the foot of the hill to the south of Kīrtipūr.

an Ahīr, from the plains of Hindustān, came and ruled over the country. His name was (1) Bara Sinha. His son (2) Jayamati Sinha succeeded him; and he was followed by his son (3) Bhuvana Sinha. This Rājā was conquered by the Kirātīs, who came from the east.

The Rājās of the Kirātī dynasty were :—

1. Yalambar, who reigned 13 years.

2. His son Pabi, in whose reign the astrologers announced that the Kali Yuga had entirely overspread the earth, and that mankind were bent on sin. The gods' period of Dwāpara ended, and the first quarter of Kali Yuga commenced.

3. His son Skandhara.

4. His son Balamba.

5. His son Hriti.

6. His son Humati.

In this reign the Pāndavas were destined to reside in forests, and one of them, named Arjuna, fought with Mahādēva, who was in the form of a Kirātī, and pleased him by his skill in archery.

7. Humati's son Jitēdāsti.

This Rājā, by the order of Arjuna, went to Kurukshētra[1], to fight against his enemies the Kauravas, mentioned in the Mahābhārata. During this reign Sākya Sinha Buddha came into Nepāl, from a city named Kapilabastu[2], and having visited Swayambhū Chaitya and Manjūsrī Chaitya, fixed his abode at Puchhāgra Chaitya[3]. While there, he accepted the worship and offerings of Chūda, a female bhikshu, and made 1350 proselytes, viz., Sālīputra, Maudgalyāyana, Ānanda, &c., from the Brāhman and Chhētrī castes. To several Bōdhisatwas, such as

[1] Near Pānipat.

[2] Said to be in the Terai.

[3] To the west of Swayambhū hill.

Maitrēya, and gods, such as Brahmā, who came to Nepāl expressly to see him, Sākya described the glory of Swayambhū. He then visited Guhjēswarī, and after that the Namobuddha mountain[1]. Here he discovered, and showed to his disciples, certain ornaments belonging to himself, buried under a chaitya. When he formerly existed as a prince named Mahāsatwa (the son of Mahāratha of Panāvatī[2], formerly called Pānchāla), he had buried these ornaments, after destroying himself by giving his flesh to a tiger to eat. He replaced them as they were, and repaired the chaitya. He next ascended into heaven, and returned after visiting his mother, who had died on the seventh day after his birth. Then, after preaching his doctrines to the people, he saw that the time of his death was approaching, and went to a city called Kūsī[3]. Here, while he was preaching to an assembly of gods (such as Brahmā) and bhikshus (such as Ānanda), he disappeared. Some of his followers remained in Nepāl and professed his religion.

As Rājā Jitēdāsti did not return from the wars recounted in the Mahābhārata,

8. His son Gali ascended the throne.
9. His son Pushka.
10. His son Suyarma.
11. His son Parba.
12. His son Bunka.
13. His son Swananda.
14. His son Sthunko.

In the reign of this Rājā, Asōka, the Rājā of Pātaliputra (Patnā), having heard of the fame of Nepāl as a

[1] About twelve miles east of Bhātgāon.
[2] A village in a valley about eight miles south-east of Bhātgāon.
[3] Or Kosīnār. The river Kūsī or Kosī is well known.

sacred place, and having obtained the permission of his spiritual guide, Upagupta Bhikshu, came on a pilgrimage to Nepāl, accompanied by his family, and followed by a large number of his subjects. He visited every holy place, and bathed in every sacred water, and went to Swayambhū, Guhjēswarī and eight Buddha bītarāgas or chaityas. He also built several chaityas. His daughter Chārumatī, while playing one day, saw an iron arrowhead turned into stone by a god, and determined to remain in Nepāl, having concluded from this that it was a land of miracles wrought by the gods. The Rājā, therefore, gave her in marriage to a descendant of a Chhētrī, named Dēvapāla; gave them 3,600 *rōpnīs* of land, and everything else requisite; and then returned to his own country. On the way back, his Rānī, Tikhya Lakshmī, gave birth to a son, and suckled him on the ground; whence the spot and the child were both named Mahīpāna. After this, Chārumatī and her husband Dēvapāla founded and peopled Dēva Pātan[1]. They were then blessed with a numerous family, and becoming aged, they determined to pass the rest of their lives in retirement. They therefore resolved each to build a bihār. That of Chārumatī was first completed, and she died in it, after living the life of a bhikshunī[2]. Dēvapāla died in great distress, from not being able to complete his bihār before his death. All this happened in the reign of the Kirāti Rājā Sthunko.

15. His son Gighri.
16. His son Nanō.
17. His son Luk.

[1] A town west of and adjacent to Pashupati temple.

[2] Chārumatī Bihār still exists at Chabāhil, a village north of and close to Dēva Pātan.

18. His son Thōr.
19. His son Thoko.
20. His son Barma.
21. His son Guja.
22. His son Pushka.
23. His son Kesū.
24. His son Suga.
25. His son Sansa.
26. His son Gunan.
27. His son Khimbu.

These Kirātī Rājās lived in an inaccessible durbār, built in the jungles of Gokarna. The Kirātīs began to kill the jackals which infested the place, and these animals took refuge at Guptēswara, on the banks of the Bāgmatī; they raised a small mound, which was called Jambuka Dobhanī, or the Hillock of Jackals[1].

28. His son Patuka.

This Rājā was attacked by Somabansī Rājpūts, from the west, and, leaving the durbār at Gokarna, removed to a distance of four kōs to the south, across the Sankha Mūla Tīrtha, where he built another durbār.

29. His son Gasti.

He, being hard pressed by the Somabansīs, fled from the new durbār. Then the Somabansīs, having subdued the Kirātīs, built a durbār near Godāvarī, at the foot of the Phūlochcha mountain.

1. The first Somabansī Rājā was Nimikha.

In his reign, an inspired devotee found at Godāvarī his rosary, club, bag, gourd, tiger's skin, and ball of ashes, all of which had been washed away in the river Godāvarī (in Madras). This gave rise to the Mēlā which is held every twelfth year at Godāvarī, when Jupiter is in Leo.

[1] A hillock near Gokarn, between it and Pashupati.

2. His son Matāksha.

3. His son Kāka-barmā.

4. His son Pashuprōkhadōva.

This Rājā peopled his country with people of the four castes (Hindūs), and rebuilt the temple of Pashupati, which had become dilapidated, roofing it with golden plates, and finishing it with a *Gajura* on the top. The temple, being thus higher than before, was now seen from a distance. This happened in the 1234th year of the Kali Yuga.

5. His son Bhāskara-barmā.

This Rājā went with a large army to the four quarters of the world, and up to the ocean, *i.e.* Sētubandha Rāmēswara[1]. By the assistance of Pashupati mantras he subdued many countries, and brought back much gold, which he dedicated to Pashupati. He also caused Pashupati to be bathed with water containing gold, which ran down to the Bāgmatī. He enlarged into a town the village of Dēva Pātan, which was founded by Dēvapāla, a Rājbansī Chhētrī, who was a follower of Asōka Rājā. This town he named Subarna-purī, or the golden town. He entrusted the daily worship, and the ceremonies accompanying it, to Bauddhamārgī householder Āchāryas.

The rules and ceremonies to be observed he caused to be engraved on a copper-plate, which he lodged with the bhikshus of Chārumatī Bihār. He dedicated Subarnapurī to Pashupati, and prayed to Pashupati that he might have no children. He therefore appointed as his successor one Bhūmi-barmā, a Chhōtrī of the solar race of Rājpūts, of the Gautama gōtra, who had been one of the followers of Sākya Ṣinha Buddha of Kapilabastu, and

[1] The extreme south of India, where Rāma built the bridge between the mainland and Ceylon.

had remained in Nepāl after his departure. Shortly after this Bhāskara-barmā died.

Of the new solar dynasty the first Rājā was

1. Bhūmi-barmā, who was crowned in the Kaligata year 1389. He quitted the Durbār at Godāvarī, and established his court at Bānēswara.

2. His son Chandra-barmā.

3. His son Chandra-barmā.

4. His son Barkha-barmā.

5. His son Sarba-barmā.

6. His son Prithwī-barmā.

7. His son Jyēshtha-barmā.

8. His son Hari-barmā.

9. His son Kubēra-barmā.

10. His son Siddhi-barmā.

11. His son Haridatta-barmā.

This Rājā was in the habit of paying a daily visit to the four Nārāyanas, viz., Chāngu, Chainju, Ichangu, and Sikhara Nārāyana, who in Dwāpar Yuga disclosed themselves to an inspired devotee. One night Jalasāyana Nārāyana appeared to this Rājā in a dream, and said that he was the original of the four Nārāyanas, and that he was buried under earth and stones, washed down by the Rudramatī from the Satarudra mountain. He told him to remove the earth and stones, and uncover him, which the Rājā did; but while doing so, he struck the Nārāyana on the nose with the spade, and broke it. To the present day the nose remains in this mutilated condition. The Rājā then made a tank for the Nārāyana, and called him Nīlakantha, and built a temple for him[1].

12. His son Basudatta-barmā.

[1] This god with the broken nose is still to be seen at Buddha Nīlkantha, a place at the foot of the Sivapūri hill, four miles north of the Residency.

13. His son Pati-barmā.
14. His son Sivabriddhi-barmā.
15. His son Basanta-barmā.
16. His son Siva-barmā.
17. His son Rudradēva-barmā.

In this reign a certain Sunayasrī Misra Brāhmana, from Kapilabastuka, arrived here, and took up his abode near Sarbēswara[1], who had appeared to Sarbapādāchārya from a jar of water, when he was worshipping. Being in search of a spiritual guide, to ensure his salvation (which ought to be sought after by every man who distinguishes between right and wrong, and without which a man has to be reborn several times), and finding no one to answer his purpose, Sunayasrī Misra went to Lhāsā, to take as his spiritual guide the inspired Patlā (or Bhikshu) Lāmā, one of the three sacred Lāmās, the other two being named Grihastha and Srāvaka. This Lāmā was in the possession of the six essential attributes; viz. the power of flying in the air; of hearing sounds from the distance of thousands of miles; of seeing for thousands of miles; the knowledge of what is in the minds of others; the knowledge of all past events; and freedom from sensual and worldly desires. Besides these, he possessed power to live and die at his own pleasure, and to be reborn when he pleased. He could also tell the events of present, past, and future times. These powers he had acquired by conducting himself according to the rules, and performing the penances imposed on him by Sākya Sinha Buddha. Sunayasrī Misra made the Lāmā his spiritual guide, and received instruction in the various matters connected with religion. He then returned to Nepāl, with the

[1] A temple in Pātan, also called Kumbhēswara.

intention of fixing on a place of residence, and building a bihār; but for a long time he could not select a spot. At last he fixed on one of the four chaityas built by Rājā Asōka of Patnā, during his visit to Nepāl, each of which was founded on the anniversary of the commencement of one of the four Yugas. He examined the ground occupied by each, and at last his choice fell on the one built on the anniversary of the commencement of Kali Yuga[1]. He then presented a bidōl (crystal) jewel to Rājā Rudradēva-barmā; and having bought the ground, he built a bihār and fixed his abode there. Having received directions in several dreams, he put a bidōl jewel in one of the four great Asōka chaityas, and repaired them all[2]. His disciples, Gōvardhana Misra and Kāsyapa Misra, came from Kapilabastuka to Nepāl, in search of their Guru; and having found him, they became converted and lived here, each in separate bihārs, which were built by their Guru and named Dunta Bihār and Lalibana Bihār.

Not having heard anything of Sunayasrī Misra, nor of the two disciples who had been sent in search of him, his mother and sons came and found him here. He built for them a house called Chōkā, near his own bihār. When a grandson was born, he made his son become a bhikshu also. His wife placed an image of Kulisēswarī to the south of the bihār. He made it a rule for his descendants, that, on the birth of a son, they were to

[1] This bihār is in Pātan, and the descendants of Sunayasrī Misra still live there. I bought a copy of the Asokāvadāna from one of them.

[2] These are: (1) Sunayasrī Misra's in Pātan; (2) the large mound on the parade-ground, south of Pātan, founded on the anniversary of the commencement of the Satya Yuga; (3) the mound opposite Thāpatalī, west of Pātan, founded on the anniversary of the commencement of the Dwāpar Yuga; and (4) the mound to the east of Pātan, south of Imādo Chaitya, founded on the anniversary of the commencement of the Trētā Yuga.

(Plate X.) MATIRAJYA CHAITYA. (pp. 16, 116)

leave their homes and live a life of celibacy in the bihār. Sunayasrī's bihār is now called Yampi Bihār, and those of his disciples are called Kōntibahī Bihār and Pinta Bihār. In Pinta Bihār there are still preserved specimens of a large rice without husk, and of rice with husk, such as grew in former ages[1].

18. Rudradēva-barmā was succeeded by his son Brikhadēva-barmā.

This Rājā was very pious. He daily fed Bajra Jōginī, before taking his own meals. He repaired the chaitya, built by Dharmadatta, and built several bihārs for bhikshus to live in. He went one day to visit that one of the four large chaityas which was built on the anniversary of the commencement of the Satya Yuga, and being attacked by a severe illness, he died there.

The servants of Yama took him to their master's kingdom; but Yama, when he saw him, chided them for having brought such a virtuous man to Hell. He was therefore released, and restored to life again. He then compared what he had seen in Hell with what was written about it in the Kāranda-byūha, and finding that they agreed, he was pleased. He attributed his curious adventure and his release to Lokēswara Padma-pāni, who, as he learned from books, had caused by his presence the cessation of the tortures of those in Hell. He therefore erected an image of Dharma-rājā Lokēswara, and one of Yamāntaka Āgama. He left his brother Bālārchana-dēva there, and himself returned and placed an image of Pancha-Buddha near Godāvarī, calling the place by the name of Bandyagāon[2]. Shortly afterwards he died at his palace.

[1] These specimens of rice are still in existence, and are shown in the month of Sāwan. The grains are as large as small nutmegs!

[2] Now called Bandēgāon, a village about two miles west of Godāvarī.

His brother Bālārchana-dēva paid great attention to the images of the deities erected by his brother. Up to this time no one had cultivated land or grown corn in these regions, but grain was brought from a great distance. Every one was afraid to be the first to dig the earth. Bālārchana therefore selected a strong young man, called Balbala, who had no family, to drive the first spade into the earth; in return for which service he was to receive a share of the corn grown by every one thereafter. He performed this service, and in course of time died, after having erected a stone image of himself, to which Bālārchana caused religious honours to be paid, and bread made of rice to be offered, on the day of the full moon in Aghan[1]. The land which Balbala dug is called Sāvāya-matēva-bhūmi, and no plough dragged by oxen is ever used on it[2].

At this time the incarnation Shankarāchārya was born in the Deccan of an immaculate Brahmanī widow. This Shankara in his six former incarnations had been defeated in religious discussions by the Bauddhamārgīs, and had been cast into the fire. At the time of his seventh incarnation there were no learned Bauddhamārgīs there, but only sixteen Bōdhisatwas (or novices), who, hearing of the advent of this great reformer, fled to the North, seeking refuge wherever they could find it, and there they died. Shankarāchārya, finding no clever Bauddhamārgīs with whom to argue, and hearing that the sixteen Bōdhisatwas had fled to Nepāl, pursued them, but could not find them. On his arrival he saw that there were no learned Bauddhamārgīs in Nepāl. The four

[1] This image of Balbala still stands near the temple of Machchhindra-nātha in Pātan, south of the durbār.

[2] This *khēt* or field lies south of the parade-ground at Pātan.

Hindū castes were Bauddhamārgīs. Of these some lived in bihārs as Bhikshus; some were Srāvakas, also living in bihārs; some were Tāntrikas, and called Āchāryas; and some were Grihasthas, following the Buddhist religion. Shankara found that of the three Bauddhamārgī sects, viz., the Bhikshus, Srāvakas, and Grihasthas (as is written in the *Sambarārnava*), the first two had no clever men to argue with him. Therefore some of the Grihastha Āchāryas, when preparing to argue with him, brought a jar of water, in which they invoked Saraswatī (the goddess of speech) to aid them. While contending with them, Shankara somehow became aware that Saraswatī had been invoked to help them against him. He therefore entered the temple at the southern door and dismissed her, after which the Bauddhamārgīs were soon defeated. Some of them fled, and some were put to death. Some, who would not allow that they were defeated, were also killed; wherefore many confessed that they were vanquished, though in reality not convinced that they were in error. These he ordered to do *hinsā* (*i. e.* to sacrifice animals), which is in direct opposition to the tenets of the Buddhist religion. He likewise compelled the Bhikshunīs, or nuns, to marry, and forced the Grihasthas to shave the knot of hair on the crown of their heads, when performing the *chūrā-karma*, or first shaving of the head. Thus he placed the Bānaprasthas (ascetics) and Grihasthas on the same footing. He also put a stop to many of their religious ceremonies, and cut their Brahmanical threads. There were at that time 84,000 works on the Buddhist religion, which he searched for and destroyed. He then went to the Manichūra mountain, to destroy the Buddhists there. Six times the goddess Mani Jōginī raised storms, and prevented his ascending the mountain, but the seventh time he succeeded. He then decided that Mahākāla, who was a Buddha and abhorred *hinsā*, should have animals sacrificed to him. Mani Jōginī or Ugra Tārinī was named by him Bajra Jōginī. Having thus overcome the Buddhists, he introduced the Saiva religion in the place of that of Buddha. Thus ends Shankarāchārya's triumph over the Bauddhamārgīs of Nepāl.

At the time of his coming into Nepāl, Brikhadēva Rājā had died, leaving his Rānī pregnant. His brother Bālārchana, being uncertain whether the issue would be a son or a daughter, remained at Matīrājya[1] and worshipped Dharma-rājā Lokēswara, whose statue had been consecrated by his brother, though he was desirous of living as a bhikshu. The Rānī in due season gave birth to a son. Shankarāchārya, when searching after great men who followed the Buddhist religion, caught Bālārchana; and as he refused to be converted, his head was shaved, and his Brahmanical thread taken away from him. Having thus in mockery made a perfect bhikshu of him, he forced him to marry a bhikshunī.

Shankarāchārya thus destroyed the Buddhist religion, and allowed none to follow it; but he was obliged to leave Bauddhamārgīs in some places as priests of temples, where he found that no other persons would be able to propitiate the gods placed in them by great Bauddhamārgīs. He then returned to the sea-side, leaving the northern parts of the world unconquered.

Very few Bauddhamārgīs were left in the country now, and the Bhikshus began to intermarry with the Grihasthas.

[1] Name of the chaitya which was built on the anniversary of the commencement of the Satya Yuga.

Pingalā Rānī had consecrated images of a god and goddess, and worshipped them with Ganges water, and fasted for a month, through the influence of which penance her husband had come to seek her, and been reconciled to her. At the time of her departure she had left Bauddhamārgī priests to continue the worship of her deities in the Pingalā Bahāla Kōt. The descendants of these priests, being desirous to perform the chūrā-karma, began to reflect thus: "Shankarāchārya has destroyed the Bauddhamārgīs. He has turned out the Bauddhamārgī Grihastha Brāhmans, who hitherto worshipped Pashupati, and has appointed in their stead Brāhmans from the Deccan; and those Bauddhamārgīs, who have accepted Shankarāchārya's doctrines have been made priests of Guhjēswarī and other places. Our fathers, however, did not accept Shankarāchārya's doctrines, and they remained firm in the worship of their deities as before. How then can we leave these deities and relinquish our former creed? If we remain in our former creed, however, we cannot discharge the duties of Āchāryas without performing the chūrā-karma, as ordered by Shankarāchārya. Our fathers died, leaving us as infants, unable to perform any action ourselves. There is no image of a god here, without which chūrā-karma cannot be performed; and we cannot go to any bihārs for chūrā-karma, except those of Kulisēswara and Kulisēswarī. Nor can chūrā-karma be performed without our first being Bhikshu Āchāryas, and no god can be consecrated without Bhikshu Āchāryas." Being thus at a loss how to act, they went to their uncles[1], the Bhikshus of Chārumatī Bihār, who had

[1] *Uncle* and *aunt* are often merely terms of respect, not of actual relationship.

married their aunts through fear of Shankarāchārya. After consultation, these Bhikshus said: "O nephews! what can we do? The people of this place, contented with their scanty means of livelihood, have kept the things they know in their hearts, and have remained silent through fear of Shankarāchārya; for which sin they will all be afflicted with goître[1]. What are we to do? Those who were living as bhikshus have been forced to live as grihasthas. The rules established by Bhāskara-barmā Rājā for this place, and written on a copper-plate, kept in this bihār, have been replaced by others made by Shankarāchārya; and a rule for sacrificing animals has been added to the copper-plate, which is now ordered to be kept here. If we are obliged to live as grihasthas, and to obey the rule about sacrificing animals, we shall commit a great breach of the rules of our own religion. We have therefore made up our minds to go elsewhere, and live in a new bihār. Let those remain here who wish to remain; but we will not stay. You too have made up your minds to remove, and we will accompany you."

They then went to Pingalā Bahāl, and worshipped with great ceremonies the Īswarī Nairātmā. Then they made a chaitya for Swayambhū and an image of Sākya Sinha Buddha; and to keep up the worship of these, they took bhikshus (living now as grihasthas), the descendants of those who had followed Sākya Sinha into Nepāl, and appointed them as priests. They made these follow the Tantra Shāstras, and settled down along with them. They did not make any change in the grihastha priests,

[1] This origin of goître is still believed in. Similarly I have heard intelligent and educated Nepalese assert that hydrocele (which is very prevalent there) originated with the introduction of the potato as an article of food.

who had been appointed by Rānī Pingalā of Mārwāra to worship her Nairātmā Guhjēswarī, but made a rule that every bhikshu, living as gribastha in the Bahāl, should in turn take charge of the Swayambhū Chaitya and the image of Sākya Sinha.

At the time when Shankarāchārya appeared, a son of Rājā Brikhadēva-barmā was born, and was named after Shankarāchārya.

19. This was Shankaradēva Rājā.

In the reign of this Rājā, a trisūl (trident) of iron, weighing a maund, was made, and placed at the northern door of Pashupati's temple, and dedicated to him[1]. There was a well near Rājēswarī[2], by looking into which people saw the shape which they were to assume when reborn. Thinking that this would cause great distress to the people, the Rājā had it filled up, and in front of it he erected a large emblem of Siva, which he called Āpānsa-jāti-smarana-birātēswara[3]. In this reign an image of Nandi, or the bull on which Mahādēva rides, was placed at the western door of Pashupati. From the day this image was erected, it was no longer a sin to pass in front of the Jalaharī, or stone on which the emblem of Siva is fixed. In the reign of this Rājā there was a Brāhman[4] named Jayasrī, who refused to become a convert to the doctrines of Shankarāchārya, and married a daughter of a bhikshu of Chārumatī Bihār, who, through fear of Shankarāchārya, had himself entered into matrimony.

1 This trisūl is still a very conspicuous object in front of the temple, as seen from the opposite bank of the river.

2 A temple south of the large temple at Pashupati, below the bridges.

3 This linga, of enormous size, still stands on the bank of the Bāgmatī at the place mentioned.

4 Explained by the Pandit to mean a person of Brahmanical descent, but by religion a Buddhist.

The Rājā told him to remain as a Bandya, or Bānrā, if he did not wish to renounce the Buddhist religion, and he would make a bihār for him on the other side of the Bāgmatī. While they were uncertain where to build the bihār, and where to place the image of the deity, a peacock came and alighted on a certain spot, and when this was dug, an image of Vishnu was found and taken out. On this spot an image of Bhagavān Sākya Sinha was placed; and for this reason the bihār built there was called Mayūra-barna (*Mayūra*, a peacock). Some people call it Vishnuksha Bihār[1].

20. The son of Shankaradēva was Dharmadēva.

This Rājā repaired the Dhanado Chaitya, built by Rājā Dharmadatta.

21. His son Māndēva.

Some say that Khāsā Chaitya was built by this Rājā[2]. He built Chakra Bihār, near Matirājya, known now by the name of Mandēva-sanskārit-chakra-mahā-bihār[3].

22. His son Mahādēva.

23. His son Basantadēva-barmā.

He was crowned in the Kaligata year 2800.

24. His son Udayadēva-barmā.

25. His son Māndēva-barmā.

26. His son Gunakāmadēva-barmā.

27. His son Sivadēva-barmā.

This Rājā was crowned before he was married. In his reign the Durbār near Bānēswara was abandoned, and one of nine stories in height was built in Dēva Pātan, where the Rājā established his court. After removing to Dēva Pātan, he brought Nritya Nātha,

[1] This building is at Pātan.

[2] Now called Bodhnāth.

[3] In Pātan, near the statue of Balbala.

known as Bhukuns, from the Satarudra mountain, and established him on the western side of Pashupati Nātha. This Nritya Nātha is possessed of great gifts. The Rājā built nine new tōls, or divisions of the city, and erected nine Ganēshas. He also brought Kāmēswara Bhīmasēna from the west, and established him to the west of Pashupati. For the protection of the country he caused to be brought from Sivapurī a round stone image, called Bhairava Silā, which he placed in his Durbār. To free the country from debt he caused to be brought an Arinī Silā, or debt-payer stone. When using this as a weight, the Bhairava appeared, but he was unable to complete the task of paying all the debts of the country.

He founded and peopled the place known as Navatōl, after performing all the requisite ceremonies, and establishing four Ganēshas, four Bhairavas, four Nritya Nāthas, four Mahādēvas, four Kumārīs, four Buddhas, four Khambas, four Gaganachārīs, and four chatushpathas or crossways with Bhūta images. Then, after establishing an Avarna deity in each tōl or division of Dēva Pātan, he erected an image of Siva. He invoked Mahāmrityunjaya to protect men from untimely death. He founded and peopled Mahānagara and other places.

After making one dhokā (gate), two wells, three dhārās, four Nritya Nāthas, five davalis[1], six tōls, seven Īswarīs, eight Āgamas, and nine Ganēshas, at Subarnapurī, he named it Gōl, because its shape was round. He caused to be uncovered Banakālī, who in the reign of Rājā Dharmadatta had eaten up the army and concealed

[1] A platform for dancing at festivals, and where images are brought to be washed.

herself in a wood. The flesh of the human bodies was still sticking to her teeth. He also erected near her a large image of Bachana Bināyaka Ganēsha. Being a wise monarch, he caused to be uncovered in the city a chaitya which Shankarāchārya had concealed. He also caused burning-ghāts to be built, for the dead bodies of each caste, to the east of Bajrēswarī Bachhlā Dēvī, on the banks of the Bāgmatī[1]. Leading to these he made a special street, along which the dead bodies might be carried.

He also established the custom of assembling the people and offering a human sacrifice to Bachhlā Dēvī, the principal deity of Nepāl, on the 12th of Chait Badi. On the 13th, unmarried boys and virgins were fed. On the 14th, which is called Pisācha-chaturdasī, a fire was kept lighted all night wherever there was an image of Mahādēva, and the next morning the Dēvī was carried in a ratha, or car, round the city to celebrate the jātrā.

Being aware that Bachhlā Dēvī was the principal deity of Nepāl, that he might be able to perform all her numerous religious rites, he ordered that, after worshipping Pashupati Nātha, a cloth should be tied by one end to his temple, and by the other to the palace. This cloth was left for four days, and then taken down[2]. In this manner he revived the worship of Bachhlā, Bhuvanēswarī, Jayabāgēswarī, Rājēswari, and many other deities. . .

This Rājā entrusted the ceremony of invoking and

[1] This temple is close to the principal bridge at Pashupati, on the right bank of the Bāgmatī. It is covered with horribly indecent figures.

[2] These cloths are constantly seen tied to the tops of temples, or extending across rivers, with flowers, small flags, etc., attached to them at intervals. The attributes of the deity are supposed to pass from the shrine or temple to the place where the cloths are fastened.

worshipping Bachhlā and other deities to Āchārs. He instituted the custom of sacrificing a human being every year to Bachhlā, to propitiate the goddess. At the end of the ceremony he used to distribute gifts in money and clothes. The Āchārs, after invoking the principal deity of Nepāl, propitiated Kshētrapālēswarī and other deities with annual offerings of money and other things. Hence arose the custom in Nepāl of offering sacrifices and presents of money, flowers, etc.

Having one day learned from a certain good man that a saint came daily to bathe in the Swapnā Tīrtha[1], the Rājā hurried there to satisfy his curiosity. He found on his arrival a hideous fakīr, whom, after much persuasion, he succeeded in bringing back with him, and lodged him near Tāmrēswara. The Rājā, having first repainted the image of Grāmadēvī Jayabāgēswarī, employed the fakīr in performing the ceremony of Jīvana-nyāsa, or bringing the goddess to life again[2]. While thus employed the fakīr informed him that he was an incarnation of Durbāsā[3]. He then caused the goddess to be very powerful in working miracles. He also soothed the restless image of Bhairava Nava-lingēswara, and discovered Gaja-karnaka (*i.e.*, Ganēsha, he with the ears of an elephant). The Rājā then proceeded with the fakīr to Bajra Jōginī, and, having repainted the image, performed the ceremony of Jīvana-nyāsa. He ordered that this ceremony should be performed only once in twelve years, instead of annually, as heretofore had been the custom.

[1] A pond near the Vishnumatī, in which people bathe on the Mesh Sankrānti.

[2] The spirit of the image, before repainting, is supposed to be extracted, and to be kept in a jar of water till the work is finished, when it is restored. A *hōm* is then performed, and Brāhmans are fed as usual.

[3] An incarnation of Siva.

The Rājā, now thinking that his Guru would soon be becoming old and decrepit, built a Dharma-sālā at Tāmrēswara, and revived the Mahādēva by daily worship. He then reigned for a long time, and at last had his brother Narēndradēva-barmā anointed as king, and he himself lived with the fakīr.

One day, when these two were going to Godāvarī, they came to a place where, in the Trētā Yuga, Manjusrī Bōdhisatwa had founded a city; and where Brahmā, Vishnu, and Mahēswara (who had come to visit Swayambhū and Guhjēswarī), were seen strolling in Mrigasthalī; and where Vishnū entered the mountain. They stopped at this place, and the fakīr expounded all its glories to the Rājā. Then, at the mountain where there was a Sāligrāma Lakshmī Nārāyana[1], the fakīr invoked Vishnu Nārāyana, and was about to disappear, when the Rājā thus addressed him: "O Guru! Thou art now about to disappear, and what will be my condition then? Pray show me the path by which I may obtain salvation, and not be subjected to being born again." The fakīr replied: "There is nothing that cannot be obtained by man. Everything can be gained, provided the requisite exertion is made. Now I am going to tell thee the way. It is difficult to obtain salvation after this birth by worshipping other deities. Therefore worship Buddha alone; obtain a knowledge of the five elements; become a bhikshu; perform devotions to and meditate on Buddha; and thou wilt then obtain salvation after this birth." Having thus spoken, the fakīr vanished. From that day this mountain was named Vishnugun, or the mountain of Vishnu.

After this Sivadēva-barmā went roaming about, and

[1] This is a spur of the hills, north of Godāvarī.

one day met a bhikshu, who was living in the Bānprastha state. He made this bhikshu his Guru, and built a bihār, in which he placed images of Swayambhū and Sākya Sinha Buddha, and then he himself became a bhikshu. Four days after becoming a bhikshu, the Rājā told his Guru that it was impossible for a man, who had enjoyed the comforts and luxuries of a king, to lead that kind of life. He therefore begged him to show him some means, by which he could live comfortably in this world, and yet obtain salvation in the next. "It is written," replied the Guru, "in the Dharma-shāstra, that a bhikshu can return to the grihastha mode of life, and is then called a Bajradhrik or Bajrāchārya. Also, that those who are descendants of Sākya Muni, are, after the ten sanskāras or ceremonies, Bandyas or Bhikshus, and they can also worship Kulisēswara, and still lead a grihastha life." Having said this, the Guru took off the ochre-dyed cloth from the Rājā's body, and performed the ceremony of Āchāryābhishēka. The Rājā then, with the sanction of the Guru, built a bihār near his own, and lodged the Guru in it. For his maintenance he assigned some land, which up to the present time is given only to those who live as bhikshus in that bihār[1]. The Rājā then, with his Guru's sanction, placed an Āgama-dēvatā or Buddha in his own bihār, meditated there daily, and performed his devotions and worship there. He then married, and many sons and daughters were born to him. It was his daily custom to sit before the Kulisēswara or Buddha, which he had erected; and one day, while thus meditating, his skull burst, and his soul escaping, he obtained salvation.

[1] Sivadeva's bihār is in Pātan.

At the time his skull burst, a mani, or jewel, came out of it. Only one person at a time is allowed to enter that Āgama, lest, if more entered together, they should begin to discuss among themselves the size and shape of that jewel.

Narēndradēva-barmā had been placed on his brother's throne, and Punyadēva-barmā, the son of Sivadēva-barmā by the wife whom he married after becoming a Bajrāchārya, performed his father's funeral rites, and led the same life as his father.

28. His brother Narēndradēva-barmā.

29. His son Bhīmadēva-barmā.

30. His son Vishnudēva-barmā.

31. His son Viswadēva-barmā.

This Rājā once said that the human sacrifice to Bachhlā was a piece of cruelty, whereupon the Nara-sivā[1] made a great noise. The Rājā went to see what was the matter, and the Nara-sivā came to seize him. The Rājā, being pleased at this, gave him a large jāgīr (grant of land), which remains to the present day.

This Rājā made a large stone image of Vishnu on the northern side of the Bāgmatī and Vishnumatī. In order to propitiate Jayabāgēswarī, who had come to Nepāl from Mānsarovara[2], across the Silā river[3], the Rājā erected an image of Nava-Durgā and Kumārīs, and offered many sacrifices on the Chandī pūrnimā, or night of the full moon in Chait.

This Rajā had no male issue, so he gave his daughter in marriage to a Thākurī, or legitimate Rājpūt, named Ansu-barmā, and shortly afterwards he died.

[1] Literally "man-jackal"; perhaps the sacrificing priest. The Pandit cannot explain this passage.

[2] A lake in Tibet.

[3] Another name for the Gandakī.

At this time Vikramājit, a very powerful monarch of Hindustān, became famous by giving a new Sambaṭasara, or era, to the world, which he effected by liquidating every debt existing at that time in his country. He came to Nepāl to introduce his era here. While searching for a suitable place for his abode, he thought of a certain spot on the first range of mountains, where there still lived the descendants of the people of Dīpāvatī, who came to Nepāl in search of Rājā Ṣarbānand, who lived in the Dwāpar Yuga. This Rājā had left his bihār in Dīpāvatī, where he worshipped the image of Dīpankar Buddh, who died in the Satya Yuga. The people in search of Sarbānand came to Nepāl, but hearing of the Rājā's death, they halted at the first range of hills and lived there, worshipping an image of Dīpankar, which they made exactly like one in Dīpāvatī. Vikramājit, knowing these people to be descended from very ancient families, took up his abode with them. One day, while he was wandering alone on the mountains, meditating on a subject which preyed on his mind, viz., how he was to pay off the numerous debts of this country, Ganēsha appeared to him, but only for a moment. The Rājā took it as a lucky omen to have seen the form of Ganēsha, who is the giver of riches and success; and he became confident that he would now succeed in his object. He therefore erected an image of Ganēsha on the spot where he had seen the form, and having worshipped it, he went to Nepāl, and after clearing off all the debts of the country he introduced his Sambat. From that day Ganēsha came to be known as Sūrya-bināyaka[1].

[1] An image of Ganēsha, with this name, stands opposite Bhātgāon, on the other side of the stream.

The Rājā then, having received the permission of the gods and the people, went back to Ujjain, and having brought the god of three Shaktis, or attributes, named Harsiddhi, placed him near Nīl-tārā. From this the village of Harsiddhi took its origin[1]. The Rājā then, under the direction of the goddess[2], brought all the gods of Nepāl to that place, with great ceremonies, and dramatic performances, and vocal and instrumental music. It is well known that there is no dramatic performance equal to that of Harsiddhi. The people, in gratitude to the Rājā for having paid off all the debts of the country, promised to continue the Harsiddhi performance. After this Rājā Vikramājit obtained salvation. Being a stranger, he left no son in Nepāl, so that Ansu-barmā, who had married the daughter of Viswadēva-barmā, and was about to ascend the throne when prevented by the descent of Vikramājit, now became king, (and thus began a new dynasty).

[1] About halfway between Pātan and Godāvarī.

[2] Harsiddhi is a deity of both sexes.

CHAPTER III.

Vikramāditya's successor begins a new dynasty. The Sālivāhana era introduced into Nepāl. Founding of Pātan or Lalitpūr. Legend of Machchhīndra-nātha. Revival of Hinduism under a supposed incarnation of Shankarāchārya. Founding of Kāntipūr or Kāṭhmāṇḍū. A Thākurī Rājā founds a new dynasty, known as the Vais Thākurī.

1. THE first Rājā of the new dynasty was Ansubarmā.

He left the Durbār at Dēva Pātan, and removed to one which he had built, with many beautiful courtyards, in a place named Madhyalakhu[1]. He also caused his Kājīs and ministers to be accommodated with houses in the same place. This Rājā was very strong-limbed and restless, and people feared his power. He once went to Prayāga Tīrtha (the junction of the Ganges, Jamnā, and Saraswatī, at Allahabad), and persuaded Prayāga-Bhairava to accompany him to Nepāl. He placed him near his Durbār, and to propitiate him established a Mānsāhuti-yagya[2], to be performed every year. The image of this Bhairava is still in existence.

Down to the reign of this monarch the gods showed themselves plainly in corporeal form, but after his time they became invisible. A slōk in the Bhabishya Purāna

[1] Some ruins on the road south of Dēva Pātan.

[2] A *hōm*, in which there is a burnt-offering of flesh instead of rice, flowers, etc.

says: "Ten thousand years Vishnu will reside on the earth; the Ganges half of that time; and Grāma dēvatās (local deities) the half of that." Nepāl, however, being the city of the gods, the deities consented to remain there three hundred years longer than the time thus fixed.

In the reign of this Rājā, a certain Bibhu-barmā Rājbansī, or descendant of a Rājā, having consecrated a Buddha, built an aqueduct with seven dhārās or spouts, and wrote the following slōk on the right-hand side of one of the dhārās: "By the kindness of Ansu-barmā, this aqueduct has been built by Bibhu-barmā, to augment the merits of his father[1]."

In this reign three thousand years of the Kali Yuga had passed away.

2. His son Krit-barmā.

3. His son Bhīmārjuna-dēva.

4. His son Nand-dēva.

This Rājā, having heard that the era of Sālivāhana was in use in other countries, introduced it also into Nepāl. Some people, however, in gratitude to Vikramājit, who introduced his era by paying off all the debts of the country, were averse to giving up the use of that era. Hence some continued to use Vikramājit's Sambat, and others, out of deference to the Rājā's wishes, used the Sālivāhana Sāka.

5. His son Bīr-dōva.

In his reign there lived an ugly grass-cutter, who used every day to cut grass in Lalitban[2], sell it in

[1] This dhārā still exists on the left-hand side of the road leading southwards from the Rānī-pokhrī.

[2] A place in Pātan, where the temple of Kumbhēswara now stands, near the bank of the Bāgmatī.

Madhyalakhu (the capital), visit Mani Jōginī, and then return home. One day, while cutting grass, he felt thirsty, and having stuck into the ground his nōl (bamboo yoke for carrying loads), he went in search of water. He soon found a tank full of water, in which he bathed and drank, whereupon he lost his ugliness and became a handsome man. On returning to his nōl, he found it stuck so firmly in the ground that he was obliged to leave it where it was. Having made a bundle of his grass, he went as usual to sell it in Madhyalakhu. Here he was seen by the Rājā, who enquired how the change in his appearance had been brought about, and was told the preceding story. The Rājā asked him to point out the place, which he did; and the Rājā then said that, as he had got a new and better shape by bathing in the tank, he would give him the name of Lalit, and consider him hereafter as one of his friends.

The Rājā was desirous of erecting some memorial of this event, but was at a loss what name to give to the tīrtha, or holy place, and returned to his palace meditating on the subject. The next night he had a dream, in which he heard these words: "O Rājā! the name of that tank is Gaurī-kund-tīrtha. At the distance of eight hāths (cubits) from the south-east corner, I, Sarbēswara-ling, am buried. Dig and see. The nōl of the clown has become siddha (supernatural) and is my Kāmēswara Found a city near it, and call it Lalit-pattan."

The Rājā awoke, sent Lalit across the Bāgmatī, with much money, and founded a city, to contain twenty thousand inhabitants, which he named Lalitpur. He built and peopled it according to the following rules, observed on such occasions. In the middle of the city he made a tank underground, and in it worshipped the Nāgs and many other deities. He then covered over the tank and the watercourses for introducing and carrying away the water. Over the tank he built a chaitya and a dhārā, and erected a Siva-ling, a Ganēsha, a Mahākāla, and a Mandapa, and built a Durbār for the Rājā, all of which he consecrated. Being a devotee of Mani Jōginī, he named all these after that goddess as follows: Mani-talāva, Mani-chaitya, Mani-dhārā, Mani-linga, Mani-Ganēsha, Mani-Kumāra, Mani-Mahākāla, Mani-Mandapa, and Mani-gal-bhatta. He then built a Dharma-sālā[1], for entertaining thirty-three crores of gods, and named it Lalitāpur. He passed the rest of his life in worshipping these thirty-three crores of gods, and then obtained salvation.

At the time Bīr-dēva Rājā was crowned, 3,400 years of the Kali Yuga had passed away.

6. His son Chandrakētu-dēva.

In the reign of this Rājā, enemies from all sides attacked the country, and plundered and pillaged the people. The Rājā, overwhelmed with grief, shut himself up with his two Rānīs in a room, and lamented and shed tears over these misfortunes for twelve years. At last he received help from a certain person, whose history is as follows.

In Trēta Yuga was built the town of Manju-pattan, which, being enlarged by Sudhanwā Rājā, was named Sānkāsyā. It was again enlarged by Rājā Dharmadatta, and named Bisāl-nagara. After this Dānāsur stopped the water, and changed the valley into a lake, at which time a grihasthāchārya, residing in Manju-pattan, took shelter

[1] This Dharma-sālā stands near the temple of Kumbhēswara before mentioned.

in the mountain of Swayambhū. Among his descendants was one named Bandhudatta Bajrāchārya, who, after becoming a bhikshu, had returned to the grihastha life. He had observed great austerities, and, by constant reciting and performing devotions, had made many mantras subservient to his wishes, and gods even had promised him their help.

At this time he was roaming in the woods and forests, performing chatur-jāp[1], and visiting holy places. On his return he found the city depopulated, and, after dipping his head and body under the water of the Panchnadī[2], and performing bajra-jāp[3], the true state of affairs became known to him, and he saw Rājā Chandrakētu-dēva with his Rānīs starving in a room. He then caused a Panch-rasmi-tēj[4] to emanate from his body and illuminate the room in which the Rājā was. The Rājā, surprised at seeing the light, got up, and went in search of the object from which it proceeded. Having traced it to the bank of the river, he was about to jump into the water, when the devotee appeared, and, taking hold of the Rājā's hands, gave him hopes that he would put an end to his misfortunes. Speaking thus, he conducted the Rājā back to his Durbār; and, in reply to his entreaties to put an end to his troubles, the Āchārya told him to collect articles of worship and offerings for the goddess, whom he was going to summon to relieve him.

The Āchārya then went to the Kāmani mountain[5], and, after performing great devotions, and reciting man-

1 Recitation of mantras at morning, noon, evening and midnight.

2 The junction of the Vishnumatī and Bāgmatī.

3 Recitation of Buddhist mantras.

4 Or solar spectrum, which, according to the Nepalese, has only five instead of seven colours.

5 One of the peaks on the south side of the valley.

tras, he at last succeeded in bringing with him the goddess, whom he left in a certain place, and went to the Durbār to bring the offerings for her. To his surprise, nothing had been collected by the Rājā, so he had himself to prepare an offering. This caused some delay, and the goddess meanwhile, in the shape of a child, was crying and wandering about in search of food. Just then a Jyāpu (cultivator), on his way to his fields, saw the child, put her in his kharpun (basket), and carried her away with him to his fields, named Navalim[1]. There he gave her bread to eat and pyātho (beer)[2] to drink, and placed her under an umbrella to shelter her from the sun. The Rājā and Āchārya returned to the place where the goddess had been left, and not finding her there, they went into the fields, and after much entreaty succeeded in bringing her back. They then placed her in a suitable sacred spot, and worshipped her; and then the Rājā and Āchārya poured forth their woes, and asked how the wealth, which had been plundered, was to be recovered, and their enemies driven away. The Dēvī instantly caused a light to issue from her body, which illuminated the ten sides of the universe. The Rājās, who had carried off the riches and pillaged the country, became frightened at this sight, and restored what they had taken away, so that the Rājā and his people were made happy again. From that day the goddess was named Lomrī-mahākālī-dēvī[3].

The Rājā was blessed with a son, whom, after per-

[1] Near the Tudikhēl, now the grand parade-ground.

[2] Two kinds of liquor are made in Nepāl, *raksht*, a spirit distilled from rice or wheat, and *pyātho*, a kind of coarse beer, fermented but not distilled.

[3] Her temple stands on the eastern side of the Tudikhēl, and is much resorted to by the natives.

forming all the requisite ceremonies, he named Narēndra-dēva. He then caused his son to be crowned, and being himself old, he ascended into Heaven.

7. Narēndra-dēva reigned 7 years.

This Rājā built a bihār near Lomrī-dēvī, whom Bandhudatta Āchārya had brought and placed there for the protection of the country. After naming it Tīrtha, because the Āchārya came from Tīrtha, he gave it to the spiritual guide of his father. He then gave much away in charity, and settled down at Madhyalakhu. He had three sons, the eldest of whom was named Padma-dēva, the second Ratna-dēva, and the youngest Bar-dēva. The Rājā sent the eldest to become a bandya in the Pingalā Bahāl, where there were at one time six hundred bandyas. The second he put under the guidance of Bandhudatta in the Tīrtha Bihār. The third was anointed as Rājā.

Bandhudatta placed Padmāntaka[1] in the Tirtha-bahāl, and then brought ten Krōdha-dēvatās, or avenging deities, from Kāmunī, and also placed them there, along with Asta-pīthas and Asta-smashāns[2]. At the north-east corner of the Tīrtha-bahāl he placed Mahākāla, whom he brought from Bhōt (Tibet). Having thus placed gods on all the ten sides, the Rājā and Āchārya lived happily.

After this, the Rājā, having lost his love of the cares of state and worldly riches, went to the distance of two kōs to the east of the city, and built a bihār there, in which he lived. From his living alone there, the bihār was named Alag-bahāl, which has been corrupted into Ak-bahāl[3].

[1] A Bhairava. [2] Eight places of worship and eight burning-ghāts.
[3] At the southern end of Bhātgāon.

8. Bar-dēva.

This Rājā reigned eight years. Because his father Narēndra-dēva relinquished the world and went to live as a recluse, the Durbār at Madhyalakhu became disagreeable to the Rājā, who therefore removed his court to Manigal-bhatta Durbār at Lalit-pātan, which had been built by the grass-cutter Lalit, under the direction of the Rājā's grandfather Bīr-dēva Rājā.

In this reign Gōrakh-nātha came into Nepāl, and when there reflected thus: "In this universe Niranjana and other Buddhas, whose forms are sachchitta (existence and thought), in order to create the world, produced the pancha-tatwas (five elements), and took the form and names of the five Buddhas. The fourth Buddha, by name Padma-pāni Bōdhisatwa, the son of Amitābha, sprung from his mind, sat in a state of samādhi (deep meditation), called Lōka-sansarjana. The Ādi-buddha then named him Lokēswara, and gave him the duty of creating the world. He then created Brahmā and other gods; and because he sat in Sukhāvatībhuvana, and watched attentively Brahmā and the other gods, to ensure their protection, he was called Āryāvalokitēswara Padma-pāni Bōdhisatwa. This Buddha went from Sukhāvatī to a place called Banga, where Siva came to learn from him Yōg-gyāna (*i.e.* union with the supreme being by means of profound meditation). Siva, after learning this, was returning home with Pārvatī, when one night he stayed on the sea-shore, and Pārvatī asked him to repeat to her what he had learned. He did so, but Pārvatī fell asleep during the rehearsal, and Āryāvalokitēswara Padma-pāni Bōdhisatwa transformed himself into a fish, and performed the part of a listener. Pārvatī at last awoke, and on being questioned showed that she had not heard all that Siva had recounted. This made Siva suspect that some one else was listening, and he exclaimed, 'Whoever is lurking in this place must appear, or I will curse him.' On this Lokēswara appeared in his true form, and Siva, falling at his feet and making many apologies, was forgiven. From that day the Lokēswara, on account of his having taken the form of a fish, was known as Matsyēndra-nātha[1]." Gōrakh-nātha then knew that this Matsyēndra-nātha daily resorted to the Kāmani mountain; but he also knew that that place was very difficult to approach. At the same time he was unable to suppress his desire to see one who had been the Guru of all the gods, and the creator of the world; and he thought that his life was worthless unless he saw Matsyēndra-nātha. However, he thought of a plan to bring Matsyēndra-nātha before him. This was to catch the nine Nāgs and confine them, so that they could give no rain. There would thus be a great drought, and the people would cry out, and surely Matsyēndra-nātha would appear for their relief.

With this design, Gōrakh-nātha attracted the nine Nāgs into a hillock, and sat down upon it. The result was a drought, which lasted for twelve years. The people were in great distress, and Rājā Bar-dēva was much troubled in his mind, as he saw no means of relieving them. While seeking for some mode of relief he used to go about eavesdropping and listening to what old people were saying.

One night he went to Triratna Bihār, where old Bandhudatta Āchārya lived, and he overheard a con-

[1] Vulgarly, *Machchhindra-nātha*.

versation between him and his wife. The wife asked the Āchārya the cause of the drought and its remedy. The Āchārya replied: "The only one who is able to put a stop to this is Āryāvalokitēswara, who resides in the Kāpōtal mountain; and he cannot be brought except by the prayers of the ruler of the country. Now the Rājā is young and foolish, and the old man his father, Narēndra-dēva, is living in a lonely bihār, because he and his son do not agree."

Having overheard this, the Rājā returned to his palace, and next morning he went to his father and fell at his feet. He brought the old Rājā home with him, and having sent for the aged Āchārya, asked him to do something to relieve their distress. The Āchārya said that he would do all he could to help them, but that, as he could not be successful through a priest alone, without his yajamāna, he must take the father Narēndra-dēva with him. They then took a large supply of offerings, and taking a mālī and mālinī (gardener and his wife) with them, they took leave of Rājā Bar-dēva. They halted at the spot where Dōlana[1] has been erected, and with great ceremonies and offerings performed purascharanas, at first one thousand, and then up to ten millions in number. After this, Bandhūdatta, Narēndra-dēva, the carrier of the articles of worship, and the mālinī with the kalas[2] remained there, and Bandhudatta performed a purascharana to summon Jōgāmbara-gyāna-dākinī. After the mantra had been recited a crore of times (counting each one as a thousand),

[1] A place where there was a tree, under which Machchhīndra-nātha rested. The old tree has fallen, but some young ones have sprung up around it. The place is to the south of Pātan, between the town and the large Asoka chaitya.

[2] A pot of water carried by a gardener before marriage processions and in religious ceremonies, &c.

the goddess was pleased, and promised her assistance. The Achārya, having gained this additional power, was now able to rescue Karkōtak Nāg from the grasp of Gorakh-nātha, and started on his journey to the Kāpōtal mountain. He carried Karkōtak in his pen, and whenever they had to cross a river or a bad road, he took out Karkōtak, who carried them over it.

After encountering many frightful objects, placed in their way by gods and devils, they reached the Kāpōtal mountain, and the Āchārya began to perform purascharana to invoke Aryāvalokitēswara; whereupon the latter, in his residence at Sukhāvatī, began to think that in Nepāl (which had been a lake for the residence of Nāgs; where Bipaswī Buddha sowed a lotus seed; where Swayambhū appeared in the form of light; which Manjusrī Bōdhisatwa peopled, and gave a king to; and where he himself, after visiting Swayambhū and Guhjēswarī, stationed the gods to protect the people and country) Gorakh-nātha, in order to see him, which he could have effected by meditation, was performing Nāg-sādhana, *i.e.*, bringing the Nāgs under his control. He therefore said, "Why has he done this mischief? Have the gods not been able to rescue the Nāgs? The people, instead of assisting and protecting their fellow-creatures, must be bent on wickedness!" He accordingly determined to go to the valley of Nepāl, to station gods expressly to protect the country, and to prove that he, whose name enabled Bandhudatta to rescue Karkōtak, possessed much power. The Āryāvalokitēswara then left Sukhāvatī, and, resting on the sky, showed himself to Bandhudatta, and after giving him much insight into his secrets, again disappeared. Then he went to reside with a Yakshinī, whom he called his mother, and who was named Gyāna-dākinī, from being created by Māyā (delusion).

Bandhudatta, according to his instructions, recited mantras to summon the Āryāvalokitēswara; but when, through the influence of the mantras, he was about to go to Bandhudatta, his mother tried to prevent him. Such, however, was the power of the mantra, that he disappeared thence, and, transforming himself into a large black bee, entered into the kalas. Bandhudatta had told the Rājā Narēndra-dēva to shut the mouth of the kalas as soon as the bee entered, but the Rājā having gone to sleep, the bee entered the kalas three times without its mouth being closed. At last the Āchārya, giving the Rājā a touch with his foot, awoke him, and caused the mouth of the vessel to be closed. The Āchārya then worshipped the bee as Machchhīndra-nātha. The Rājā, however, determined to slay the Āchārya, because he had touched him with his foot.

After this, Gyāna-dākinī, with numerous gods, yakshas, and devils, came to attack Bandhudatta, who, being hard pressed, called all the gods in Nepāl to his assistance. The Nepalese gods went to the place where Bandhudatta was, and, after a consultation, decided that the office of ruler and protector of Nepāl should be entrusted to Machchhīndra-nātha; and Bandhudatta on his part promised to send occasional offerings to Gyāna-dākinī and the gods who had objected to Machchhīndra-nātha's being taken to Nepāl. Having thus satisfied every one, the Āchārya worshipped the Āryāvalokitēswara in the kalas, according to the das-karma, or ten ceremonies observed on the birth of a child.

When the Āchārya was about to depart, Gyāna-dākinī asked by what road he intended to go back.

He replied, "by any way they liked to point out." The gods and devils, who had come from the Kāmrūp mountain, then said that he should take the god by the way of Kāmrūp, and that he should leave marks along the road to enable the god to return by the same route. For this purpose, they said, they would give him a quantity of dēvadāru (deodār) seeds to scatter as he went along. The Āchārya agreed to this, but stipulated that the god should only return as far as the dēvadāru trees produced from this seed extended. The gods, bhūts, prēts, pisāchas, yakshas, and gandharbas agreed to this; whereupon, by means of a mantra, the Āchārya parched the seeds, and carried away the god, scattering the parched seed as he went, and thus he reached the Kōtpāl mountain.

This Kōtpāl mountain got its name as follows. In Satya Yuga, when Nepāl was a lake, Bipaswī Buddha had sown a lotus seed, from the flower of which the form of light had issued. In the Trētā Yuga, Manjusrī Bōdhisatwa, coming from Mahā-Chīn, had cut a passage to let out the water through this mountain, which he named Kōtpāl.

After propitiating the gods, daityas, gandharbas, yakshas, rakshasas, &c., who had come from the Kāmrūp mountain, Bandhudatta sent them back. Then he worshipped the kalas in which the Āryāvalokitēswara was, and invoking all the deities of Nepāl, he held a great jātrā on the banks of the Bāgmatī, as he entered Nepāl; and now he scattered the unparched dēvadāru seeds along the road by which they entered the country.

In this jātrā, the kalas, in which the Āryāvalokitēswara was, was carried by four Bhairavas, namely, Hayagrīva, Harsiddhi, Lutābāhā of Pachhilu village[1], and Tyāngā. Brahmā swept the road, reciting Vēdas as he did so; Vishnu blew the sankha; Mahādēva sprinkled kalas-water on the road; Indra held an umbrella; Yama-rāj lighted the incense; Varuna sprinkled water from a sankha, and rain fell; Kuvēra scattered riches; Agni displayed light; Nairitya removed obstacles; Vāyu held the flag; and Īshān scared away devils. In this manner all the gods showed their respect, while bringing in Āryāvalokitēswara-Matsyēndranātha. These gods, however, were not visible to any except Bandhudatta and Narēndra-dēva. The people only saw Bandhudatta, Narēndra-dēva, the mālī and mālinī, and the gods in the shape of birds and beasts.

A plentiful rain now fell in Nepāl. When the procession reached a certain spot they sat down to rest, and here Harsiddhi Bhairava, in the shape of a dog, barked and said "bū", which Bandhudatta explained to the Rājā Narēndra-dēva to mean "birth-place", and that they were to consider that Machchhīndranātha was born on this spot.

In honour of the Amaras, or gods, who came so far in company with them, and of the spot thus mysteriously pointed out by the dog, Bandhudatta, after consultation with the Rājā, determined to build a town and name it Amarāpur[2], and here he placed the kalas containing Āryāvalokitēswara-Machchhīndranātha. They then appointed two priests to worship him in turn. One of these was a distant cousin of Bandhudatta, and a descendant of a priest of Swayambhū, who lived in the

[1] On the road between Kōtpāl and Pātan.

[2] Or Bogmatī, about three miles south of Pātan.

Triratna Bihār. The other was a resident of Tō Bahāl[1]. They assigned to these lands for their maintenance.

After this, Bandhudatta, Narēndra-dēva, and the mālī, went on their way to the place where Rājā Bar-dēva had remained. As they went along, they talked, and decided that they would institute a rath-jātrā[2] with an image of the god. Each of them, however, wished to have it held at the town in which he himself lived; that is to say, Bandhudatta wanted it at Kāntipūr (or Kāṭhmānḍū), Narēndra-dēva at his residence, and the mālākār (or mālī) at Lalitāpur. While thus disputing, they arrived at Ikhātōl in Lalitpattan, and seeing a great crowd of people, they agreed to abide by the decision of the oldest person there. They therefore called the Nāikyā (or head man) of the whole district belonging to Lalitpattan, and having put sacred things on his head[3], asked for his decision. The Nāikyā reflected thus: "There is no town where Narēndra-dēva lives, nor where the Āchārya lives. These three people have all taken equal pains and trouble, but it is Mahārāj Narēndra-dēva who has been put to expense. However, I shall give my decision in favour of Lalitpattan, because it is a large town with many inhabitants; and Rājā Bar-dēva has come from Madhyalakhu to reside here;

[1] There seems to be some mistake here, for Tē Bahāl is said to be the same as Triratna Bihār.

[2] A festival in which the images of the gods are drawn in a *rath* or chariot. A *rath* consists of a platform with wooden shafts, 30 or 40 feet in length, and ponderous wooden wheels, six or eight feet in diameter and a foot thick. On the platform an erection of wood or bamboo is run up to a height of from 30 to 50 feet. The shrine of the gods is placed on the platform, and the upper part of the erection is adorned with flowers and green branches. The *rath* is drawn along by the worshippers.

[3] This ceremony is performed when a person is put on his oath. Buddhists place the book called *Pancharaksha* on the head; Hindūs use for the same purpose gold, leaves of the *tulsī* plant, a *sāligrām*, and the book named *Harivansa*.

and besides, it is my own dwelling-place. In showing this partiality, and doing this injustice to Rājā Narēndra-dēva, I shall however, I am sure, be swallowed up by the earth." Having formed this resolution, he caused seven *ukhals* [1] to be brought and piled one upon another. He then ascended to the top of them and spoke thus: "Hear, O Āchārya Bandhudatta, Mahārāj Narēndra-dēva, Mālākār, and all you people! Anything to be done for Padmapāni - Āryāvalokitēswara - Machchhīndranātha [2] should be referred to Mangal-bhatta, where reside the gods of the whole three worlds." Having thus spoken, he was swallowed up by the earth, and so died. This spot is still well known to the people[3].

The audience, being contented with the decision, went to the bihār in which Sunayasrī Misra once lived as a bhikshu; and as they considered it a very sacred spot, they performed a purascharana[4] at a place called Chōbhu. Then, taking possession of one-third of the bihār which was built by Sunayasrī Misra, they caused an image to be made of Āryāvalokitēswara-Machchhīndranātha. This, after consecration, they took to Amarāpur, and worshipped it; and after this the spirit of the god, brought from Kāpōtal mountain in the kalas, was transferred to the image. This image was

[1] A wooden block like a butcher's block, about two feet high, with a small hole in the centre, in which rice is pounded with a wooden pestle, about four feet long, grasped by the middle so that either end can be used. The object of the pounding is to remove the husk.

[2] On the Buddhist prayer-machines is written *Om mani padmē hūm*, i.e. "hail to him with the jewel and lotus." The Pandit and Munshī say that this is Machchhīndra-nātha, and not Sākya Muni. The Nepalese do not use prayer-machines, although they are found round the temples at Bodhnāth and Swayambhūnāth for the use of the Bhotiyas.

[3] It is near the Poḍhiyatol in Pātan, to the south of the durbār.

[4] When a person wishes to attain any object, he makes a vow to recite mantras a certain number of times, either himself or by proxy. The mantras vary with the deity to be propitiated.

made of earth brought from the Hmayapidō mound[1], with the earth of which also the Swayambhū Chaitya was built by Prachanda-dēva Rājā, in accordance with the directions of Sāntikar Āchārya. This earth was taken from its place after many ceremonies and the worship of Jōgāmbara-gyāna-dākinī. This hillock was considered very sacred, because, after the depopulation of Bisāl-nagara, when the two countries of Matirājya and Irkhārājya were peopled, the Rājās used to take earth from it to use in the worship of Pūrnachandī-dēvī.

After the consecration of the image, whatever offerings and presents were necessary were given to the descendants of Sunayasrī Misra.

Bandhudatta, who knew everything of present, past, and future times, established the rites of worship in the following order. The image of the deity was brought from Amarāpur, when the sun was in the northern hemisphere, and kept in a temple built in Tau Bihār[2]. He was bathed on the 1st of Chait Badi. On the 8th he was put in the sun. On the 12th and 13th the *das-karma* was performed[3]. On the 1st of Baisākh Sudi he was put on the rath, and after being taken round the city (of Lalitpattan) he was conveyed back to Amarāpur, or Bugmatī, when the sun was in the southern hemisphere. From the time the rath-jātrā of Machchhīndranātha began, the rath-jātrās of Dhālāchhē Lokēswara, Swattha-nārāyana, and others, which used to take place in Lalitpattan, were discontinued; except that of Mīnanātha-dharmarāj, who is Sānu (or junior) Mach-

[1] A wooded knoll on the left bank of the Vishnumatī, where it is crossed by the road to Bālājī.

[2] In Pātan, to the south of the Durbār, on the left-hand side of the street leading to the parade-ground.

[3] Ten ceremonies, commencing from the time of the conception of a child.

chhīndra. From this year too the rath-jātrā of Chaubahāl was discontinued, which used to take place in Dēva-pātan every year, because the rath, in returning from Dēva-pātan, was sunk in the Dānāgāl Khōlā.

After this, the son of Rājā Narēndra-dēva removed from Madhyalakhu Durbār with his court to that of Mangal-bhatta, and Narēndra-dēva returned to his own residence. Narēndra-dēva's wife had died, and her two daughters he had given in marriage, the elder at Pātan, the younger in a village near his residence. He now called these two daughters before him, and said: "I have become old. Ye have no brothers, and your mother is dead. Your gōtīyā brothers (step-brothers) may invite you to their houses, or not, according to their pleasure. I have no wealth to give you. All I have to give you is my crown with its appurtenances, and the book *Pragyā-pāramitā*. She who comes to me first on the morning of the fourth day from this, after bathing, will get the crown, and the other the book." The two sisters did as they were told. The elder came first and got the crown, and the younger got the book. This crown and book are still in existence[1].

Bandhudatta Āchārya, sometime after this, went to Narēndra-dēva, and asked him whether all his wishes had been accomplished, and nothing left unfulfilled. The Rājā replied, that the Āchārya, with great kindness, had taken much pains and trouble to fetch Āryāvalokitēswara-Machchhīndranātha to this *Khas*[2] country, and had relieved the poor people from the distress of a drought, which had lasted for twelve years, by a plentiful

[1] If so, the Pandit does not know where.

[2] The *Khas* are, strictly speaking, the children of Brāhmans and Chhētrīs by women of the different hill-races, such as Bhotiyas and Newārs. They now rank as Chhētrīs.

rain, which had pleased the gods of Nepāl. Every wish of his had been fulfilled, and there was nothing more remaining to be done. The Āchārya then told him to think well, because there was one thing wished for in the Rājā's mind, which still remained to be fulfilled. The Rājā, however, could think of nothing. Whereupon the Āchārya said: "When Āryāvalokitēswara came in the form of a black bee to enter the kalas, I awoke you by touching you with my foot, and you then resolved to kill me. That is the one thing still undone, and you ought to perform it." The Rājā begged to be forgiven, and said that he, being a descendant of kings, was easily enraged, and hence thought of such a thing, which he begged the Āchārya would forget. The Āchārya told him that it was not from any ill-feeling that he mentioned this, but that it was incumbent on him to carry out any resolution made at the moment when he was in the presence of Īswara. The Āchārya then made a figure of himself with boiled rice, at which the Rājā struck, and thus accomplished his vow.

On returning home that same night Bandhudatta died, and, being absolved, was incorporated with the right foot of Machchhīndranātha.

The Rājā Narēndra-dēva was much grieved, and after four days he too was absolved and incorporated with the left foot of the deity. For this reason, any one going to see Machchhīndranātha looks at his feet, in order to see Narēndra-dēva Rājā and Bandhudatta Āchārya.

Seeing such devotion on the part of the Rājā and Āchārya, the people became very much attached to the worship of Āryāvalokitēswara-Machchhīndranātha, who in return always gave plentiful rain and protected the people. Machchhīndranātha came into Nepāl in the

Kaligata year 3623[1]. Here ends this brief history of Machchhīndranātha.

Bar-dēva Rājā, the son of Narēndra-dēva, now lived in the Mangal-bhatta Durbār at Pātan, and followed his father's advice in worshipping Machchhīndranātha. The Harsiddhi Nāch, introduced by Rājā Vikramājit, had been discontinued; so Bar-dēva revived the deity Harsiddhi and the Nāch, and made a rule that the Nāch should be first of all performed before Machchhīndranātha.

In the reign of this monarch, a Brāhman, an incarnation of Shankarāchārya, came to see whether the rules and customs established by that great reformer were still in force in Nepāl. He found them observed everywhere, even at the place where Machchhīndranātha was, owing to the directions of Bandhudatta Āchārya, who knew all the events of the present, past, and future times. The Brāhman then went to Pingalā Bahāl, where he found that the Bandya Āchāryas had acquired great influence by reciting mantras and worshipping Āgama. After eating their meals they used to throw the remainder into the enclosure around Pashupati. Seeing this, he determined to destroy these impious people. He therefore entered their service, and one day, when throwing away the remnants of their meal, he also threw away their Mrigthuchā (a small golden bull, supposed to supply the food)[2]. The next morning, the Bandyas came as usual for their meal, but found no food and no Mrigthuchā. They said that this was a great sin which had been committed, and therefore they went to live elsewhere.

[1] This date is given in a slōk, of which the figures are *sūla* (3), *dwandwa* (2), *ras* (6), *agni* (3). According to rule, these figures must be inverted, giving 3623.

[2] The Mrigthuchā is not used nowadays in Nepāl.

The Brāhman then went towards Bhōt, and arrived at a place called Khāsā. The Lāmā of Bhōt, knowing that such a one had arrived, came in the disguise of a poor Bhōtiya, and while the Brāhman was bathing, relieved the calls of nature before him. Thereupon the Brāhman used bad language towards him, calling him an Asur and a Chandāl. The Lāmā then ripped open his stomach with a knife, and asked the Brāhman to do the same, so as to see which of them was purest internally. The Brāhman, being afraid, transformed himself into a kite and flew away; but the Lāmā transfixed him to the ground by piercing his shadow with a spear. The Lāmā then placed a stone on him, and performed Sādhana over him. The spot where this occurred is still pointed out, where Khāsā Khōlā is crossed.

At this time a son was born to Bar-dēva Rājā, who attributed this happy event to the advent of the Brāhman, whom he considered to be Shankarāchārya himself, after he had heard the history of that great reformer. He therefore named this son Shankara-dēva, in honour of Shankarāchārya.

9. Shankara-dēva reigned 12 years.

This Rājā built a village in the shape of a sankha, or shell, and named it Sānkhu. It was dedicated to Ugra-tārā-dēvī.

10. His son Barddhamān-dēva reigned 13 years.

11. His son Balī-dēva reigned 13 years.

12. His son Jaya-dēva reigned 15 years.

13. His successor Bālārjuna-dēva reigned 17 years.

14. His successor Vikrama-dēva reigned 12 years.

15. His successor Guna-kāma-dēvā reigned 51 years.

While this Rājā was fasting and worshipping Mahālakshmī, the goddess appeared to him in a dream, and told him to found a city at the junction of the Bāgmatī and Vishnumatī rivers. This was the sacred place where, in former times, Nē Muni had performed devotions and practised austerities, and here was the image of Kāntēswara dēvatā. To this spot Indra and other gods came daily, to visit Lokēswara and hear purānas recited. The new city was to be built in the shape of the kharg or sword of the Dēvī, and to be named Kāntipur; and dealings to the amount of a lākh of rupees were to be transacted in it daily. The Rājā, being thus directed, founded the city at an auspicious moment, and removed his court from Pātan to Kāntipur (Kāṭhmāṇḍū). This took place in the Kaligata year 3824.

The city contained 18,000 houses. Lakshmī gave her promise that, till the traffic in the city amounted to a lākh of rupees daily, she would reside there. By her kindness the Rājā was enabled to build a suvarna-pranālī or golden dhārā[1], and hence he named the city Suvarna-pranālī-kāntipur. He then peopled it with various castes.

He also went towards the East, and brought Chandēswarī, and placed her in the centre of the country for its protection. In like manner he made Karbīra-smashān on the banks of the Vishnumatī. At the same place he erected an image of Bidyādharī-dēvī, who had shown herself in the sky to a pandit named Bajrapāda.

He also brought from Dakshina-Kālī the goddess Rakta-Kālī, and revived her worship as Kankēswarī. He also revived the worship of two sets of Nava-durgās, the one inside, the other outside, of the country. To

[1] This dhārā is on the street leading from the Durbār in Kāṭhmāṇḍū to a bridge over the Vishnumatī on the old road to Thānkōt.

the west of the country he renewed the worship of Panchlinga Bhairava, whose jātrā takes place on the 5th of Āswin Sudi. This Bhairava had come to play with a Kharginī, or Kasāinī.

He also brought from Indrānī-ghāt the goddess Manāmaijū-pītha, and placed her in the east of the country, at a place called Āgama-chōka. To the east is the Lomrī-dēvī, brought by Bandhudatta Āchārya from the Kāmrūp mountain. Then he established, or rather revived, the Hīlyā jātrā, Krishna jātrā, and Lākhyā jātrā. The last of these was in honour of Sākya Muni having obtained a victory over Namuchi-māra[1], when the latter came to distract his attention, while he was sitting under a *bodhi* tree[2] in profound meditation for the purpose of becoming a Buddha. After his victory Brahmā and other gods came to pay their respects to Sākya Muni, for which reason the gods are represented in these jātrās.

He also instituted the Matayāta and Sringabhērī jātrās. The Hīlyā, Krishna, and Lākhyā jātrās were in existence before the time that Kāntipur was founded. He then instituted the Indra jātrā by erecting images of Kumārīs. Then, in imitation of the Lokēswara jātrā of Pātan, he made an image of Khasarppa Lokēswara, and caused his jātrā to be celebrated every year. He then founded a village named Thambahīl, at the place where formerly Vikrama-sīla Bihār stood. The image of Thambahīl, consecrated by Sinhal Baniyā, the survivor of the party of 501 baniyās, had been destroyed when the waters of the Bāgmatī had been stopped up by Dānāsur, but it had been replaced by the descendants of Sinhal.

[1] Another name for Kāmdēva, or more likely for Indra.

[2] The Bhotiyas use the seeds of this tree as beads in their rosaries.

The Rājā took a large army with him, and brought much wealth from all quarters. He caused Pashupati to be bathed with golden water, poured from two golden dhārās, for a fortnight, and instituted a jātrā to be continued ever after. He also made a new roof of gilt copper for the temples of Pashupati and Bālasukī[1].

In the reign of this Rājā some one consecrated the image of Ganēsha in Kāntipur, and named him Asōka Bināyaka, from the circumstance of there being many Asōka trees at that spot. A hithi was also built near the place known by the name of Maduhiti-dhārā.

What remained of the wealth of the Rājā he caused to be stored up in rooms, which he built in the Indrāchal mountain[2]. The wealth amounted to fifty-two crores, and he made Bālasukī the guardian of it. This Rājā ruled over both cities, *i.e.* Pātan and Kāntipur.

One night Srī Skandaswāmī appeared to the Rājā in a dream, and told him that he would be much pleased if all the boys of the city were assembled and kept at a place near Kankēswarī-kālī. If he did this, his subjects would never revolt, and his enemies would be destroyed. The god added, that he was taught by his parents from his boyhood to play at Siti (stone-throwing) from the beginning of the month Jēth to Siti-khashtī. The Rājā, taking this to be a warning from Īswara, assembled the boys, and established the custom of their pelting each other with stones[3].

16. His son Bhōj-dēva reigned 8 years.

17. His son Lakshmī-kāma-dēva reigned 22 years.

[1] So the MS., instead of *Bāsukī*.

[2] The hillock north of the temple at Pashupati.

[3] This custom was originally carried out with great rigour, the prisoners on each side being sacrificed. The sacrifices were however discontinued long ago, and the festival (if it may be so called) was abolished by Sir Jung Bahādur, on the occasion of the British Resident, Mr Colvin, being struck by a stone whilst looking on.

This Rājā, thinking that his grandfather had acquired so much wealth and conquered the four quarters of the world through the aid of the Kumāris, resolved to do the same. With this intention he went to the Pātan Durbār, and having worshipped as Kumārī the daughter of a bandya, living in a bihār near the Durbār, known by the name of Lakshmī-barman, he erected an image of Kumārī and established the Kumārī pūjā.

18. His son Jaya-kāma-dēva reigned 20 years.

This Rājā, in order to put a stop to theft and snake-bites, revived the worship of the Bālasukī Nāg, and made offerings to him of musical instruments. From that day no cases of robbery or snake-bite took place in the city.

This Rājā had no issue, so after his death the Thākurīs of the Noākōt mountain came and elected a Rājā from among themselves.

1. This Rājā's name was Bhāskara-dēva.

In his reign the Bānrās of Pingalā Bahāl removed to other places. Their descendants, who were Āchāryas, became Bānrās, and lived in Gnākhā-chōk in Lalitpattan[1]. The Bhikshus of Dēvapātan and Chābahīl came to these people, and told them that they had heard from some people, who were working in the fields, that they had seen the god of Pingalā Bahāl. They accordingly went to see, and found the god buried under the ruins of the Pingalā Bahāl, and brought him to Pātan. While they were taking him thither, when they had arrived at a bowshot north of Mangalbhatta, they saw Lakshmī-dēvī of Lagankhēl in the form of a kite; and one of the devotees, by the influence of his mantras, brought her down, and the Dēvī became stationary there in the road. After this, they took the god to Gnākhā-chōk, but he said

[1] Close to the western gate of the town.

he would not like to live there. This having been brought to the notice of Rājā Bhāskara-dēva, he caused a new bihār, named Nhūl-bahāl, to be built for the god. This new house also being disapproved of by the god, the Rājā went to ask where he would like to fix his residence. The god said he would like to live in a place where a mouse attacked and drove away a cat. The Rājā himself then went in search of such a place, and one day at a certain spot saw a golden mouse chasing a cat. Here he built a bihār, and named it Hēma-barna (*i.e.* golden-coloured)[1], and having placed the god in it, with Āgama-dēvatās, just as they were in Pingalā Bahāl, he assigned lands as guthīs[2] for the maintenance of the establishment. The Bānrās, who came with the god to reside here, were those of Thyākāyēl and Hatkhātōl.

2. His son Bal-dēva.
3. His son Padma-dēva.
4. His son Nāgārjuna-dēva.
5. His son Shankara-dēva.

In the reign of this Rājā, some people, from a village named Jhul[3], had gone to the Gaur country (Bengāl) and lived in a city named Kāphī, whence several persons returned to Jhul. These men performed yagya daily in a hollow consecrated place, where a perpetual fire was kept alight. The hollow place is called yagya-kund, and he who undertakes this fire-worship is obliged to perform the yagya with his wedded wife sitting by his side, as Siva and Sakti. The yagya is never performed by a single person.

[1] It is a little to the east of Gnākhā-chōk.

[2] A *guthi* is land assigned for a religious purpose, which cannot be resumed by the donor nor seized by creditors. Rent may or may not be paid for it. A *birtā* is a grant of land in perpetuity, for which rent is paid. A *jāgīr* is a grant of land for a term, which may be resumed by the donor. No rent is paid for it. Soldiers and officials are usually paid in this way, the grant terminating with the service.

[3] It lay between Kīrtipur and Mātātīrtha.

One of these Brāhmans, having no lawful wife, took with him a Brāhmanī widow, named Yasōdharā, instead of his wife; and one day, as he was performing the yagya, the fire increased, and, after burning him up, consumed the whole village.

Rājā Shankara-dēva then established a yagya-kund in Pātan; and in Kāntipur he make known the Tānā-dēvatā as Kul-dēvatā; and he made it a rule that no house should be built higher than the gajura of the Dēvī.

At the time when the village of Jhul was burning, Yasōdharā, the Brāhmanī widow, fled to Pātan with a small model of a chaitya, the book Pragyā-pāramitā (written in golden letters in Vikrama-sambat 245[1]), and her infant son Yasōdhara. She repaired the bihār in Gāla-bahāl, built by Bidyādhara-barma, and placed the model chaitya inside the one in the bihār. She caused her son Yasōdhara, after his chūrā-karma, to be made a bandya; and in order to conceal this from her relatives, who were Agnihotrīs, she did not allow the ceremonies attending the chūrā-karma to be performed in front of the Āgama-dēvatās of the bihār. To this day the bandyas of this bihār only follow this custom. In other bihārs the custom is different. Previously this bihār was called Bidyādhara-barma-sanskārit-mahā-bihār, but after the chūrā-karma of Yasōdhara it became known as Yasōdhara-mahā-bihār, and also as Buyā-bahāl[2].

Long before this time, out of hatred to Shankarāchārya, a party of one thousand Bānrās murdered seven hundred Brāhmans residing in Bisālnagara. The wives of these Brāhmans immolated themselves as Satīs, and their curses were so powerful that the thousand murderers were burned to ashes. The spirits of these Satīs then became so tur-

[1] V. S. 245 = A.D. 188.

[2] West of the Durbār in Pātan.

bulent, that no one would venture to pass that way. The Rājā, therefore, in order to put a stop to this trouble, caused an emblem of Siva to be placed there by venerable pandits. This emblem, having been erected for the Sānti, or peace, of the Brahma-pisāchas, was called Sāntēswara. It is also called Nandikēswara[1], from its having been erected by a Brāhman of Bisāl-nagara, named Nandi, who himself after death was deified as Moptā-dēva or Bhātbhatyāni.

This Rājā, to establish peace on a more secure footing, instituted the custom of a yearly jātrā of the Navasāgara Bhagavatī of Bisāl-nagara, on the anniversary of the Prētachaturdasī. The original image of this Dēvi, made by Viswa-karmā, was so frightful, that no one would pass that way. The people therefore buried it, and covered the place with stones.

After the seven hundred Brāhmans had been massacred, the rest left Bisāl-nagara, and went to live at Dēva-pātan, where they built a house having seven courts.

The dynasty of the Vais Thākurīs of Noākōt ends here. A descendant of a collateral branch of the solar race of the former Rājā Ansu-barmā, by name Bāma-dēva, having gained over the nobles of Lalitāpur and Kāntipur, succeeded in expelling the Vais Thākurī Rājās, and made himself king.

[1] A large temple on the north side of the Pashupati road.

CHAPTER IV.

A new Rājpūt dynasty. Founding of Kīrtipur and of Bhaktapur or Bhātgāon. Introduction of the Nepāl era, and legends connected with it. Arrival of Newārs in the country under Rājā Nānya-dēva from the south Kārnātaka, who expelled the Malla Rājās and founded a fresh dynasty. Legend of Kēschandra. Nepāl invaded from the west by Mukunda-sēna. The Khas and Magar castes enter the country. Pestilence, and destruction of the invaders. The Vais Thākurīs of Noākōt again seize the throne, and hold the country for 225 years. Country invaded by Hari-sinha-dēva of Ayōdhyā, who founded a dynasty. Legends connected with his conquest of the country. Turjā Dēvi. Invasion by and defeat of the Bhotiyas. Legend of the Baid and Karkōtak Nāg.

Of the new dynasty the first Rājā was

1. Bāma-dēva.
2. His son Harkha-dēva.
3. His son Sadāsiva-dēva.

This Rājā founded a town near Kāntipur and Lalit-pātan, at the south-west corner of the valley, near the hills. On account of the great *kīrti* (celebrity) attached to this place, from a cow belonging to it having been the means of discovering Pashupati-nātha, it was named Kīrti-pur. The children of the cowherds of this town used to go to the forests to feed their sheep, and amused themselves by making a clay figure of a tiger. One day the children, thinking the figure incomplete without a tongue, went to fetch a leaf to supply the defect; and on their return were dismayed to find their sheep devoured, and a real tiger in the place of the image, a Bhairava having entered into it. The images of the Bāgh (tiger) Bhairava and the deified children are still to be seen at this place.

The Rājā, having gone to the four quarters of the world, and conquered all countries, brought back a great quantity of gold, and made with it a new roof for the temple of Pashupati-nātha in the Kaligata year 3851. He was the first to introduce into the currency the *Suki*, a coin of copper and iron mixed, with the figure of a lion on it.

4. His son Mān-dēva.

He reigned for ten years, and then abdicated in favour of his eldest son, and lived the life of a bandya in a bihār, and so obtained salvation. This bihār, having on it numerous chakras, was called Chakra Bihār.

5. His son Narsinha-dēva reigned 22 years.

6. His son Nanda-dēva reigned 21 years.

This Rājā, after consultation with Sunandāchārya, an Āchār of Dēva-pātan, built three apartments, one within the other, for Bhuvanēswarī, into which only the initiated are allowed to enter.

7. His son Rudra-dēva reigned 7 years.

This Rājā entrusted the government to his son, and employed himself, after having become a Bauddha-mārgī, in acquiring a knowledge of the elements.

8. His son Mitra-dēva reigned 21 years.

9. His son Ari-dēva reigned 22 years.

A son having been born to this Rājā, while he was engaged in wrestling, he gave the child the title of Malla.

10. His son Abhaya Malla.

This Rāja had two sons.

11. The elder, Jaya-dēva Malla, reigned 10 years.

12. The younger, Ānanda Malla, reigned 25 years.

This younger brother, being very generous and wise, gave up the sovereignty over the two cities; and having invoked Annapūrnā Dēvī, from Kāsī, founded a city of 12,000 houses, which he named Bhaktapur (Bhātgāon), and included sixty small villages in his territory.

After this, the Rājā, having obtained the favour and directions of Chandēswarī, founded seven towns; viz. Banēpur, near Chandēswarī Pītha; Panāvatī, near the Prayāga Tīrtha of Nepāl, celebrated in the Shāstras, on the site where Pānchāla-dēs formerly stood; Nālā, near Nālā Bhagavatī; Dhaukhēl, near Nārāyana; Khadpu, near Dhanēswarī; Chaukōt, near the residence of Chakōra Rishi; and Sāngā, near Nāsikā Pītha[1].

He established his court at Bhaktapur, where he built a Durbār; and having one night seen and received instructions from the Navadurgā, he set up their images in proper places, to ensure the security and protection of the town both internally and externally.

It was at this time, when Ānanda Malla reigned in Bhaktapur, and his elder brother in Pātan and Kāntipur, that a certain astrologer of Bhaktapur found out an auspicious moment, at which he said that sand, taken from a certain place, would turn into gold. The Rājā Ānanda Malla, having ascertained the exact time, sent a number of coolies, to take up sand at that particular moment, from the place called Lakhu Tīrtha, at the junction of the Bhatīkhu and the Vishnumatī, and to convey it to the Rājā's palace. The coolies did as they were directed, but,

[1] Banēpur, now called Banēpa, is a village outside of the great valley, eight or nine miles east of Bhātgāon. Panāvatī (now Panautī) lies five or six miles south of Banēpa, in another valley. Nālā is between Banēpa and Bhātgāon. Dhaukhēl and Khadpu lie east of Banēpa. About Chaukōt I have no information. Sāngā stands where the road from the Nepāl valley crosses the low hills into the Banēpa valley.

as they were going back with their loads, a Sudra merchant of Kāntipur, named Sākhwāl, prevailed on them to take their loads of sand to his house; and then the coolies filled up their baskets again with sand from the same place as before, and took it to Bhaktapur. Their second loads, however, not being taken up at the auspicious moment, did not turn into gold, and the Rājā, being enraged at the imposition practised on him, burned the book[1].

On the other hand, Sākhwāl, having obtained so much wealth, with the permission of Jaya-dēva Malla, paid off all the debts existing at that time in the country, and thus introduced a new era into Nepāl, called the Nepāl Sambat[2]. He then established a chaitya near his house, and placed a stone image of himself at the southern door of the temple of Pashupati-nātha. Thus he obtained salvation.

Mahārāj Ānanda Malla, finding that his heap of sand did not turn into gold, was very angry; and going to the astrologer, told him that what he had said about the sand turning into gold was false. Having said this, the Rājā returned to his palace, and the astrologer in his mortification kindled a fire, and put his book into it to be burned. The Rājā, however, on his return to the palace, happened to observe the baskets in which the sand had been brought, and saw some grains of gold at the bottom of them. He ran back to the astrologer to tell him that he was right, and seeing the fire, asked what was being burned in it. The astrologer's wife told him that it was the false Shāstra

[1] *I.e.*, the book by reading which the astrologer had been led to make the prediction. Further on the astrologer is said to have done this.

[2] This era begins in October, A.D. 880. The present year, 1876, is therefore N.S. 996—7.

which her husband was burning. The Rājā was very sorry, and snatching the unburned portion of the book out of the fire, put it into milk. He then took the astrologer to his palace, and after showing him the grains of sand which had become gold, told him that the Shāstra was true, and that it was their own haste which was in fault. The astrologer advised him to enquire from the coolies how they had carried out their orders, and they said that the first loads of sand had been taken by a merchant of Kāntipur, and that those brought to Bhaktapur had been collected afterwards.

Rājā Ānanda Malla was then sitting in his court, surrounded by his courtiers and astrologers. On hearing what had happened they exclaimed: "There is nothing so powerful as luck or destiny in this world. High birth and wealth are its servants. It is also written in the Shāstras, 'Luck everywhere begets fortune; neither learning nor strength can do it. In the churning of the ocean Hari got Lakshmī and Hara got poison.' Oh Mahārāj, in the Satya Yuga the thirty-three crores of gods, dēvatās, and daityas, churned the ocean, and first of all there came out the Uchchaisravā, which Indra took, saying that it was his luck. After the horse came out Lakshmī, whom Vishnu took. Then came out the Kālakūta poison, and began to destroy the world. The thirty-three crores of dēvatās then began to pray to Mahādēva, who alone was able to destroy the power of the poison. Mahādēva, being easily propitiated, appeared, and asked what they wanted from him. They replied that the Kālakūta poison was destroying the world and themselves, and they sought protection, and implored it with joined hands and tears in their eyes. Mahādēva said that he would instantly destroy its power; and so saying, he put it into his mouth, but, instead of swallowing it, he kept it in his throat, which became blue from the effects of the poison, and hence Mahādēva is named Nīla-kantha. Feeling now very hot, he went close to the snowy range of mountains, but the cold there was not sufficient to cool him. He then struck his trisūl into the mountain, from which sprang three streams of water, and he laid himself down and let the water fall on his head. There lies Sadāsiva, who takes away the sins of man, and exempts him from having to be reborn. The good things that came out of the ocean, after churning, were appropriated by dēvatās and daityas; but when Kālakūta came out, these all fled, and so it fell to the lot of Mahādēva. Such is destiny, oh Mahārāj! The astrologer foretold an auspicious moment, and you sent coolies to fetch gold, which all went to Sākhwāl, who took no pains or trouble to get it. Be content therefore with your fate."

Rudra-dēva Chhētrī Rājā, who, being learned in Tatwa-gyāna, or the knowledge of the elements, had after a brief reign abdicated in favour of his son Mitra-dēva, and occupied himself in acquiring religious merit, at this time first practised Bauddhacharyā, then Mahāyānikacharyā, then Tribidhībōdhi. After this he repaired the old Ōnkulī Bihār, built by Rājā Siva-dēva-barmā, and after performing the chūrā-karma he lived in it as a bandya, the sure way of obtaining *mukti*, and thus he earned salvation. This Rudra-dēva Rājā on one occasion sent an image of Dīpankar Buddh to receive pindapātradān instead of himself. He also kept a guthī, by name Bēpār Madhi, in the name of his ancestors, Bāma-dēva, Harkha-dēva, Sadāsiva-dēva, Mān-dēva, Narsinha-dēva, Nanda-dēva, and of himself Rudra-dēva, for his own bihār, in order that people living in it might be allowed to follow any trade[1]. To make this more secure, he informed his grandson Jaya-dēva Malla of his having established this custom.

At the time when Rājā Jaya-dēva Malla was ruling over Lalit-pātan and Kāntipur, and Ānanda Malla over Bhaktapur, in the Sākā year 811, and Nepāl Sambat 9 (A.D. 889), on the 7th of Srāvana Sudi, a Saturday, Nānya-dēva Rājā came from the south Kārnātaka country and entered Nepāl. He brought with him the Sāka Sahkāla era, and introduced it. Among the troops that were with him were Newāras, from a country called Nāyēra, who were Brāhma-putra Chhētrīs and Āchārs. He brought two dēvatās with him, named Māju and Swēkhū, and having defeated the Malla Rājās, he compelled them to flee to Tirhūt. He established his court at Bhaktapur, and ruled over it as well as over Lalit-pātan and Kāntipur. The kings of this dynasty are as follows.

1. Nānya-dēva reigned 50 years.
2. His son Gangā-dēva reigned 41 years.
3. His son Narsinha-dēva reigned 31 years.

In his reign, in Nepāl Sambat 111 (A.D. 991), on the 6th of Phāgun Sudi, Rājā Malla-dēva and Kathya Malla, of Lalit-pātan, founded the village of Chāpāgāon, then called Champāpurī.

4. His son Sakti-dēva reigned 39 years.
5. His son Rāma-sinha-dēva reigned 58 years.

All went well in his reign.

6. His son Hari-dēva.

He removed his court to Kāntipur, in which city at this time lived a Thākurī, named Bhāskara Malla, who had a son called Kōschandra, who was a minor when his father died, and unable to take care of his own

1 This passage is rather obscure.

affairs, so that his father had appointed a guardian. Kēschandra, however, being of a truant disposition, used to give his guardian the slip and go gambling here and there. One day he went to Thambahīl, where he saw the dēvatā being repaired by the descendants of Sinhal. This dēvatā had been erected by Sinhal, but was destroyed when Dānāsur flooded the valley. He began gambling there, and as it was late, instead of returning home, he went to the house of his sister, who lived at Thambahīl. His sister reproved him for playing to so late an hour, but he paid no attention to her, and after taking his meal, he again went out to gamble. He lost heavily, and returned to the house of his sister, who again reproved him, but with so little effect that Kēschandra now took away and staked the plate off which he had eaten his meal, and lost it also. When he returned his food was served to him on the ground, which so affronted him that he tied up the rice in his clothes, and going home he put it in a corner. To relieve his mind from the feeling of degradation he then went to Nīla-kantha-Gosāīn-Thān, and having bathed in the lake, prayed to the deity, and asked for help. Nīla-kantha's voice replied from the sky, that he should visit Pashupati and Kritimukha Bhairava, and his misery would be ended. Kēschandra did as he was directed, and seeing that the offering of rice before Kritimukha was so rotten that the grain had become full of maggots, he gathered it up, and took it home. His curiosity then led him to go and see in what condition the rice was which he had brought from his sister's house. This also was rotten, and Kēschandra, not knowing what to do with it, begged for and obtained a quantity of rice from some other people, and mixing the rotten rice with this, he went to sell it. He exchanged it for some marchā (the refuse rice that remains after distilling spirit), and went to a place named Bakhunchhā, where he spread it out to dry, as it was wet, and then went to sleep. While he slept pigeons came and ate the marchā, and being told by Kritimukha Bhairava to give something in return, they left golden dung on the spot. Kōschandra, having awoke, was gathering the gold, when a Rākshasa, named Gurung Māpā, came by, and was about to devour him; but being addressed as Māmā (maternal uncle), the Rākshasa was appeased, and helped Kōschandra to carry the gold to his home. Kēschandra then married the daughter of Rājā Haridēva.

As for the Rākshasa, he kept him in his house, and told him that he might have the bodies of all the persons who died there for his food. This gave much annoyance to the people, and caused a great deal of misery, for when parents, to frighten their crying children into silence, said "Gurung Māpā take thee," the Rākshasa took them at their word, and soon devoured them. The people therefore complained to Kēschandra. He had bought 360 rōpnīs of land, which he had levelled into a khēl or plain, and called Tudi-khēl, because he had purchased the land with gold begotten by *tudi*, or maggots produced in rotten grain. He therefore now gave this plain to Gurung Māpā as his residence, on condition that he was not to devour any one, and was never to allow three bricks to stand on one another on the Khēl. In return for this service Kōschandra promised to send him every year an *āra* of rice[1] and a buffalo for his food.

[1] About 80 lbs.

Kēschandra's son having died in his youth, he took his body to burn, and having ascended into the sky by means of the smoke, he saw his son above him in the clouds mounting upwards. Having come down again, he performed the funeral rites. He then returned home and built a bihār, in which he placed a bauddha, and assigned a guthī for feeding pigeons with 102 āras of dhān (unhusked rice), because all his wealth was derived from pigeons. The bihār he named Pārāvata-mahābihār[1], from *pārāvata*, a pigeon. He also assigned a guthī to place on the Tudi-khēl one āra of boiled rice, and one cauldron full of flesh, for Gurung Māpā on the anniversary of the 14th of Phāgun Badi. He then caused a picture of all these circumstances to be made, and put it in his bihār, where he lived as a devotee of Buddha. This picture is shown to those who wish to see it in the month of Sāwan[2]. People afterwards named his bihār Itum-bahāl.

In the reign of Hari-dēva Rājā, the ministers, people and troops of Pātan revolted, and the Rājā with his ministers and the troops of Kāṭhamāḍon (*sic*), going to suppress the rebellion, was defeated, and pursued as far as Thambahīl.

At this time there was a Magar in his service, who, through the machinations of the ministers, was dismissed as being no longer required. This man returned to his home, and praised Nepāl as having houses with golden roofs and golden pranālīs (or dhārās). The Rājā Mukunda-sēna, a brave and powerful monarch, having heard of this, came to Nepāl from the west, with a large number

[1] In the centre of Kāṭhmāṇḍū, west of the Indra-chok or main bāzār. Pigeons are still fed here at certain times. They inhabit the temples in great numbers, and are very tame, at least in the streets.

[2] A copy of this picture still exists, and is exhibited as mentioned in the text.

of mounted troops, and subdued Rājā Hari-dēva, the son of Rāma-sinha-dēva. Of the Nepalese troops some were slain, and others fled. Great confusion reigned in the three cities. Through fear of the troops the people buried their radishes, and having cut their rice, stacked it and concealed it by heaping earth over it. The victorious soldiers broke and disfigured the images of the gods, and sent the Bhairava placed in front of Machchhīndranātha to their own country, Pālpā and Butawal.

On the day that Rājā Mukunda-sēna arrived at Pātan the priests were performing the Snāna-jātrā, or ceremony of bathing Machchhīndranātha. Seeing the troops, they ran away, leaving the god in the Davalī (bathing-place). At this moment the five Nāgs, which were in the golden canopy of Machchhīndra, poured forth five streams of water on the head of the deity. Mukunda-sēna saw this, and, out of respect for such great power, he threw upon the image the golden chain which adorned his horse's neck. Machchhīndra himself took it up, and put it round his neck, and this chain is never removed from the neck of the image.

With this Rājā the Khas and Magar castes came to Nepāl. These men, having no mercy, committed great sins, and the Aghōra Mūrti (the southern face) of Pashupati showed its frightful teeth, and sent a goddess named Mahā-mārī (pestilence), who within a fortnight cleared the country of the troops of Mukunda-sēna. The Rājā alone escaped to the east, in the disguise of a Sannyāsī. On his way back from thence to his own country he arrived at Dēvī-ghāt[1], and died there. From

[1] At the junction of the Taddi and Trisūl-gangā in the Noākōt valley.

this time the Khas and Magars came into the country; and sinkī and hakuwā rice were made[1]. The Kārnātakī Rājās reigned for five generations. In the sixth Haridēva was subdued by Mukunda-sēna, whose troops were destroyed by pestilence. For seven or eight years after this there was no Rājā in Nepāl.

Seeing that the throne was vacant the Vais Thākurī Rājās of Noākōt came and began to rule. In Lalitpātan every tōl (division or quarter of the town) had its own Rājā. In Kāntipur there were twelve Rājās, who were called Jhinihmatha-kula. Bhātgāon had also a Thākurī Rājā.

At this time Bhīmasēna, being desirous of living in Nepāl, came in the form of a man to the house of a Thākurī of Kwātha Bahāl. This person, having recognised him by some of his supernatural deeds, built a temple for him, the walls of which he caused to be painted. In this temple he established Bhīmasēna.

To the west of the city (*i.e.*, Kāṭhmānḍū), at a distance of fifteen kōs, was a place called Majīpāta, where a Rākshasa used to visit a Kshipānī (a female dyer of chintz, &c.). The twelve Thākurīs persuaded him to take part in the annual Indra-jātrā, and established him in the Majīpāta-tōl.

From this time the Thākurīs ruled the country for 225 years; but, as they were very numerous, their names have not been recorded. They left numerous Bauddha temples, with lands assigned for their maintenance, in

[1] Sinkī is radishes buried in the ground till they ferment. They are then taken out, dried, and eaten. The smell is atrocious and utterly abominable. Hakuwā is made by stacking the rice when not perfectly ripe, covering it with earth, and allowing it to heat and become slightly malted. It is then dried. It is considered very light and wholesome.

Lalitāpur (Pātan), Kāntipur (Kāṭhamāḍon), and Bhaktapur (Bhātgāon).

The descendants of the Jhūl-bahāl Thākurīs used to worship the das-pāramitā-bauddha-dēvatās by washing their feet and feeding them in their houses with kshīra (rice boiled in milk)[1]. To maintain this custom lands or guthīs were set apart. One of the descendants of these Thākurīs had married a woman of Bhātgāon, and used to go to his father-in-law's house. One day, while conversing with his father-in-law, he told him that he worshipped the das-pāramitā-bauddha-dēvatās. The father-in-law said he would like to see them, and for this purpose went to Pātan, and while his son-in-law was serving them with food, he mixed poison in something and laid it before them to eat. They, however, were aware of the treachery, and escaped the effect of the poison by repeating a dhārani, or mantra. The Thākurī, who had given the poison, became affected by it, and no physician could cure him; but an astrologer told him that his disease was the work of some great deity. The son-in-law then entreated the Bauddha-dēvatās for his cure, and by their advice, the water with which their feet had been washed was given to him to drink, and he was cured. From that day the dēvatās came no more, and the Thākurīs worship ten old bhikshus who represent them.

A descendant of the same Thākurīs of Tihrū-bahāl, named Bharī-bharāo, being poor, used to store cakes of cow-dung (fuel) in his dhukutī or treasury, and revealed to no one what he had there. He used to carry the key with him wherever he went; but one day he forgot it,

[1] Any ten old men from any bihār are taken and worshipped as gods. Their feet are washed and they are fed as described. The names of the original dēvatās were: Dāna pāramitā, Sīla p., Kshānti p., Bīrja p., Dhyāna p., Pragyā p., Upāya p., Bala p., Pranidhi p., and Gyāna p.

and his wife, finding it in his absence, opened the door, and saw that the room was full of ingots of gold. She told her husband, who was much surprised to find gold instead of cow-dung. Both of them, out of gratitude, became desirous to employ a portion of the gold for religious purposes. The wife however wished to do something for Nārāyana, and the husband for Buddha; and they could not agree which to prefer. At last they determined to sow the seed of bhīmpātī and tulsī[1], the former as an emblem of Buddha and the latter of Nārāyana; and whichever sprang up first was to decide which was to be the god of their worship. The Bhīmpātī came up first, so they followed the Buddhist religion. They invited the Bauddha-mārgīs of the three cities, on the 3rd of Phāgun, entertained them the whole night with feasting and an illumination of the house, and gave them leave to go away on the 4th. They then assigned lands for the maintenance of this custom, which is kept up to the present day.

The Thākurī Rājās built many Bauddha temples, pātis[2], and other religious houses. They were the first to introduce the Ghorā-jātrā.

At this time Rājā Hari-sinha-dēva of Ajōdhyā (or Oude), a descendant of Srī Rāma-chandra, being hard pressed by the Musalmāns, fled to Simāngarh[3] with his four ministers, family and servants, and treasure. His Rānī had a kētī (slave girl), whose paramour was a Rākshasa of Ceylon, who was a skilful architect. One night, when the slave girl was going to sweep the floor of the

[1] Tulsī is a kind of basil, held sacred by the Hindūs. Bhīmpātī is a shrub with bunches of small whitish blossoms, held sacred by the Buddhists.

[2] A *pāti* is a *dharmsāl* or house of rest for pilgrims. One of large size is called a *powah*.

[3] Now called Simroungarh.

(Plate XI.) VARIOUS FORMS OF CHAITYAS. (p. 174.)

palace, her paramour gave her, without her knowledge, a golden broom, with which she swept, and left some golden fragments on the floor. The Rājā, having seen these, was curious to know how they came there. After a long inquiry, he at length heard of the paramour, and calling him before him, demanded his name, caste, family, residence, etc.

The demon told him that his name was Māyābīja, and that he was a Rākshasa from Ceylon. He presented the Rājā with a diamond necklace, consisting of 108 stones, which were so brilliant that they resembled the star Venus.

The Rājā then asked him to build a temple for his household goddess Turjā (or Tuljā) Bhavānī, which Māyābīja undertook to do. In one night he erected a temple of five stories, with images of gods and goddesses, wells of water, and tanks full of clear water, crowded with the red lotus, fish, and waterfowl. He also laid out gardens, full of flowers and singing birds, which could rival the Nandana-bana of Indra in heaven. He also built a wall round the city, so thick and high that neither beasts nor enemies could penetrate it. As the cock crew before the work was completed, he was obliged to stop and leave a portion of the wall unfinished.

After some time Turjā Bhavānī directed the Rājā to go to Nepāl, which he did in the Sāka year 1245 and Nepāl Sambat 444 (A. D. 1324)[1].

On his way to Nepāl he arrived on the 9th of Pūs Sudi, a Saturday, at a jungle called Madhu-bana, where his followers could get nothing to eat, and were on the point of being starved; whereupon the Rājā prayed to his goddess Turjā for help. In the night the goddess

[1] This was when Simroungarh was destroyed by Tughlak Shāh of Dihlī.

told the Rājā, in a dream, that they might eat whatever they could find early in the morning. Early next morning the Rājā saw a wild buffalo, which his people caught and brought before the goddess, who directed the Rājā to seek for a man among the bushes after sunrise to kill it. Such a man having been found, the task of sacrificing the animal to the goddess was entrusted to him, and he was called khaḍgī (swordsman). The goddess then directed that they should eat the buffalo's flesh, as her prasāda or leavings. The descendants of the khaḍgī became the caste named after him, but now called Kasāīs. Seven castes of people came with the goddess to Pādara Khārī, viz. Brāhmans, Bhadēla, Achāra, Jaisī, Baida, Rajaka (MS. Rajīka), and Khaḍgī.

The Rājā was overtaken by night before reaching Bhātgāon, and some traders, arriving where the Rājā had stopped for the night, halted there also. They asked him what was the cause of something which they felt to be supernatural in this place, where before this time they could never make up their minds to halt.

The Rājā then spoke thus: "In Trētā Yuga the monster Rāvana,—a grandson of Pulastya, who had ten heads and twenty arms, a body like a mountain, a complexion like lampblack, a burden to the earth, an enemy to gods and good men, and the ruler over fifty-two crores of cities,—having obtained the desire of his heart from Brahmā at Gokarna, (where he had observed austerities, and had made a sacrificial offering of his heads for ten thousand years, by putting them in the burning fire of the yagya-kund,) went and defeated Indra the king of heaven. Rāvana took Turjā Bhavānī, the principal Dēvī of Amarāpur, the capital, and was carrying her off to Ceylon, when he was seized with a pressing necessity, and descending to the earth, was obliged to put down the goddess. When he was going to take her up again, all his strength was insufficient to accomplish this, and he was obliged to leave her where she was. After some time, Rāma, the incarnation of Nārāyana, who was born in the house of Dasaratha, the king of Ajōdhyā, through the aid of his wife Sītā and the help of Sugrīva, the monkey king, built a bridge across the arm of the ocean, killed Rāvana, Kumbha-karna, Indrajit, Prahasta, etc., and made Bibhīkhana king of Ceylon. Then Rāma, mounting Pushpaka-bimāna, returned to Ajōdhyā. On his way thither, when he had arrived on this side of the sea, he saw a ray of light issuing from the earth and ascending to the sky. He descended to find out the cause of this, discovered Turjā-dēvī, and took her to Ajōdhyā. As he did this secretly no mention is made of it in the Rāmāyana. The goddess was brought to Simāngarh, where Māyābīja of Ceylon built a temple, garden, and city. This city was attacked by a large army of the emperor Akbar (*sic*), who succeeded in taking the city by entering at that portion of the wall which had been left incomplete by Māyābīja. Turjā-dēvī has now come to Bhātgāon, and her influence is such, that enemies are destroyed and good men exempted from being reborn. She was worshipped by Brahmā, Vishnu, and Mahēswara."

The Rājā here ended his narrative; after which, the Thākurīs and people of Bhātgāon came to see the goddess, and such was her influence that they quietly made over the Durbār to Hari-sinha-dēva. He established the goddess there, in a temple which he named Mūla-chōk.

The Bhotiyas, hearing of the renown of Turjā-dēvī,

came with a large army to carry her away; but when they arrived at the stream named Sāmpusi, instead of seeing Bhātgāon, they beheld a frightful fire blazing, and were frightened. They each threw down a clod of earth and a quantity of ashes, which formed two or three small ridges of hills, named Dandampā, and then they returned to their own country. These ridges are still in existence[1].

A person who washed the clothes of Rājā Hari-sinha-dēva at Pādara Khārī was called Rajaka, and this caste of people, his descendants, settled down at Dēva-pātan and Bhātgāon.

A Baid (physician) of this Rājā was one day preparing to bathe in the water at Tēkhudobhāna[2], when he was accosted by Karkōtak, the king of the Nāgs, who, in the form of a Brāhman, was seeking for a Baid to cure a malady with which his Rānī's eyes were affected. The Nāg, being satisfied that the man was a Baid, entreated him to go to his house and see a patient. The Baid, after finishing his ceremonies and bathing, went with the Brāhman. They arrived at a pond, at the south-western corner (of the valley), a thousand bowshots beyond Chaubahāl. The pond was so deep, and the water so black, that it was frightful to look at. It was shaded by trees, large fish played in it, and it was covered with waterfowl[3]. The Nāg told the Baid to shut his eyes, and in a moment he jumped with him into

[1] To the N.E. of Bhātgāon; but I could not ascertain which stream is the Sāmpusi.

[2] The junction of the Bāgmatī and Vishnumatī.

[3] This tank, Taudāh, is still in existence, and believed to be the abode of Karkōtak. I have been gravely cautioned against going to fish there for fear of this mighty Nāg or serpent. During the present reign an unsuccessful attempt was made to draw off the water, with the view of getting the wealth supposed to be sunk in it.

the water, and they arrived at the Durbār of Nāg-rāj in Pātālpurī. The walls of the palace were of gold, the windows of diamond, the rafters and beams of sapphires, the pillars of topaz adorned with rubies. The darkness of the subterranean place was dispelled by the light emanating from large jewels in the heads of the Nāgs. They entered the palace, and saw the Nāginī, sitting on a throne studded with jewels of several sorts, shaded with three umbrellas of white diamonds, one above the other, and surrounded by beautiful Nāginīs. Karkōtak, assuming his proper form, took the Baid by the hand, and gave him a seat near the throne. He himself mounted the throne, and showed the patient to the Baid. The Baid, having examined her eyes, took out a drug from a bag which he carried at his waist, and having rubbed it on a clean stone, applied it to the eyes, which were instantly cured. Karkōtak gave the Baid a handsome present and a dress of honour, and having expressed his gratitude, made him a promise that his descendants would be good curers of eye-diseases. The descendants of this Baid, accordingly, were renowned as good eye-doctors. Hari-sinha-dēva, having been made acquainted with these events, honoured the Baid, and gave him a place to reside in, near Sēsha Nārāyana.

The descendants of the Newāras, who came from Nāyēra, still occupy the country.

Dwīmāju-dēvī made over to Hari-sinha-dēva all the treasure which she had hoarded up from the time of Nānyadēva Rājā; and the Rājā, in return, established the yearly Dēvālī Pūjā in her honour.

The kings of this dynasty were:

1. Hari-sinha-dēva, who reigned 28 years.
2. His son Mati-sinha-dēva reigned 15 years.

3. His son Sakti-sinha-dēva reigned 22 years.

This Rājā abdicated in favour of his son Shyāma-sinha-dēva, and took up his residence at Palāmchōk[1], whence he sent presents to China, which so pleased the Emperor that he sent in return a seal, with the name Sakti-sinha engraved on it, and in addition the title of Rāma, with a royal despatch, in the Chinese year 535.

4. His son Shyāma-sinha-dēva reigned 15 years.

In this reign a tremendous earthquake was felt in Nepāl. The temple of Machchhīndranātha and all other buildings fell down, and innumerable human beings perished. This took place on the 12th of Bhādra Sudi, in Nepāl Sambat 528 (A.D. 1408).

This Shyāma-sinha-dēva had no male issue, but only a daughter, whom he gave in marriage to one of the descendants of the Malla Rājās, who fled to Tirhūt on the invasion of Nānyadēva Rājā. He then made his son-in-law Rājā.

[1] To the east of Banēpa.

CHAPTER V.

The line of Hari-sinha-dēva having become extinct, the throne is filled by a descendant of the former Malla Rājās, who founds a new dynasty. Laws of Jayasthiti Malla. Division of the kingdom. Malla Rājās of Bhātgāon. First invasion of the Nepalese territory by the Gōrkha kings. Birth and education of Prithwīnārāyana Sāh.

1. Jayabhadra Malla reigned 15 years.

Before this time these Malla Rājās had ruled over Bhātgāon, and the Navadurgā-dēvī, being much pleased (at their return), caused such a plentiful crop to be produced, that, in threshing out the rice, a large quantity was scattered about and formed a hillock of corn; which hillock still exists at the south-east corner of the town.

2. His son Nāg Malla reigned 15 years.
3. His son Jayajagat Malla reigned 11 years.
4. His son Nāgēndra Malla reigned 10 years.
5. His son Ugra Malla reigned 15 years.
6. His son Asōka Malla reigned 19 years.

This Rājā, having propitiated the Kwāthachhō-kumārī-dēvī of Pātan, defeated the Thākurī Rājās, and took their possessions. Through the influence of this Dēvī, the rivers Bāgmatī and Manmatī, which flowed near his temple and joined there, left a great space of land at their junction.

This Rājā once went to hunt in the jungle of Swayambhū, and became thirsty. While searching for water he saw Swēta Kālī and Rakta Kālī, in the middle of the space bounded by the Vishnumatī on the west, the

Bāgmatī on the south, and the Rudramatī on the east: and he determined to name this place Kāsīpur, or the northern Kāsī.

This Rājā ruled over both Pātan and Bhātgāon; and Gangā-bālakumārī being pleased with him, he was blessed with a wise and powerful son.

7. His son Jayasthiti Malla reigned 43 years.

This Rājā was very wise, through the favour of Gangā-bālakumārī, who was very much pleased with his father Asōka Malla, the sixth of the Malla Rājās, the descendants of Rājā Jayabhadra Malla, who succeeded to the throne in right of his wife, the daughter of Rājā Shyāma-sinha-dēva, the fourth in descent from Rājā Hari-sinha-dēva, of the solar race, who brought Turjā Bhavānī into Nepāl.

He made many laws regarding the rights of property in houses, lands, and birtās, which hereafter became saleable.

In former reigns criminals were allowed to escape with blows and reprimands, but this Rājā imposed fines, according to the degree of the crimes. He ordered that all the four castes of his subjects should attend the dead bodies of the kings to the burning-ghāts, and that the instrumental music of the Dīpaka Rāga[1] should be performed while the dead bodies were being burned.

To some castes he gave permission to sound the kāhāl (a long trumpet), while the bodies of their dead were being burned.

Every caste followed its own customs. To the low castes dwellings, dress and ornaments were assigned, according to certain rules. No sleeves were allowed to

[1] There are six rāgs, 36 rāginīs, and eight putras or sons of these. All these are various modes of singing.

the coats of Kasāīs. No caps, coats, shoes, nor gold ornaments, were permitted to Pōdhyās. Kasāīs, Pōdhyās, and Kullus, were not allowed to have houses roofed with tiles, and they were obliged to show proper respect to the people of castes higher than their own.

The Rājā caused a stone image of Rāma, with his two sons Lava and Kusa, to be made, and placed it on the bank of the Bāgmatī, opposite Ārya Tīrtha, where it is yearly worshipped as a patron deity. He also caused the image of Gorakhnātha to be revived with mantras by an inspired devotee. He likewise established a daily worship and ceremonies to be performed at Gokarnōswara.

He built a two-storied temple of Kumbhēswara in Lalit-pātan, and put a gajura on it. He caused the tank near Kumbhēswara to be cleaned out, and found in it eight stone images of Nārāyana, Ganēsha, Sītalā, Bāsukī, Gaurī, Sānda, Kritimukha, and the Āgama-dēvatās of Bauddha-mārgīs, which he caused to be erected in various places. To pacify Sītalā he erected Unmatta Bhairava, and to mitigate his fury he placed an Āgama-dēvatā above him. These circumstances are inscribed on a stone of the said Bhairava, which bears the date Nepāl Sambat 542 (A.D. 1422).

This Rājā, after having earned the esteem and gratitude of his subjects by making numerous religious and social laws, died on the 5th of Kārtik Badi, Nepāl Sambat 549 (A.D. 1429)[1].

In making laws about houses, lands, castes, and dead bodies, he was assisted by his five pandits, Kīrtinātha Upādhyāya Kānyakubja, Raghunātha Jhā Maithilī, Srīnātha Bhatta, Mahīnātha Bhatta, and Rāmanātha Jhā. Such laws were formerly in existence, but having

[1] There seems to be an error in this and the immediately preceding date.

fallen into disuse through lapse of time, they were again compiled from Shāstras and brought into use.

Houses he divided into three classes: Gallī, situated in a lane; Gallī bhitar, situated in a street; and Shahar, in the centre of the city. To estimate the value of houses it was to be determined how many Khā they covered. For first class houses a khā was 85 hāths (cubits) in circumference; for the second class of 95 hāths: and for the third of 101 hāths[1].

To the four principal castes, viz., the Brāhman, Kshatrī, Vaisya, and Sūdra, were given the rules of Bāstu-prakaran and Asta-barga for building houses. The ceremonies before laying the foundations were to be performed by Brāhmans, if the owners of the buildings were Brāhmans or Kshatrīs; and by Daivagyas, if they were of the Vaisya or Sūdra castes.

Lands were divided into four classes, and their value was to be determined by the number of Karkhas or Rōpnīs they contained. For the fourth class a rōpnī was 125 hāths in circumference; for the third class 112 hāths; for the second 109 hāths; and for the first class 95 hāths. A hāth was to be of the length of 24 lengths of the first joint of the thumb.

Formerly the Tāngo or bamboo measuring-rod was 10½ hāths in length, but Rājā Jayasthiti Malla reduced it to 7½ hāths. The land-measurers were made into a caste called Kshatrakāra, and the house-measurers into one called Takshakāra.

In dividing the people into castes the five councillors

[1] It may seem an extraordinary arrangement, and to a European a very absurd one, that a measure should vary in dimensions according to the quality of the thing to be measured. Such, however, is still the rule in Nepal. There is a special class of people who determine the value of houses and lands. These people are now called Chhibhandail, and they make a mystery of their trade.

had to consider that the bandyas had been converted in the Trētā Yuga, by Krakuchhand Buddh, from the Brāhman and Kshatrī castes, and had become bhikshus, and that these again had been made grihasthas by Shankarāchārya. It is, moreover, written in the Shāstras that, first of all, one should live as a Brahmachārī and read all the Shāstras; secondly, that he should live as a Grihastha; thirdly, that he should accept Pravrajyā-vrata, and live in the woods as a Bānaprastha Bhikshu; and, fourthly, that he should return to the life of a Grihastha, or householder, and instruct sons and grandsons, living himself in a state of Nirbriti (*i.e.*, free from worldly cares). He who does all this receives the title of Buddha or Bajrāchārya-arhat-bhikshu.

Now Shankarāchārya had forced these people to change from bhikshus to grihasthas, without passing through the four different kinds of lives; and being thus fathers of families, they were obliged to attend to worldly affairs; but still they were respected by the four castes. Hence it was determined to class them as Brāhmans or Kshatrīs, their customs and ceremonies being the same. Bandyas therefore are like Sannyāsīs, who are all of one class without any distinctions of caste.

The rest of the people were divided into 64 castes as follows, the first mentioned being the lowest.

(1) Charmakāra, (2) Mātangī, workers in leather: (3) Niyōgī: (4) Rajaka, (5) Dhobī, washermen: (6) Kshatrikāra: (7) Lōhakāra: (8) Kundakāra: (9) Nādichhēdī: (10) Tandukāra: (11) Dhānyamārī: (12) Badī: (13) Kirāta: (14) Mānsabikrī, butchers: (15) Mālī, gardeners: (16) Byanjanakāra, cooks (?): (17) Māndhura: (18) Natījīva: (19) Surābīja: (20) Chitrākāra, painters: (21) Gāyana, musicians and singers: (22) Bāthahōm:

(23) Natēbaruda : (24) Sūrppakāra, cooks (?) : (25) Bimārī : (26) Tankādhārī : (27) Tayōruta : (28) Kānjikāra : (29) Bhāyalāchanchu : (30) Gōpaka, cowherds : (31) Tāmrakāra, coppersmiths : (32) Suvarnakāra, goldsmiths : (33) Kānsyakāra, bellmakers : (34) Karnika : (35) Tulādhara, weighers : (36) Kumbhakāra, potters : (37) Kshētrakāra, land-measurers : (38) Srinkharī : (39) Takshaka : (40) Dārukāra : (41) Lēpika : (42) Nāpika : (43) Bhārika : (44) Silpikāra : (45) Marīkāra : (46) Chichhaka : (47) Sūpika : (48) Sajakāra : (49) Srichāntē : (50) Ālama : (51) Daivagya, (52) Ganika, (53) Jyōtisha, (54) Grahachintaka, different kinds of astrologers : (55) Āchārya : (56) Dēva-chinta : (57) Pūjita : (58) Amātya : (59) Sachiva, (60) Mantrī, state officials in olden times : (61) Kāyastha : (62) Lēkhaka, writers : (63) Bhūpa, Rājā, Narēndra, or Chhētrī : (64) Dwija, Bipra, or Brāhmana[1].

Brāhmans were of two classes, Panchagauda and Panchadrāvida, each containing five divisions with numerous subdivisions. Jaisī Brāhmans were not sacred. Among the Newāras there were four divisions of Jaisīs, viz. Āchārya, Baida, Srēshtha, and Daivagya. Āchāryas were divided into three classes; Baidas into four; and Srēshthas into many classes, of which ten were allowed to wear the Brāhmanical thread, as were also the three classes of Āchāryas and the four classes of Daivagyas.

Of Sūdras there were 36 classes, amongst which the Jyāpu had 32 divisions, and the Kumhāl four divisions. The Pōdhyā caste had four divisions.

The four highest castes were prohibited from drinking water from the hands of low caste people, such as Pōdhyās or Charmakāras. If a woman of a high caste had inter-

[1] Many of these castes are now not known in Nepāl.

course with a man of a lower caste, she was degraded to the caste of her seducer.

Thus Rājā Jayastithi Malla divided the people into castes, and made regulations for them. He also made laws about houses and lands, and fostered the Hindū religion in Nepāl, thereby making himself famous.

In Nepāl Sambat 515 (A. D. 1395), on the morning of the 10th of Māgh Sudi, having placed and worshipped a kalas, the Rājā performed a Kōtyāhuti-yagya[1]. He then made a rule that Brāhmans might follow a profession, and enacted laws for the disposal of lands and houses by sale or mortgage. He then composed the Narakāvali Slōk, got benedictions from Brāhmans, and made poor wretched people happy by conferring on them lands and houses, according to caste.

The Slōk.

"Oh sun, moon, air, fire, earth, water, conscience, day and night:—these by their conjunctions and virtues (*dharm*) know the deeds of every man. He who speaks aught but truth will lose his rectitude, his sons, the merits of his former existences, and his forefathers who are in Heaven. He who resumes a gift made by himself, or by any one else, to a god or a Brāhman, shall remain for sixty thousand years as a worm in the dust. He who disobeys the regulations now made and ordained, shall be guilty of the sin mentioned in this slōk; but he who obeys, shall be exempt from it."

[1] A *hōm* performed a crore of times. I remember this ceremony being performed in front of the new temple in the centre of Pashupati wood, which was built by Sir Jung Bahādur. On this occasion two lākhs worth of grain, ghee, etc., were said to have been burned. The burning went on for a long time in a pit surrounded by ḳanāts or tent-walls.

8. Jayasthiti Malla's son Yaksha (or Jayayaksha) Malla reigned 43 years.

This Rājā, having studied the rules made by Shankar-āchārya, appointed Bhatta Brāhmans from the south of India to worship Pashupatinātha, and made the Newāras of Dēva-pātan store-keepers.

In his reign one Padma-dēva built a temple for Dharmarāj-mīnanātha-lokēswara, in which he placed images of Samantabhadra-bōdhisatwa and Padmapāni-bōdhisatwa, together with those of other Bōdhisatwas, gods, planets, &c. This is called the Padmadēva-sans-kārit-bihār, and its history is inscribed on a stone fixed in a chaitya in front of this Lokēswara[1].

In his reign also a stone image of Ganēsha was placed at Kāṭhmāṇḍū in Tēda-tōl, which is between Āsan-tōl and Jyāthā-tōl.

This Rājā began to build a wall round Bhātgāon, and caused the following inscription to be placed on a stone to the right of the principal gate.

"Yaksha Malla Dēva made this fortification and ditch, and a high citadel, in which to keep troops and ammunition. In building this fortification the people of the four castes willingly bore loads of bricks and earth. The Kōt-nāyaka (*i.e.*, officer in charge of the fort) will see that the people clean the streets and houses every year before the 6th of Jyēshtha Sudi, and that the roofs of the premises in the fort are repaired. If the Kōt-nāyaka fail in this duty he shall be fined twelve dāms. No horses, buffaloes, cows, or swine, are to be allowed to graze on the glacis. Any one whose cattle trespass shall be fined one dām, and be made to repair any damage thus caused. Any one not attending to this shall be held guilty of the five

[1] To the east of the large temple of Machchhīndranātha in Pātan.

great sins[1]. If any rational being causes any damage he shall be fined nine dāms. For every brick, stone, or piece of wood injured in this wall, a fine of one dām shall be levied[2]. Dated the 15th of Srāvana Sudi, Nepāl Sambat 573 (A.D. 1453)."

Yaksha Malla and his son Jayarāja Malla built the temple of Srī Srī Srī Dattātrōya, in Tachapāl-tōl in Bhātgāon.

In this reign some potters, while digging for clay, found an image of Lokēswara, which had been made by Guna-kāma-dēva Rājā, but which had been buried under the ruins of the temple that fell down in the time of the Thākuri Rājās. The Rājā got the image repaired, and put it into a new temple, which he built for it in Kāṭhmāṇḍū. The image henceforth was named Yamalēswara, and the place where it was dug up was called Yamala[3].

Yaksha Malla had three sons. He died in Nepāl Sambat 592 (A.D. 1472).

9. His eldest son Rāya Malla succeeded his father at Bhātgāon, and reigned 15 years.

10. His son Suvarna Malla reigned 15 years.

In this reign a famine occurred, and the people of Bhātgāon were dispersed. This Rājā reigned over Bhātgāon and Bandēpur (Banēpa). He introduced the dance of the Navadurgā, having heard that they had been seen dancing at night; and also the dance of Mahā-lakshmī in the village of Budō[4]. He had under his rule, besides

[1] These five sins are, murdering a Brāhman, murdering a woman, murdering a child, murdering one's own gōtra (relative), and killing a cow.

[2] The fines mentioned seem very trifling nowadays, but at that time a dām was the price of 100 lbs. of rice.

[3] To the north of the Rānī-pokhrī or large tank, east of Kāṭhmāṇḍū. The temple is in Kāṭhmāṇḍū, on the right side of the street which leads to the Indra-chok.

[4] A small village north of Thēmī, which latter is half-way between Kāṭhmāṇḍū and Bhātgāon.

Bhātgāon, the villages of Thēmī, Nakadēsa, Budē, Sankhapur and Chāgu.

11. His son Prāna Malla reigned 15 years.

12. His son Biswa Malla reigned 15 years.

This Rājā went to Dēva-pātan, and in consultation with the Rājā of Kāntipur invoked the Nārāyanas, and placed their images on the four sides of Pashupatinātha. In the place of Jalasayana Nārāyana he set up Bālasukī (Bāsukī). In the same year the Ichāngu Nārāyana[1] was buried under a rock that fell from the Yamālaya mountain. Sivānanda Brāhman erected in its place an image, which had been carried thither by the stream of the Vishnumatī.

This Rājā built a three-storied temple for Dattātrēya in Tachapāl; and having assigned lands for supporting the daily worship of the deity, he made it over to Sannyāsīs, for whose residence he built a matha (or bihār).

13. His son Trailōkya Malla reigned 15 years.

14. His son Jagatjyōti Malla reigned 15 years.

In this reign some Indian corn (maize) was by chance brought from the east, mixed up among a quantity of mās or urd-dāl (a kind of pulse). The clever people of the country were immediately assembled, and decided that this new grain would cause a famine, so that it was thought best to send it back whence it had come; and to destroy all the ill luck it might have left behind, Brāhmans were fed, and the gods worshipped[2].

Jagatjyōti Malla was once playing at dice with Turjādēvī, when a sinful thought passed through his mind, whereupon the goddess vanished.

[1] Ichāngu is a village S.W. of Swayambhū.

[2] This proceeding is exactly what would take place under similar circumstances at the present day.

This Rājā introduced at Bhātgāon the custom of holding the rath-jātrā of Ādi-bhairava on the anniversary of the Mēsh Sankrānti, when a tall pole was erected in his honour as a flagstaff. He also introduced this jātrā at Thōmī. Having on one occasion suspected that the Bhairava of Bhātgāon had improper desires regarding a certain Sakti or female deity, he punished him by bringing the rath of Kālī into violent collision with the Bhairava's rath. The wheels of the Bhairava's rath were made of wood, brought from the Pashupati forest by permission of the Rājā of Kāntipur.

15. His son Narēndra Malla reigned 21 years.

16. His son Jagatprakāsa Malla reigned 21 years.

This Rājā, hāving made sādhan of Bara-bīrja-hanumān, built a brickwork ghāt on the river to the east of Bhātgāon, and erected many monuments there.

In the reign of this monarch, Dara Sinha Bhārō and Vā Sinha Bhārō built a temple in Tachapāl-tōl in honour of Bhīmasēna. The stone lion in it has the following inscription:

"In Sambat 775, 3rd of Pūs Badi" (A.D. 1655)[1].

In Nepāl Sambat 782 (A.D. 1662) this Rājā built the Bimala-snēha-mandapa, and having composed five hymns in honour of Bhavānī, he caused them to be inscribed on a stone on the 6th of Mārgasira (Aghan) Sudi. He also caused an inscription to be placed on a stone to the effect that "twenty-four rōpnīs of land have been assigned to furnish oil for lighting the Mandapa." He built a Basantapur Durbār[2], and called it Nākhāchhē-tava-gōl-kwātha. He erected a pillar for the Garur of the

[1] Here again there seems to be some error in the date.

[2] A sort of pleasure-house for the Rānis. The two lions which stood at the gate of this Durbār are still to be seen to the west of the present Durbār in Bhātgāon.

Nārāyana of Nārāyana-chōk, and had the following inscription placed on it:

"Srī Jaya Jagatprakāsa Malla Rājā, the master of many arts and sciences, composed hymns in honour of Garuda-dhwaja for the benefit of the people, on the 3rd of Jēth Krishna, Sambat 787 (A. D. 1667), being a Friday, when the moon was in the 26th mansion or Uttarabhādra, and in the 11th kumbha[1], and in the sōbhana-yōga."

In the same year he erected an image of Bhavānī Sankara.

17. His son Jitāmitra Malla reigned 21 years.

This Rājā, in Nepāl Sambat 802 (A.D. 1682), built near the Durbār the two-storied Dharmasālā, in which there is the golden Mahādēvā. To the east of this he built the Dharmasālā with the temple and statue of Nārāyana. He also erected the temple of Dattātrikāsa, and the temple with Nārāyana, below the temple of Mahādēva built by Kājī Bhagīratha-bhaiyā; as well as the two-storied temple called the temple of Pashupati. In the Dharmasālā there is a stone with the following inscription:

"The overseers of the water-course do not give water fairly to the people, therefore the following arrangement is being made. At the time of planting rice the people are to make a watercourse, and every one going to work at this, after doing a day's work, must come and get a certain royal token (to entitle him to a share of the water). He who cannot produce this token shall be fined 3 dāms, but not more than that amount. The overseers are not to levy any duties for allowing water to be taken from the channel. The rank of people is not to be taken

[1] A mistake, for Uttarabhādra is in Pisces, the 12th sign, and not in Aquarius, the 11th.

GATEWAY OF BHŪPATĪNDRA MALLA'S DURBĀR

(Plate XII) AT BHĀTGĀON (p 133)

into account in distributing the water, but every one is to get a supply in turn. If the overseers do not allow water to be taken in turn, the head-officer shall be fined six mohars. By obedience to the above rules Īswarī will be pleased; by disobedience she will be displeased. Srī Srī Ugra Malla, Srī Srī Bhūpatīndra Malla, and Chautārā Dukhibhāgirāma have assisted in making this arrangement. The 15th of Jēth Sudi, Nepāl Sambat 803" (A.D. 1683).

Rājā Jitāmitra Malla built the temples of Pashupati and Nārāyana, and erected many other memorials.

18. His son Bhūpatīndra Malla reigned 34 years.

This Rājā built a Durbār with 55 jhāls, or windows, in one of which he put a small pane of glass, presented to him by a man from the plains of India[1]. This piece of glass was considered so rare and valuable that the Rājā placed it in the window as an object of wonder for the people. To the right and left of the principal door of the Durbār he erected stone images of Hanumān and Narsinha. He made 99 chōks, or courtyards, in the Durbār. In the Mūla Chōk he placed a golden door[2], and set up many images of gods; and in other Chōks he made tanks. In one Chōk, which he named Mālatī Chōk, he placed a window of sandal wood, and a stone with the following inscription. "In Nepāl Sambat 817 (A.D. 1697)[3], on the 9th of Phāgun Sudi, having placed these deities in the Durbār, Srī Srī Jaya Bhūpatīndra Malla, and Srī Srī Jaya Ugra Malla Dēva, of the solar race and of the Mānava gōtra, assign the land named

[1] The position of this pane of glass may be seen in one of the plates. Even at the present day glass is very scarce in Nepāl, and only used by a few of the wealthiest people.

[2] Very handsome, and still well preserved.

[3] In the MS. originally 818, but corrected with a pencil.

Dōlkhā Khēt, consisting of seven rōpnīs, and another piece of land named Khāpi Khēt, consisting of four rōpnīs, as guthī. From the annual income arising from these, Hanumān and Narsinha are to be each rubbed with one kurwā (1½ seers) of oil, on the 9th of Phāgun Sudi, the 9th of Asārh Sudi, and the 9th of Kārtik Sudi, in every year. On the 9th of Phāgun Sudi, Talēju (*i.e.*, Turjā) is to be worshipped. On the following days worship is to be performed, and offerings made: on the Makara Sankrānti, Basant panchamī, Sivarātri, 15th of Phāgun-Sudi, Ghōrā jātrā chaturdasī, Mēsha Sankrānti, Rāma navamī, Kārtik chaturdasī, Akshaya-tritīyā, 14th and 15th of Baisākh Sudi, 6th, 10th, and 15th of Jēth Sudi, Ghantā-karna chaturdasī, 15th of Sāvan Sudi, Kaliyugādi, 4th and 15th of Bhādon Sudi, 9th of Āswin Sudi, Dēvālī, Sukharātri, 9th and 15th of Kārtik Sudi, and Saptabrīhi chaturdasī. The Rājā in person is to attend and assist at the ceremonies. The woman who prepares the articles of worship is to get a share of the offerings. The Āchārya priest is to get 22 pāthīs of rice. The roof of the Mālatī Chōk is to be repaired annually. The Āwāl (tiler) is to get 3 pāthīs of rice, the Lōhār (blacksmith) 2 pāthīs, and the Lōhankarmī (stone-mason) 2 pāthīs. It is the duty of the holder of the guthī to attend to the above."

Bhūpatīndra Malla built a three-storied temple, the length of which ran north and south, and placed in it, facing west, a Bhairava for the protection of the country, and the removal of sin and distress from the people. This Bhairava gave much trouble, and the Rājā in consequence consulted clever men, who told him that, if the Īswarī of the Tantra Shāstra, whom the Bhairava respected, were placed near him, he would be appeased. He therefore, at an auspicious moment, laid the foundation of a five-storied temple, with a flight of stairs, and with images of lions, griffins, elephants, and Jaya Malla (and) Phattā. The pillars were of carved agrās (or sāl) wood, and there were five stories of roofs. This temple is the most beautiful, as well as the highest, in the whole city[1]. In building it the Rājā set an example to his subjects by himself carrying three bricks, and the people brought together the whole of the materials in five days. When the temple was finished he secretly placed in it a deity of the Tantra Shāstra, who rides on Yama-rāj (supposed to be a Bauddhamārgī-dēvatā), whom no one is permitted to see, and who is therefore kept concealed[2]. After this the Bhairava became tranquil.

On the 10th of Jēth Sudi, Nepāl Sambat 823 (A.D. 1703), at an auspicious moment, the Rājā placed a Chūḍāmani in the temple[3]. At the moment that the foundation of the temple was laid, a Jyāpu sowed some rice, and when he went to take it up, he found he could not pull out the plants, but had to use a spade to dig them up[4].

The Rājā made *kausīs*[5] in the Durbār, and having built temples there, he placed in them beautiful images of Vārāhī, Kaumārī and Vaishnavī, on the 10th of Bhādon Sudi, Nepāl Sambat 828 (A.D. 1708).

On the 3rd of Baisākh Sudi, Nepāl Sambat 827 (A.D.

[1] This temple is really a beautiful work of art, covered with magnificent carvings in wood. A picture of it by a native artist forms one of the plates.

[2] Even to this day.

[3] The *chūḍā-mani* is a jewel worn on the top of a head-dress.

[4] An omen showing the stability of the foundation of the temple.

[5] A *kausī* is an open platform at the roof of a house, on which people take the air. Nepalese houses are not flat-roofed (as in India), but with sloping roofs and tiled.

1707), he placed a Bhairava and Ugrachanda in the Nāyakhāchhē-tava-gōl-kwātha, built by his grandfather Jagatprakāsa Malla.

Again, he built a temple in the Durbār, and placed his Dēvatā in it, that those persons who fast during the month of Kārtik might worship there. This temple contains the following inscription.

"O thou whose lotus-feet are worshipped by gods and the king of gods, thou who art the husband of Gaurī, the destroyer of Manmatha, and whose forehead is adorned with the moon! I dedicate the faculties of my mind to thy two lotus-feet. Be thou propitious to thy humble devotee Bhūpatīndra. On Saturday the 10th of Bhādon Sudi, Nepāl Sambat 828, Bhūpatīndra Malla, to please his patron-goddess, placed Siva in this temple. May Sadāsiva be gracious to him."

The Rājā and his son Ranjīt Malla put a golden roof on the temple of the Bhairava in Nepāl Sambat 838 (A.D. 1718).

On the 3rd of Phāgun Badi, Nepāl Sambat 841 (A.D. 1721), he dedicated a new bell for the temple of Batsalā (or Bachhlā) Dēvī, near the Durbār, the old one, dedicated in N. S. 820, after a Kōtyāhuti-yagya, having become damaged.

19. His son Ranjīt Malla.

This Rājā was very prudent and economical. He sent a great quantity of his coin to Lhāsā, in exchange for which he got a large quantity of gold and silver. He collected a great many rare and curious articles, and made numerous Chōks in the Durbār, and also a golden door.

Being desirous of erecting a stone-pillar, like the one in Kāntipur, he requested Jayaprakāsa Malla, the Rājā of Kāntipur, to send oil-men to put it up. Jayaprakāsa

Malla complied with his request, but privately told the men to spoil it. They went to Bhātgāon, and prepared to set up the pillar, but while doing so they let it fall, and broke it into three pieces. Seeing that the Rājā was displeased at this, they joined the pieces together again and put up the pillar. Ranjīt Malla and Jaya-prakāsa Malla both gave the men dresses of honour.

Ranjīt Malla dedicated a large bell to Annapūrnā Dēvī on the 1st of Phāgun Badi, Nepāl Sambat 857 (A.D. 1737).

At this time the Rājās of Bhātgāon, Lalit-pātan, and Kāntipur, were on bad terms with each other. Hence Narbhūpāla Sāh, Rājā of Gōrkhā, laid claim to the throne of Nepāl, and crossed the Trisūl Gangā to invade the country. Being, however, opposed and defeated by the Vaisya-rājās of Noākōt, he was obliged to return to Gōrkhā, after burning the bridge over the Trisūl Gangā.

A jyāpu, who owned a field, near a plain to the south of Machchhīndrapur (Bogmati), called Dēva-khēl, was one night sleeping in it, when he saw a strange sight. Some one came and lighted a lamp, and then others came and spread carpets, on which several persons sat down. At the bidding of one of these, another person went to call some one, but returned with the answer that he would come to-morrow. On this the meeting broke up. Next night the same events took place, but the vacant seat on the carpet was occupied by Machchhīndra-nātha, who, it seems, was the person who had promised to come the night before. A Bhairava then came forward and asked for food. Machchhīndra told him to go to Gōrkhā, and enjoy the sovereignty of the country where Gorakhnātha resided.

The Bhairava then said that, if he would give him the sovereignty over Nepāl also, he would go. To this Machchhīndra-nātha agreed, and then the meeting broke up. From this the Jyāpu learned that henceforth the Gōrkhas would rule over Nepāl.

Rājā Narbhūpāla Sāh had two wives, of whom the senior was pregnant at this time. The junior dreamed one night that she swallowed the sun, and, awaking, she told the Rājā. He however only abused her, which so hurt her feelings that she did not sleep all the rest of the night. In the morning the Rājā told her that it was merely to keep her awake that he had abused her, because, if she had slept again, the effect of the dream would have been lost, and he considered this dream was as good as a promise that his kingdom would be enlarged. After this the junior Rānī became pregnant, and after seven months gave birth to a son, who was named Pṛithinārāyana Sāh.

When Prithinārāyana came of age he went to see Nepāl, and lived at Bhātgāon with Rājā Ranjīt Malla, who, being pleased with his guest, promoted a friendship between him and his son Bīr-narsinha Malla. In this way Prithinārāyana lived three years in Nepāl, with the object of making himself acquainted with everything regarding the country.

On the Vijaya dasamī, when the Navadurgās were being taken to the Mūla Chōk, Rājā Ranjīt Malla and Prithinārāyana Sāh stood together at the ḍoor of the Kumārī Chōk. When passing, the Bhairava gave the prasāda to Prithinārāyana instead of to Ranjīt Malla; and in like manner the Kumārī presented him with a blue lotus. A few days after this Prithinārāyana took leave and returned to Gōrkhā.

Ranjīt Malla had several illegitimate sons, who conspired against the life of Prince Bīr-narsinha Malla, and consulted some ill-disposed persons as to how they might remove him. These people said that he might be destroyed by performing a Kōtyāhuti-yagya and pronouncing the mantras so as to produce a bad effect. The sons then told the Rājā that, if he would have a Kōtyāhuti-yagya performed, the country would be prosperous and he would have done a meritorious act. The Rājā consented, and Prince Bīr-narsinha died suddenly at the age of 32, and with him the dynasty of the solar race in Bhātgāon became extinct.

CHAPTER VI.

Ran Malla, king of Banēpa. The Malla Rājās of Kāntipur or Kāṭhmāṇḍū, down to the time of the Gōrkha invasion. Repairing of the Swayambhū temple. Taking of Kāṭhmāṇḍu by the Gōrkhas.

9. RAN MALLA, the second son of Rājā Yaksha Malla, became king of Banikāpur (Banēpa) and seven adjacent villages. He reigned 21 years, and died without issue.

Dēvī gave a golden head of a buffalo to a certain oilman of Banikāpur, who, in consequence, made an offering to Pashupatinātha of a kavacha[1] ornamented with precious stones, and an ēk-mukhi-rudrāksha[2], in N. S. 622 (A.D. 1502). At the time that he made this offering he presented a shawl to the Rājā, which is still preserved at Kāntipur. These riches had been given to him by the Kumārī-dēvī of Kumārī-kund, to be employed for charitable purposes.

9. The youngest son of Rājā Yaksha Malla was named Ratna Malla, and he had quarrelled with his eldest brother Rāya Malla. It was the custom at that time for the Rājā, when dying, to impart to his eldest son the mantra by which Turjā-dēvī was made subservient; but

[1] Formerly a coat of mail, now any loose coat.

[2] A rudrāksha is the seed of the Eleocarpus ganitrus. It is used by fakīrs to make rosaries. The seed in general has from two to eight or more lines, marking its divisions. Seeds with only one line are very rare, and considered especially sacred. There are two such *ēk-mukhi-rudrākshas* at Pashupati temple. Rudrāksha means literally "the eye of Rudra or Siva."

Ratna Malla, the youngest son, treacherously got this from his father, when dying, to the prejudice of the eldest brother.

Through the influence of this mantra, the Nīla-tārā-dēvī, being pleased with him, informed him in a dream that, if he went to Kāntipur, he was sure to become Rājā there, through the help of a certain Kājī. He therefore rose early in the morning, and, having seen the Dēvī, went to the house of the principal Kājī of the twelve Thākurī Rājās, and told him his dream.

The Kājī said he would assist him, and concealed him. Then, having invited the twelve Thākurī Rājās to dinner, he gave them poison. After this he made Ratna Malla king, who, when firmly established on the throne, put the Kājī to death, as he feared that one who had killed all the Thākurī Rājās for his sake, would not be likely to hesitate about killing him too, if a quarrel arose at any future time. "Kings, serpents, and tigers are never to be trusted; he who trusts any of them is soon ruined."

The Thākurīs of Noākōt having had the image of Rājyēswarī painted, without getting permission from Ratna Malla, he was offended, and defeated them in a battle, N. S. 611. He then brought a large quantity of fruit and flowers from Noākōt, and offered them to Pashupati-nātha. From this time the custom was introduced of bringing fruit and flowers for offerings from Noākōt.

The Rājā being at one time hard pressed by the Bhōtiyās, called Kuku, and others from the country of the Dēva-dharma, four Tirhutiyā Brāhmans, having brought a number of troops from their spiritual disciple Sena Rāja of Pālpā, assisted Ratna Malla in driving off the

Bhōtiyās. From this time the place where the Bhōtiyās were defeated became known as Kuku-syānā-jōr, and the Tirhutiyā Brāhmans were rewarded with grants of land and dresses of honour.

At this period the Yavanas (Musalmāns) first entered Nepāl.

In this reign a Swāmī (prior or abbot), by name Somasēkharānanda, from the Dakhan, who was well versed in Khōdhā-nyāsa[1], came to Nepāl, and was made a priest of Pashupati-nātha. To assist him in the performance of the ceremonies two Newāras of Bandēpur were appointed as Bhandārīs. Two other Newāras from Kāntipur were appointed to take care of the property and treasures in the temple, and were called Bisētas. A Ditthā (overseer) was also placed over the Bhandārīs and Bisētas. This Swāmī got the title of Guru, and the Rājā caused Dakshina-kālī to be invoked by him and placed at the south-west corner of Pashupati, along with the seven planets and eight Mātrikā-ganas. By the directions of the Swāmī, the Rājā showed a Dēvī in the Ādi-bauddha to the Bhandārīs, who every year perform Dēvālī Pūjā to her. To the Bisētas he entrusted the annual Pūjā of Matīlī-dēvī, in the temple of Panchlinga Bhairava. After this the Swāmī went to heaven.

Rājā Ratna Malla, having perfected the mantra of Turjā-dēvī, consecrated her image in a small temple, which he built near Tānā-dēvatā, on the 10th of Māgh Badi, N. S. 621 (A.D. 1501).

Ratna Malla conciliated the people of Kāntipur and Lalit-pātan, and having brought copper from Tāmbā

[1] A form of worship consisting in making certain gestures with the hands and arms, while repeating mantras. A full performance of this ceremony occupies at least three hours.

Khānī[1], he introduced pice (*paisā*) into the currency instead of Sukichās[2]. The Ditthā Nāīkyā (overseer) employed in this work was Madhana, a Bauddhāchārya of Ōnkulī Bihār in Lalit-pātan[3].

After reigning 71 years, Ratna Malla died.

10. His son Amara Malla reigned 47 years.

In this reign the potters of Banikāpur wished to place an image of Ananta Nārāyana in the temple of Pashupati, but failed to get permission. They then managed in one night clandestinely to build a temple of tiles near Bakshalā (Bachhlā) Dēvī[4], and placed the image of Nārāyana in it, without any one knowing what was being done.

In this reign the descendants of one Muni Āchārya, a worshipper of Bhuvanēswarī, instituted an annual jātrā of Kumārs and Kumārīs (nine in number), mounted on nine different sorts of raths, with rice-pestles, iron chains and trisūls, attended by people undergoing tortures[5]. The whole procession goes round Īsānēswara. This jātrā takes place on the 8th of Asārh Badi. In Nepāl Sambat 677 (A.D. 1557) this Muni Āchārya had set out to obtain the Mrit-sanjīvanī (elixir of life), and had disappeared. His descendants heard of his disappearance while performing the jātrā, and they caused his horoscope to be carried behind the raths in the shape of a dead body. While this was going on, Muni Āchārya returned to Dēva-pātan with the elixir, and hearing that his horoscope was going to be burned with such pomp in

[1] In the Chitlong valley, at the foot of the Sisagharī hills.

[2] Sukichā or Suki, an ancient coin, worth eight pice.

[3] An ancestor of the Pandit who assisted in translating this book.

[4] This temple stands between the two bridges at Pashupati, on the right bank of the river, close to its margin.

[5] Children placed so that the trisūls appear to have transfixed their bodies.

place of his corpse, he left the two pitchers and the basket containing the elixir at that place, and made himself invisible by entering into the horoscope. There are two hillocks at the place where he left the elixir, which are called Kubkudō[1].

A Rāj-baid had come with Turjā and settled down at Pharphīng, and afterwards removed to Lalit-patan. The Rājā brought this man to reside at Dēva-pātan, and built a place for his family god.

In this reign the beautiful dances of the gods and goddesses were instituted in Lalit-pātan and Kāntipur.

In this reign there lived a Bauddhāchārya, by name Abhayarāj, clever and devoted to his religion[2]. He had three wives, two of whom had been fruitful, one having two sons and the other four. He then married a fourth wife, and seeing that his elder sons were displeased at this, he left the wife with four sons at Ōnkulī Bihār, and the other with two sons at a house which he had recently built, and he himself went to Bauddha Gayā with his newly-married wife. He remained there three years as a devotee of Buddha. One day he heard a voice from the sky, telling him that Mahābuddha had accepted his service and worship, and that he should now return to his home, where Mahābuddha would come to visit him, and where he would receive the royal favour. The voice also told him that she who spoke was Bidyādharī-dēvī, a handmaid of Mahābuddha. At this time, however, Abhayarāj's wife was pregnant, and they therefore could not undertake the journey. In due season a son was born, and named Bauddhaju. After this they returned home, taking with them a model Bauddha image from that

[1] To the south-east of Dēva-pātan.

[2] This paragraph contains part of the family history of the Pandit.

place. On arriving at home, Abhayarāj built a three-storied Buddhist temple, and erected a Bauddh with an image of Sākya Muni, in which he placed the model image. To the east of the temple, in his former house, he built an Āgama, and placed there an image of Bidyādharī-dēvī. Rājā Amara Malla called him before him, and told him that, as his (the Rājā's) father had appointed Madhana, Abhayarāj's father, as Ditthā Nāīkyā, to superintend the making of pice, he now appointed him to the same post.

This Amara Malla reintroduced the Harsiddhi dance, but, thinking that the elephant (one of the dramatis personæ) caused scarcity of grain, in order to counteract this he introduced the dance of Mahā-lakshmī of Khōknā. He introduced also the following dances:

The dance of Halchōk-dēvī of the Jamāl mountain,
" of Manā-maiju-dēvī,
" of Durgā-gana of Pachli Bhairava,
" of Durgā-gana of Lumrīkālī,
" of Kankēswarī-gana, and
" of Gnatēswarī.

In this last dance it was found necessary to have the Bāgh-bhairava of Kīrtipur represented, with the sheep which he devoured, and the performers had to go to Kīrtipur to perform their dance. In the dance of Kankēswarī, on one occasion, a man, who had disguised himself as a beast, was eaten up by Kankēswarī, and after this the dance was discontinued, because the performance would have required a human sacrifice. The other dances were continued, some being performed annually, others only every twelfth year.

He also instituted the rath-jātrā of Kankēswarī, Luchumbhōlu, etc., to take place on the Prēta-chaturdasī.

This Rājā's sovereignty extended over the following

towns: 1. Lalitāpur, 2. Bandyagāon, 3. Thēchō, 4. Harsiddhi, 5. Lubhu, 6. Chāpāgāon, 7. Pharphing, 8. Machchhīndrapur or Bugmati, 9. Khōknā, 10. Pāngā, 11. Kīrtipur, 12. Thānkōt, 13. Balambu, 14. Satangal, 15. Halchōk, 16. Phutum, 17. Dharmasthalī, 18. Tōkhā, 19. Chapaligāon, 20. Lēlēgrām, 21. Chukgrām, 22. Gōkarna, 23. Dēva-pātan, 24. Nandigrām, 25. Namsāl, 26. Mālīgrām or Māgal.

The Rājā once inquired when these villages were founded, and he was told that some were given as marriage-portions to daughters of Brāhmans by Rājās; some were founded by rich men, three generations before this time; some were peopled by persons seeking refuge, when driven by disaster from their former abodes; some were of greater antiquity, such as Namsāl, Nandigrām[1] and Mālīgrām, which were the remnants of Bisāl-nagara. Mālīgrām being destroyed by fire, the people settled down near Nandigrām, calling the new village by the name of the old one. Rājā Sankara-dēva founded Chāngu Nārāyana, a village of 700 houses, and peopled it. He also dedicated a town to Bajra Joginī, which he built in shape of a sankha (shell). The above was told by respectable men to Amara Malla.

11. His son Sūrya Malla.

This Rājā took Chāngu Nārāyana and Sankhapur from the Bhātgāon Rājā. He went to live at Sankhapur, and in order to please the goddess Bajra Joginī, he instituted her rath-jātrā. He lived there six years, after which he returned to Kāntipur and died.

12. His son Narēndra Malla.

13. His son Mahīndra Malla.

[1] Nandigrām is the first village on the road from Kāṭhmāṇḍū to Pashupati, where the temple of Nandikēswar stands.

This Rājā placed Mahīndrēswarī and Pashupati-nātha in temples to the north of his Durbār. He went to Dihlī with a present of a swan and hawks for the Emperor, who, being much pleased therewith, granted him permission to strike coin in his own name, in weight six māshās. He struck this coin, and called it mohar, and made it current in every part of his country[1].

He induced many families to reside in Kāntipur, by giving them houses, lands and birtās.

He went to Bhātgāon and lived with Rājā Trailōkya Malla, and daily worshipped Turjā-dēvī. At last she was pleased, and directed him to build a high temple in his Durbār in the form of a jantra[2]. He then returned to Kāntipur and told the architects to build the temple on the plan he proposed, but they were at a loss how to build it. At last they were enlightened by a Sannyāsī, and built it. It was completed in N. S. 669 (A.D. 1549), on Monday the 5th of Māgh Sudi; and Turjā Bhavānī entered it in the form of a bee. The Rājā caused the temple to be consecrated with great rejoicings, and gave the Brāhmans many birtās. From this time people were allowed to build high houses in the city.

In this reign Purandara Rājbansī, son of Vishnu Sinha, built the large temple of Nārāyana in Lalit-pātan, in front of the Durbār, in N. S. 686 (A.D. 1566).

Mahīndra Malla had two sons, the elder named Sadāsiva Malla, and the younger, by a Thākurī mother, named Siva-sinha Malla.

14. Sadāsiva Malla kept many horses, and the people

[1] This is the first silver coinage of Nepāl. The copper pice, stamped with bulls, lions and elephants, were current long before.

[2] A most indefinite direction, as jantras (charms or amulets) are of all shapes, square, oval, round, etc.

were much annoyed by his letting them loose to graze on their crops.

In this reign, one Jīvarāj, the son of Bauddhaju, the son of Abhayarāj, the great devotee of Buddha, who was born at Bauddha Gayā, visited that holy place, and after returning home built a large temple, like the one at Gayā, consisting entirely of images. It was named Mahābuddha-dēvālaya[1]. This Jīvarāj, after performing a great pūjā, and thinking of taking some prasāda of the Mahābuddha to the Lāmās of the north, went to the Lāmā of Sukim and told him how he built the great temple. The Lāmā gave him a plateful of gold, and he returned home and made golden luthām (shafts) for the rath of Machchhīndra-nātha, and assigned land for their maintenance, which is called Luthām-guthī. Jaya-muni, the son of Jīvarāj, seeing that the Bauddha-mārgīs of Nepāl were deteriorating, for want of clever Pandits, well versed in the Bauddha-mārgī shāstras, and for want also of good books, disguised himself as a Dandī and went to Kāsī (Benāres), where he studied Vyākarana (grammar), etc., and then returned to Nepāl, with a great collection of Bauddha-mārgī books. Thus he promoted the Bauddha religion, and himself became famous as the great Pandit of Mahābuddha.

Sadāsiva Malla was a licentious man, and many handsome women, who came to see the jātrās, fell into his snares[2]. His subjects, seeing his wickedness, determined to take vengeance. So one day, as he went towards

[1] This temple is in Pātan, and is the family-temple of the Pandit. It is built of tiles, on each of which is the figure of a god.

[2] Such conduct on the part of the rulers is still common. I have heard of several instances in which girls, seen at the jātrās by high officials, have been taken to their houses and kept there as concubines. The Newārs, in consequence, consider it a great misfortune if their girls are good-looking and escape being marked by the small-pox.

the Manōharā, they assaulted him with nōls and mudgars (sticks and clubs), and he was compelled to take refuge at Bhātgāon. The Rājā of Bhātgāon, knowing him to be a wicked man, kept him in confinement in one of the Chōks. After sometime he disappeared from that place[1], and the Chōk was after this called Sadāsiva-malla-chōk.

The legitimate solar dynasty thus became extinct in Kāntipur.

15. The people, after having expelled Sadāsiva Malla, made his brother Siva-sinha Malla king.

This Rājā was a wise man. He caused Dēgutalē (gods) to be set up by a Mahārāshtra Brāhman, and gave him the title of Guru. In order to secure for the country the protection of Panchlinga Bhairava, who is the Chhētrapāl of the southern side of the universe, he caused a well to be filled with many articles of worship in honour of him, and instituted his rath-jātrā on the 5th of Āswin Sudi.

In the time of this Rājā, a certain powerful Tāṇtrika of Kāntipur, by name Surat-bajra, went to Lhāsā, which journey was considered a difficult undertaking; and one day, as he was taking tea with the Lāmā of Bhōt, he saw his house in Nepāl on fire, and succeeded in extinguishing the flames by throwing the tea on them!

Siva-sinha had two sons, the elder named Lakshmī-narsinha Malla, and the younger Harihara-sinha Malla, the latter of whom went to reign at Lalit-pātan during the life of his father. His father and his mother, Gangā Rānī, were both afraid of this prince's violent temper. Gangā Rānī made a large garden, at a spot midway between Kāntipur and Buḍhā-nīlakantha, which she called Rānī-ban[2], and planted in it all sorts of fruit-trees.

[1] A habit prisoners had, and still have, in Nepāl.

[2] Close to the British Residency. The remains of the garden, still known as

One day, when Siva-sinha Malla was absent on a hunting expedition, Harihara-sinha Malla expelled his elder brother Lakshmī-narsinha from the durbār, on pretence of some quarrel. Lakshmī-narsinha, being in great fear, took refuge at Dēva-pātan, in the house of a washerman, and lived there in concealment. The two daughters of the washerman, by name Phikunchā and Parunchā, rendered him great service and became intimate with him. Hence Lakshmī-narsinha Malla promised that, if he became Rājā, he would make water pass from the hands of the washerman caste (*i.e.*, would raise their caste to a higher position among the castes). Gangā Rānī meanwhile searched for her son, but in vain.

At this time a certain Brahmachārī Khōdhānyāsīswāmī, by name Nityānanda-swāmī, from southern India, came to Pashupati-nātha, and was made a priest of the temple by Gangā Rānī. The middle roof of the temple of Pashupati being in very bad repair, she caused it to be taken off, leaving the temple with only two roofs. The gold of the one taken off was made into a gajura and placed on the top of the temple, which was thoroughly repaired.

In N. S. 705 (A.D. 1585) she repaired the temple of Chāngu Nārāyana.

In N. S. 714 (A.D. 1594) the temple of Swayambhū was repaired by the Rājā, and the principal timbers renewed. The above is inscribed on a stone, placed on the west of Swayambhū.

By the direction of Nityānanda-swāmī, Gangā Rānī offered a flag to Pashupati-nātha, one end of which was tied to the top of his temple, and the other to the top

Rānī-ban, are enclosed by a high wall, and the place was used some years ago as a deer-park by Sir Jung Bahādur.

of the durbār at Kāntipur (a distance of nearly three miles).

After this, both the Rājā and Rānī died. At the time of the Rānī's death, a dreadful noise was heard at midnight at the south-west corner of the temple of Pashupati-nātha. So loud was it, that the hearers became deaf. This Rānī also built a temple at Bhātgāon.

16. After the death of Siva-sinha Malla and Gangā Rānī, Lakshmī-narsinha Malla became Rājā, and ruled over Kāntipur. In this reign, on the day of Machchhīndra-nātha's Lagan-jātrā (*i. e.*, the day on which his car reaches Lagan-tōl), Kalpa-briksha (the tree of Paradise) was looking on in the form of a man, and, being recognized by a certain Bisēta, was caught by him, and was not released until he promised the Bisēta that, through his influence, he would be enabled to build a satal (pātī) with the wood of a single tree. On the fourth day after this, the Kalpa-briksha sent a sāl tree, and the Bisēta, after getting the Rājā's permission, had the tree cut up, and with the timber built the satal in Kāntipur, and named it Madu-satal. From its being built of the timber of one tree, it was also named Kāṭhmāḍō[1]. This satal was not consecrated, because the Kalpa-briksha had told the Bisēta that, if it were, the wood would walk away.

This Rājā had a Kājī, by name Bhīma Malla, a relative of the Rājā's younger daughter's husband, who was a great well-wisher of his master. He established thirty-two shops in the city, and sent traders to Bhōt. He himself went to Lhāsā, and sent back to Kāntipur a large quantity of gold and silver. Owing to his exertions, the property of Nepalese subjects dying at Lhāsā was made

[1] It stands on the right-hand side of the road leading from the Durbār over the Vishnumati.

over to the Nepalese government; and he brought Kuti under the jurisdiction of Nepāl.

While this Kājī was in Bhōt, some mischief-maker told the Rājā that Nityānanda-swāmī never bowed to Pashupati-nātha, and the Rājā went to see if this were the case. Nityānanda-swāmī guessed his purpose in coming there, and after the ceremony of worship had been finished, and Chandēswarī had been worshipped, he bowed to Kāma-dēvatā, whose foot broke and fell off. He then bowed to the Dharma-silā, and it cracked in two. Next he bowed to a stone inside the southern door, which also fell in pieces. After this, he was on the point of rushing inside to bow to Pashupati-nātha, when he was forcibly stopped by the Rājā. From this day it was the custom of the Swāmī, after the ceremony of worship had been finished, to stand at the south-western corner of the temple and cry "Pakḍo" three times. He died shortly after this.

Bhīma Malla returned from Lhāsā, and rendered many services to the Rājā. He caused the cracked Dharma-silā to be covered with a plate of copper. He was desirous of extending Lakshmī-narsinha's rule over the whole country, but some one persuaded the Rājā that he was aiming at making himself king, and hence the Rājā caused him to be put to death. His wife became a satī, and uttered the curse, "May there never be bibēka (sound judgment) in this durbār[1]."

The Rājā afterwards expressed great sorrow for what he had done, and, owing to the curses of the Kājī's family, he became insane, and unfit to manage the affairs of state.

17. His son Pratāpa Malla then took the reins of

[1] And her curse seems to have stuck to the country to the present time!

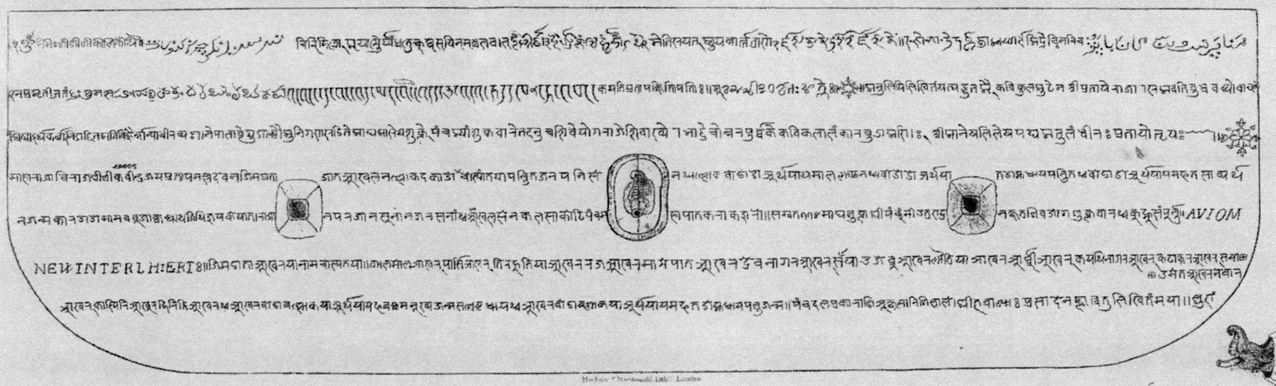

(Plate XIII) PRAYER OF RĀJĀ PRATAPA MALLA (p.215)

government into his hands, and ruled for 61 years. He kept his father in confinement, and the old man died insane, and thus the mantra of Turjā was lost.

Pratāpa Malla took his seat on the gaddī (throne) in N. S. 759 (A.D. 1639). Though he did not get the Turjā mantra, still he was possessed of great ability, talent, and learning. He brought two Rānīs from Tirhūt, and married them. He introduced the annual rath-jātrā of Sēnā (or Sānu) Machchhīndra, who was dug up by potters and placed in a temple by Rājā Yaksha Malla.

This Rājā brought together many Pandits from other countries, and learned many things from them. He composed prayers for different Pītha-dēvatās of Nepāl, and after getting them inscribed on stones, placed them in many holy places, such as Pashupati, &c. He made himself master of all the Shāstras, and amassed four crores of rupees, which he buried in a place according to Bāstu-chakra[1], and having placed four flags, he built the Mohan-chōk over it[2]. In order to keep away evil spirits, witches, and epidemics, such as smallpox, he made a principal gate to the palace, and set there an image of Hanumān, whence it was called Hanumān dhōkā. To perfect these precautions, he placed a Hanumān with five faces in a three-storied temple. He built Nāsala-chōk, and put in it the furious images of Narsinha and Nritya-nātha, to which he afterwards added several others. He built Indrapur and a Jagan-nātha-dēvala in front of the durbār, and on the 5th of Māgh Sudi, N. S. 774 (A.D. 1654) he composed a prayer to Kālikā, and had it inscribed on stones in fifteen differ-

1 A ceremony used in laying the foundations of houses, etc.

2 One of the courts in the palace at Kāṭhmāṇḍū.

ent characters, all of which he had studied. These he placed in different temples and in the durbār[1].

He made a beautiful image of Nritya-nātha, exactly like one in a conical-shaped temple, and placed it in a large pātī, newly built for the purpose, which was named Madu-nāsala-dēva. He got made a metal image of Biswarūpa, to be placed outside of the durbār during the Indra-jātrā, for the people to see. He caused the jalharī (or stone on which the emblem of Siva is fixed) and the greater part of the emblem of Panchlinga Bhairava to be covered up, because people from the plains of India, seeing the jalharī, used to laugh at the Nepalese for sacrificing animals to Mahādēva. He built Bhandārkhāl (in the durbār), and made a tank. He went to consult Jalasayana Nārāyana, and was told not to make an image for this tank, so he brought an old image, which was lying in a pond near Gyānēswara, and placed it in the tank. Being desirous of supplying water to the tank from Nīlakantha, he got permission from the deity, and brought the water in a narrow channel. When it reached Rānīban it stopped[2], and the Rājā made a vow that he would not go to the durbār till he went along with the water. He remained there for a whole year, and the Indra-jātrā was celebrated at that place. During this time an embankment was made to the level of the watercourse. The places which supplied earth for this work were named Tāpāīnājōl. In the Navarātri, or Dasahrā festival, the work was completed; the water reached the tank,

[1] This inscription forms one of the plates. The date 774 is in the fifth line, between the second and third devices.

[2] There is a break in the Tār or table-land here. The mound mentioned is close to the Residency, and indeed the Residency garden and grounds are supplied with water from this channel. The embankment is about a quarter of a mile long and thirty feet high.

and with it the Rājā returned to the durbār and worshipped Nārāyana. On the same night the Rājā had a dream, in which he was told by Buḍhā-nīlakantha that he or any of his descendants or successors who went to visit Nīlakantha would die. Hence, from that time, no Rājā ever visits Buḍhā-nīlakantha.

After a few days the Rājā heard that there was a frightful stone image in a tank, near the place from which he had brought the image of Jalasayana Nārāyana. He went there and recognized it as Bhīmasēna, who played in a stone-boat in the water, when the valley was a lake. He caused it to be dragged out and placed to the west of the durbār. This Bhairava possesses great powers.

He then set up in the Sundara-chōk an image of Nārāyana, in the attitude of riding on the Kālā Nāg after vanquishing him, and along with him he placed an image of Garuḍa. Both of these images had been found in a place called Sākōnhā in the Sānkāsyā-nagarī. This Garuḍa gave much annoyance to the Rājā, who in consequence removed him to a spot near the Nārāyana of Nārāyana Hiti.

Syāmārpā Lāmā came from Bhōt, and renewed the *garbha-kāth* of Swayambhū (the main timber round which the mound is built), and gilt the images of the deities. This was done in N. S. 760 (A.D. 1640), and this date and the name of Rājā Lakshmī-narsinha are inscribed under the arch of the southern side (of the temple).

Rājā Pratāpa Malla then composed a prayer to Swayambhū, which is inscribed on a stone at the temple. It is dated N. S. 770 (A.D. 1650). In like manner he composed many verses, and set them up in different places, inscribed on stones. At last he inscribed his name on his coinage, with the affix Kavīndra (poet), and obtained great celebrity.

Being a young man, he was very amorous, and the number of his concubines amounted to three thousand. At this time a girl, not yet arrived at puberty, fell a victim to his lust and died. Afraid of the consequences of this great sin, he went to Pashupati, and remained there three months, during which time he erected emblems of Siva, named Kōti Linga, built a temple in the middle of the space, and performed a Kōtyāhuti-yagya. He then repaired the gajura of the temple of Pashupati-nātha, and erected a pillar at the southern door of the temple. He and every member of his family then performed the ceremony of Tōlā-dān[1]. Next, statues of all of them were placed in the temple. On the fourth day after this he made solemn vows, and gave many fields north of Dēva-pātan as *gōchar* or common grazing grounds. He then placed emblems of Siva, with temples built over them, at intervals of a pace, all the way from Pashupati to Kāntipur, and hung up a *patākā* (flag) of cloth, extending from the temple of Pashupati to the temple of Mahādēva in Mohan-chōk in the durbār at Kāntipur. By doing all this, he obtained absolution for the sin he had committed.

At this time a Mahārāshtra Brāhman, by name Lamba-karn Bhatta[2], came and lived at Kulēswara. He paid a visit to the Rājā, who, on being made acquainted

[1] This consists in weighing the person against gold, silver, or whatever the offering is to be.

[2] So named from one of his ears being very long. He obtained a promise from the Rājā of as much land as he could walk round in seven days. He might easily have walked round the entire kingdom in less time; so the sardārs persuaded him that it would be beneath his dignity to walk, and that he must be carried in a pālkī. They then provided cripples and blind men as bearers, and lame men to cook his food, and sent them off to the north-west corner of the valley, which is hilly and wooded. Of course he did not make very rapid progress, but still he got over a good deal of ground, much of which is held by his descendants to the present day. They are a wealthy family.

with his merits, gave him the title of Guru. By his advice the Rājā built a high temple near Dōgutalō, with three golden roofs, and placed his own and his son's statues on a pillar (in front of it).

At this time a Nāg of Chaubahāl, by name Kōināhasī, came to Pashupati, along the Bāgmatī, and having caused the water to rise, entered the temple by a drain and stole the *ēk-mukhi-rudrāksha*, which Nārāyana, in the disguise of a Sannyāsī, had given to Mohan Sinha Sālmī of Banikāpur, who sewed it on a coat which he offered to Pashupati. Bāsukī, having heard of the robbery, jumped into the river, killed the Nāg, brought back the rudrāksha, and put it on the jalharī. When the river had risen near Rājyēswarī, a great crowd came to see it, and the Rājā with his Guru and priests also came there. Then Lamba-karn Bhatta, having put a stop to future inroads of Nāgs, rebuilt the temple of Bāsukī with a new gajura, and, to insure the security of the temples, he put in them musical instruments, called Dhapānī, to be played on when one quarter of the night remained. From this time, through the favour of Bāsukī, no acts of violence have been done by the Nāgs.

In this reign a Tirhutiyā Brāhman, by name Narsinha Thākur, who had for three years repeated the mantra of Narsinha, and thereby secured his aid when needful, came to Kāntipur. He went to live at Panchlinga Bhairava, where the Rājā visited him, and, becoming acquainted with his powers, gave him the title of Guru. Sometime after this, having perused the book *Mahākāla Sanhitā*, the Guru went to a place north of Slēkhmāntak-ban, and having found there a khaḍgī (kasāī) and a tail-kār (oilman), and examined the marks on their bodies, he came to the conclusion that that spot was the abode of Īswarī. He communicated this intelligence to the Rājā, who employed all his subjects to dig a tank there, and an Īswarī appeared. Then he put iron beams in the shape of a jantra, to cover the subaqueous fire and prevent it from rushing up, and over these he placed a jantra of the shape of eight lotus leaves. He then placed there a Bhairava, the Nava-durgā-gana of the Slēkh-māntak-ban, and Hinsā-Narsinha. He next enclosed the place with a wall, within which he erected pillars, one surmounted by a lion and the other by a statue of a man. Having thus discovered Guhjēswarī-Kālī-Mahā-māyā, he caused a prayer to be inscribed on a stone, which he put in the temple. Under this prayer is the following inscription:

"Glory to Srī Srī Srī Rājādhirāj Rāmachandra, of the solar race, whose descendant Srī Pratāpa Malla Rājā, in order to secure his welfare, has erected a pillar, surmounted by a lion, in front of the temple which he has built and consecrated with burnt offerings and sacrifices. On Thursday, the 6th of Baisākh Badi, Uttara nakshatra, Subha yōg, he has dedicated them to Guhjēswarī Bhavānī."

This inscription is in Sanskrit, and under it is the following in the language of Nepal (Parbatiyā):

"These slōks have been composed by Srī Srī Kavīndra Jaya Pratāpa Malla Dēva, and are dedicated to Srī Srī Srī Guhjēswarī."

In this reign, in N. S. 774 (A.D. 1654), Sumaraj Sākē Bhikshu built the Lagan Bahāl in Kāntipur.

In N. S. 777 (A. D. 1657), on the day of the full moon in Māgh, the Rājā placed a gilt image of Biswarūpa in Lāyakul-bahāl. In Pau-bahāl he placed a painting, representing figures engaged in churning the ocean, and he directed that it should be taken out on great festival days. He assigned a guthī for this purpose.

On the 13th of Bhādon Badi, N. S. 777, the insane Rājā Lakshmī-narsinha Malla died, after being in confinement for sixteen years. His remains were burned at Pashupati, at the Dēva-ghāt, on the Rāj-smashān. One of the widows of the Rāja, by name Bhavānī Māī, performed satī on this occasion.

Pratāpa Malla had four sons: Pārthipēndra Malla, Nripēndra Malla, Mahīpēndra (or Mahīpatēndra) Malla, and Chakravartēndra Malla.

A Swāmī Khōdhānyāsī from the south of India, by name Gyānānanda, came to Pashupati. The Rājā went to see him, and, having examined him, appointed him priest of the temple. By the Swāmī's advice, the Rājā made an umbrella of gold with the Panchāyana-panchapatra mantra, and having caused an inscription to be put on it, of slōks composed by himself in the Bhujanga measure, to which the Swāmī added the abstruse Tāndava-mantra, made by Mahākāla, he offered it to Pashupati-nātha. Then the Swāmī, to propitiate Pashupati-nātha, on the 14th of Sāvan Sudi, made an offering of cotton thread, seven dhārnīs and one seer in weight, after going through a long purifying ceremony, which is called Pabitrārohana. This ceremony lasts for four days, and on the last day the prasāda is offered to the king.

The Rājā then built a house for the Swāmī in Dēvapātan, in which to perform his daily religious ceremonies, and in the middle of it he made a raised platform. The Swāmī built another house adjacent to it, in which he placed a deity of the Swatantra-mūla-mūrtti-urddhāmnāya for his daily worship.

By the Swāmī's advice, the Rājā left his throne for a

time to be filled in turn by his four sons, for one year each. Nripēndra Malla, when acting as Rājā, made a coat for the Nandi of Pashupati-nātha. During the reign of Mahīpēndra Malla, Pratāpa Malla placed a large bajra (thunderbolt of Indra) in the Dharmadhātu mandala in front of Akshōbhya Buddha, on the eastern side of Swayambhū, in N. S. 788 (A. D. 1668). To the right and left of Swayambhū he built two temples, in which he put secret Āgama dēvatās. Chakravartēndra Malla reigned only for one day and then died, but the other three sons reigned for their three years.

The inscription on Chakravartēndra's coin, devised by the Swāmī, consists of a triangular Bānāstra (bow and arrow), Pās (a noose), Ankus (the iron hook for driving an elephant), Kamal (a lotus), Chāmar (a yāk's tail), and Sambat 789. This device caused his death[1].

The deceased son's mother was inconsolable for the loss of her youngest born, and the Rājā, to comfort her, caused a tank to be dug, and built in the middle of it a temple, containing the family deity. This tank was filled with water brought from every Tīrtha or holy place. On its southern bank the Rājā placed a stone elephant bearing his own and the Rānī's statues. This tank is called the Rānī Pōkhrī.

There was a Gubāhāl (or Buddhist guru), by name Jāmana, who advised the repairing of the Itum Bahāl, built by Kēschandra. The Rājā learned many arts from Jāmana Guru-bhājū and Lamba-karn Bhatta, and showed

[1] A bow and arrow are ominous of death, but, nevertheless, the water in which such a coin is dipped possesses the quality of causing a speedy delivery in child-bed. These coins, which are very rare, are still used for this purpose. A sword that has killed a man is also used in the same way; and the figure known among children in Scotland as "the walls of Troy" is supposed to have the same effect, if shown to the woman.

his skill by exhibiting many wonderful sights to the people[1]. He died in N. S. 809 (A.D. 1689).

18. His son Mahīndra Malla, or Bhūpālōndra Malla, succeeded him. He instituted the jātrā of Swēta-bināyaka, and the guthī, or lands assigned for its support, were given in charge to the Bandyas of Chābahīl. He died in N. S. 814 (A.D. 1694).

19. His son Srī Bhāskara Malla succeeded him at the age of fourteen, and reigned for eight years. He had two wives and two concubines. He built a beautiful Dharmasālā in Kindōl[2], and remained always in the society of his women. In the year in which the Rājā reached his 22nd year there were two months of Āswin[3], and the Rājā determined to hold the Dasāīn (Dasahrā festival) during the intercalary month. The people of Bhātgāon and Pātan refused to celebrate it in that month, but the Rājā persisted in doing so, and the goddess, being angry, sent a plague called Mahā-māī, which appeared now after an interval of 120 years.

The symptoms of this disease were that the patient was seized with a pain in the head near the ear, and death ensued in an instant. The daily mortality amounted to between 30 and 40. This lasted for two years, but at length the frightful teeth of Pashupati were seen, and the daily number of deaths increased to between 80 and 100. At this time Jhangaltharī Kājī kept the Rājā, his two wives, and a servant, with a store of provisions, in Kindōl Bahāl, to prevent the disease being communicated to them. He kept them there for six months, while the plague was raging in the country.

[1] Among other feats, he is said to have made the statue of a Bhairava in front of the palace smile and move its head.

[2] South of Swayambhū.

[3] The time for festivals and religious ceremonies is calculated by the lunar month, and no festivals are celebrated in the intercalary month.

At this time a Jōgī came, and told the Kājī that the Mahā-māī would not be appeased by any small ceremony. If he was desirous of appeasing the goddess, he should give every man in the country, whether a native or a stranger, an ample meal of such food as he liked best. The Kājī therefore distributed food at Hanumān Dhōkā, and in four days the plague began to abate. The Rājā inquired about the plague from a cultivator, through a hole in a window of the Dharmasālā at Kindōl; and being assured that the mortality had abated, he jumped out of the window, and ran to the durbār. He died that same night, on the 15th of Bhādōn Sudi, N. S. 822 (A. D. 1702). The cause of his death was that the eye of Mahā-māī had fallen upon him. In him the solar dynasty at Kāntipur became extinct. The Rānīs and Maijus (concubines) sent for a distant relative, on the side of a daughter, and having made him Rājā, the four became Satīs.

20. The new Rājā was named Jagajjaya Malla. He built a temple to Rādhā-Krishna and another to Mahā-Vishnu. There was a drought in his reign, and as the Rājā thought that it was the result of the resumption of charitable grants of land, he caused lands to be assigned to Pashupati-nātha to supply the Mahābalī-bhōg[1].

He had two sons, Rājēndra-prakāsa and Jaya-prakāsa, born before he became Rājā. After becoming Rājā, he had three sons born in Mohan-chōk, viz. Rājya-prakāsa, Narēndra-prakāsa, and Chandra-prakāsa. Nine years after he became Rājā, the eldest son Rājēndra-prakāsa died. The Rājā was so grieved at this that he shut himself up in his palace for three months. The Khas sepoys came and comforted him, saying that he had four sons

[1] Food offered to the gods and afterwards distributed to fakīrs.

left and ought not to give himself up totally to grief. The Rājā told them that it was his wish that, after his death, Jaya-prakāsa should be made king; but the sepoys said that they would make Rājya-prakāsa king, who was born in Mohan-chōk. This avowal of their intention made Jaya-prakāsa their enemy.

After a time, Chandra-prakāsa the youngest son died, and his father made a tank in his name on the other side of the Tukhuchā, which he named Mīhma-juju-kā-pōkhrī.

At this time the Rājā heard from a fakīr that the Gōrkhālī Rājā, Prithwīnārāyana, had extended his rule as far as Noākōt; and being grieved also by the resumption of chantahli lands[1], which was sure to bring ruin on his kingdom, he died in N. S. 852 (A. D. 1732).

21. Jaya-prakāsa Malla succeeded him, and reigned for 39 years. Being afraid that the Durbār officials wished to make his brother, Rājya-prakāsa, king, he expelled him from the durbār during the time of mourning for his father. Rājya-prakāsa then went to live at Pātan, where the Rājā, Vishnu Malla, treated him well, and said that, being childless, he would adopt him as his heir.

The Tharīs (Durbār officials), being offended by the Rājā not allowing them a near approach to his person, took Narēndra-prakāsa to Dēva-patan, and made him king over five villages, viz. Sānkhu, Chāngu, Gōkarna, Nandi-grām and Dēva-pātan. After four months, Jaya-prakāsa deposed him, and he took refuge at Bhātgāon, where shortly afterwards he died.

Jaya-prakāsa imprisoned some of the mischief-making Tharīs and restored order to his kingdom. The Tharīs however gained over to their party the Rānī Dayāvatī,

[1] Lands given as gifts to temples.

and proclaiming her infant son, only 18 months old, as king, they obliged Jaya-prakāsa to flee from the durbār. The Rājā first went to Mātā-tīrtha, but being driven out from there after eight months by six Pradhāns (state officials) of Lalit-pātan, who had espoused the cause of Rānī Dayāvatī, he went to Gōdāvarī. He was expelled thence also, and took refuge at Gōkarnēswara; but being obliged to leave that place too, he went to Guhjēswarī, where a devotee gave him a khaḍga or sword. After two years and six months had been spent in exile, he was one day worshipping at Guhjēswarī, when a fish, an offering to the goddess, came into his hand[1]. He accepted this as a good omen, and mounting his horse Khurāsān, with his sword in his hand, he met the troops from Kāntipur and defeated them. He killed a great many of them, and returned to his durbār in Kāntipur. Here he took up in his arms his infant son Jyōti-prakāsa, and put to death those who had made him king. Some of the Kājīs took poison to escape punishment, and Dayāvatī Rānī hanged the Kājī who had been the chief instigator of the rebellion. She herself, however, was shortly made to end her life in imprisonment at Lakshmī-pur (one of the chōks in the durbār).

Jaya-prakāsa, having disposed of his enemies, and confiscated their property, assembled a court of good men and Brāhmans. He now invaded Noākōt, and Prithinārāyana was obliged to return to his own country, leaving Noākōt in the Rājā's hands. Eight years after this, the Rājā was informed that Kāsīrām Thāpā had promised the

[1] At Guhjēswarī there is a small well, with eight lotus leaves of silver around it, and three kalasas of gold, silver and crystal. When a man has worshipped, he takes up a kalas, and puts his hand into the well to draw water; and if any of the things that have been offered come into his hand, it is regarded as a good omen.

Gōrkhālī Rājā to get possession of Noākōt for him. The Rājā therefore summoned him on some pretext, while he was performing sandhyā at Gaurī-ghāt, and put him to death at Chābahīl, in spite of the Thāpā's protestations of innocence. The Rājā said that Thāpās Buḍhāthōki, Bist, Bāglī and Basnyāt were his enemies, because they had said to his father that they would not take him, Jaya-prakāsa, as king.

Prithwīnārāyana, having heard of the death of Kāsīrām, came to Noākōt, and took possession of the lands of thirty-two Tirhutiyā Brāhmans, who fled to Nepāl. From that day Jaya-prakāsa's fortune began to decline. He ought not to have put Kāsīrām Thāpā to death.

He now heard that the six Pradhāns of Lalit-pātan had deprived his brother of his eyesight, and having got them into his power he imprisoned them. They were taken round the city, and were made to beg a handful of *chūrā*[1] from every shop for their food. Their wives came to see them and brought food to them, but the Rājā caused them to be dressed as witches, and after making them go round the city with their husbands, and treating them very ignominiously, he let them go. These Pradhāns after their release endeavoured to dethrone Jaya-prakāsa. The Gōrkhālī Rājā was very glad to hear of all these events.

The Rājā, in return for the favour which he had received from Guhjēswarī, built the Guhjēswarī ghāt and the houses around the temple. He turned the course of the Bāgmatī, which formerly ran northwards at that place. He also assigned lands for the expenses of the daily *ārati*[2], and for keeping a lamp constantly burning

[1] Rice partly boiled and then pounded flat and dried.
[2] Five wicks lighted in a vessel, which is turned round before a shrine.

during the two Navarātris every year (*i.e.*, nine days and nights from the first of Kuār Sudi and Chait Sudi). He established the custom of feeding people in the Guhjēswarī jātrā, introduced by his father. At Pashupati-nātha he built a high platform, and caused Kōti-pārthiva-pūjā to be performed[1]. He caused 21 dhārās to be made at Bālā or Lhuti-kōt (Bālājī), and appointed priests there, the water having been ascertained to come from Gandakī[2]. He caused numerous Sāligrāmas to be brought from Kālī Gandakī and placed in the temple of Pashupati-nātha and Bāsukī. From this time Sāligrāmas became known in Nepāl.

The ornaments of Guhjēswarī were stolen, and Kājī Gangādhar-jhā traced the thief and recovered the property. Rājā Ranjīt Malla (of Bhātgāon), being actuated by envy, sent some Bhotiyā thieves, who entered the temple of Guhjēswarī, broke the large bell, upset the Bhairava, and took away the Mūla-kalasa; but no sooner had they done this than they were struck blind, and were obliged to throw away the kalasa and make their escape. It was found six months afterwards and restored to its place.

There was a Kājī of Lalitpur, who once said that he would never permit himself to be imprisoned by Jayaprakāsa. The Rājā heard of this, and having got hold of him, by means of a Guru, named Dēvānanda-bhājū, he put him in prison, where he died. The Gōrkhālī Rājā was glad to hear of all these things.

At this time Prithwīnārāyana Sāh attacked Kīrtipur with a large force. His main camp was at Naikāp[3].

[1] One crore of emblems of Siva are made of clay and worshipped in this pūjā.

[2] The water comes from several springs at the foot of the Nāgarjun mountain. This is where the fish-tanks now are.

[3] The rocky range on which Kirtipur and Chaubahāl stand.

The Nepalese Kājīs, noblemen, and sardārs wore armour. In the battle the troops of Dēva-pātan, being encouraged by their local goddess Jayabāgōswarī, struck the first blow. On the Gōrkha side, Surpratāp lost one of his eyes, and Kālu Pānrē was killed. The battle lasted for twelve gharīs (nearly five hours), and both sides lost many men. On the Nepalese side twelve thousand sepoys, brought from the plains of India by Saktiballabh Sardār, were killed. Mahārāj Prithwīnārāyana Sāh was in a dōlā (palanquin), and a sepoy raised his khoḍā to cut him down, but his hand was held by another, who exclaimed that he was a Rājā and not to be killed. A Duān and a Kasāī then carried the Rājā in one night to Noākōt. The Rājā praised the Duān and said *Syābās pūt* ("Well done, my son"), and from that day the people of his caste came to be called Putwār and had access to the king's person.

Jaya-prakāsa now thought that the Gōrkhālīs were annihilated, and made great rejoicings. In this way the Nepalese repulsed the attacks of the Gōrkhālīs for eighteen years.

At this time the Rājā had put a stop to the yearly stonethrowing at Kankēswarī; but having heard a great noise at midnight, he was obliged to allow the custom to be continued. He built a house in Kāntipur for the Kumārīs to live in, which was constructed according to bāstu-chakra, and instituted their rath-jātrā.

After some time Sītalā, the goddess of small-pox, to bring ruin on Nepāl, entered Mohan-chōk, and Jyōti-prakāsa, the son of the Rājā, died of that disease. The Rājā took the dead body with great pomp to the Rāj-ghāt at Pashupati and burned it.

The four Tharīs, being jealous of the Tirhutiyā Brāhmans, went over to Prithwīnārāyana, and surrendered to the Gōrkhālīs some places which were in the jurisdiction of Nepāl.

Ranjīt Malla, the Rājā of Bhātgāon, was glad that Jaya-prakāsa had become childless and would soon be ruined. He now detained some people of Kāṭhmānḍōn who had gone to see the Biskyāt-jātrā, on the pretext that they were too proud of their dress; but released them again, when threatened by Jaya-prakāsa. Jaya-prakāsa, out of revenge, confined for six months, in the kōt at Dēva-pātan, some people from the other side of the Manōharā, who had come to perform the ceremony of scattering grain at Pashupati, and only released them after they had paid heavy ransoms. He took into his service Nāgā sepoys to fight against the Gōrkhālīs, and for the support of these he took away the jalharī of Pashupati-nātha, which had been given by Vishnu Malla, the Rājā of Lalit-pātan. This not being sufficient, he got information from one Malēbhatā-dhanjū of Dēva-pātan, and took away the treasure of Pashupati-nātha and also that of Jayabāgēswarī. He even took away the gajuras of the temples to support the sepoys, vowing at the same time that he would repay double of what he took, if he were successful against his enemy.

He repaired the foundation of Talēju, and the ceremony of consecration was performed with great pomp and rejoicing. Images of Bhīmasēna and others were placed in the temple amidst grand musical performances and dances.

He also renewed the principal timber of the Swayambhū mound. The following inscription on a stone contains an account of what was done[1].

[1] A copy of this inscription is in the University Library of Cambridge.

"Obeisance to Triratna, the protector of all Satwas! also obeisance to all Buddhas and Bōdhisatwas! Obeisance to the lotus of the never-dying Sadguru, whose protection I ever seek! This Sadguru, in order that prosperity and happiness may attend the gods and mankind, has appeared in the Swayambhū Chaitya in Nepāl, which is always surrounded by crowds of people, and lighted by the jewels which shine on the heads of Brahmā, Vishnu, Mahēswara, Indra, and other gods and lōkpāls, who in constantly bowing and raising their heads spread variegated light around. He is born the never-dying jewel to reward the merits of mankind. He exempts from the wheel of the world (*i.e.*, from being born again) those who bow to him with sincerity. He is the noose by which are successfully drawn the three sorts of Bōdhi-gyān, namely, Srāvaka-yāna, Pratyēka-yāna, and Mahā-yāna. He fulfils the desire of every one, like the Bhadra-kalasa. He is the ocean of good qualities and the sparsa-mani of Jambu-dwīpa. The great Swayambhū Chaitya, possessing such attributes, having been rendered uninhabitable by the sin of the Kali Yuga, requires to be repaired. To repair it, Karmāpā Lāmā, the most talented, the jewel of men of arts and sciences, having a mind as clear and enlightened as the sun and moon, came from the north, in order to give happiness to the king, kājīs and people; and in N. S. 871 (A.D. 1751), in the year (of the Jupiter-cycle) named Prajāpati, by the Bhōtiyās Kēdā, and by the Chinese Simu-u, he commenced the work, on an auspicious day, at a place between the Himālaya and Bindhyāchala mountains. At the moment that the repairs were begun, Mahādēva, Ganapati, and Kumār appeared in their true forms, and said that the charge of procuring the gold and other things requisite for the work belonged to them, and that they would provide them. Vishnu, in the form of a Brāhman, came and described the kind of beam which would be required. Through the interest taken in its completion by such great gods, Srī Srī Jayaprakāsa promised to carry out the repairs, and the Rājā of Gōrkhā, Srī Srī Srī Prithwīnārāyana promised to have the large beam dragged to its place. A war having broken out between the Mayūratō country and Lāhōr, and it being necessary to conclude a treaty between Bhōt and Nepāl, the Lāmā was obliged to return to his own country. On arriving at Kērōn, he said that he would not be able to return to Nepāl, but that one of the five Karmāpā Lāmās would come in his place and be as good as himself. If this could not be arranged, a disciple of his would come, whom the people should trust, and through him complete the repairs. He then returned to Bhōt. Then came Brug-pā-thyāng-chikhyēmpā, the omniscient, the disciple of the former Lāmā, who, assisted by Sākya Bhikshu and Sāsanadhara, completed the repairs according to the directions of Karmāpā Lāmā, suffering great hardships. It was completed in N. S. 878 (A. D. 1758), and was consecrated by Brug-pā-thyāng-chikhyēmpā and Bīr-ratna Lāmās.

Account of Expenditure.

1,382 dhārnīs of copper.

2,045 tōlās of gold. The whole gold expended on it was 3,344 tōlās and ten māshās.

Sāhī rupees 4,775.

1 dhārnī, 1 seer, and 2 pāōs of silver.

2 dhārnīs of pure copper.

14,106 charit mohars.

If all the khātās, kōchin (kinds of silk), tea, ghī, salt, oil, and flesh, be taken into account, the total cost comes to 43,639 rupees, besides 67 horses and 21 pieces of kōchin. The musk used in applying to the deity was worth 1,000 rupees.

May the temple extend its protection to every living creature!

The inscription on this stone was formerly cut on another one, but Karmāpā Lāmā, coming on a pilgrimage to Akshōbhya Buddha at Swayambhū, saw the stone broken, and took it to Bhōt; and this one is a copy of the former one. May the king, kājīs, and every living creature of this country obtain salvation, and be endowed with the title of Samyak Buddha by being absorbed into the Srī Srī Srī Bajradhara-bajrasatwa-sachchit-buddha."

In N. S. 887 (A.D. 1767) there were 21 shocks of earthquake felt in twenty-four hours, on the 1st of Asārh Sudi.

Prithwīnārāyana, when a youth, had obtained the prasāda of Kumārī at Bhātgāon, and this helped his fortunes. He was also called by Pashupati-nātha, and came with his troops and visited the temple. He assigned a guthī to Pashupati-nātha for the Panchāmrita for bathing the images[1]. It was not the custom to bathe with Panchāmrita previously to this time. This was the only religious endowment made by Prithwīnārāyana to the temple of Pashupati-nātha.

Eight months after this, on the 14th of Bhādōn Sudi, N.S. 888 (A.D. 1768), Prithwīnārāyana entered Kāntipur with his troops. Jaya-prakāsa sat in the Talēju temple, and his troops fought for an hour or two[2]. At last he

[1] A mixture of cows' milk, curd, ghī, sugar and honey.

[2] The troops and most of the people were drunk, as is the custom at the Indrajātrā festival.

spread gunpowder on the steps of the temple, and fled to Lalitpur, and taking the Rājā of that place, Tēj-Narsinha, with him, he took refuge at Bhātgāon. The Gōrkhālīs entered the durbār, and went to the temple of Talēju, where Tulārām Pānrē was killed by the explosion of the gunpowder, and a number of the troops along with him.

Prithwīnārāyana Sāh obtained prasāda of Kumārī on the 14th of Bhādon Sudi, and by his order the Jātrā was continued.

After two or three days, the six Pradhāns of Lalitpur came to invite the Gōrkhālī Rājā to their town. The Rājā knew them to be traitors, and therefore told them in pleasant words to wait for him the next day at Tēkhu-dōbhān. One of the Pradhāns, having guessed the fate awaiting them, gave everything he possessed in charity during that one night. The next day Prithwīnārāyana went to the river side, and caused the Pradhāns to be bound. One of them shouted like a lion and escaped, though he was hotly pursued. He afterwards went to Kāsī. The others were put to death, and their wives became satīs. The Rājā obtained possession of Lalitpur, and confiscated the property of the Pradhāns who had been put to death; but he confirmed the acts of charity performed by one of them on the night before their capture. The Rājā now lived and ruled quietly.

CHAPTER VII.

History of the kings of Pātan, in particular of Rājā Siddhi-Narsinha. Taking of Pātan by the Gōrkhas.

1. HARIHARA-SINHA MALLA went to rule over Pātan in the lifetime of his father Siva-sinha. He brought the image of Dhantalē Vārāhī to Lalitpur by floating her down the Bāgmatī. He also obtained the favour of Panchalinga Bhairava, through the influence of which he became king. He had a son named Siddhi-Narsinha, for whose welfare he dedicated a village named Bhulu, and caused the fact to be inscribed on a copper plate.

2. Siddhi-Narsinha Malla.

This Rājā was very wise, because he was conceived whilst his father, in accordance with the advice of his Kājīs, lived at Pashupati to the south of his temple; and he was born at an auspicious moment.

In N. S. 740 (A.D. 1620) he enlarged the durbār of Lalitpur. On the 10th of Jēth Sudi he consecrated an image of Talēju, by the advice of Biswanāthōpādhyāya, whom he made his Guru. He induced many merchants to reside in the town. One night he saw Rādhā-Krishna in a dream in front of the durbār, and on that spot he built a beautiful temple, and placed the deity in it. On

Thursday, the 10th of Phāgun Sudi, Punarbasu nakshatra, Āyusmān yōg, N. S. 757 (A.D. 1637), he performed a kōtyāhuti-yagya, and consecrated this temple. There was a bihār, named Hatkō Bihār, built by Lakshmīkāmadēva-barmā, near the Mūla-chōk of the durbār. This bihār Siddhi-Narsinha caused to be pulled down and rebuilt near Gāubahāl. He placed an image of Siddhi-Ganēsha and one of Narsinha at the corner, and extended the durbār over the ground thus obtained[1]. Seeing that there were not carpenters enough in the town, he made Bandyas take up the trade, and assigned guthīs to the Nāïkyās, to give them a feast on a certain day of every year.

In this reign the following bihārs existed:

Jyēshthabarn Tangal, built by Bālārchanadēva.
Dharmakīrti Tava, built by Bhuvanākar-barmā.
Mayūrabarn Vishnuksha, built by Shankaradēva.
Vaishnavabarn, built by Baisdēva-barmā.
Ōnkulī Rudrabarn, built by Sivadēva-barmā.
Hakwa, built by Lakshmī-Kalyān-barmā.
Hiranyabarn, built by Bhāskaradēva-barmā.
Jasōdhara-buyā, built by Bidyādhara-barmā.
Chakra, built by Mandēva-barmā.
Sakwa, built by Indradēva.
Datta, built by Rudradēva-garga.
Yanchhu, built by Balādhara-gupta.

Among these the following five, namely Vishnuksha, Ōnkulī, Gwākshē (or Chakra), Sakwa, and Yanchhu, had one chief Nāïkyā, who was the oldest among the five head Bauddha-mārgīs of the bihārs. The rest, namely Tangal, Tava, Vaishnavabarn, Hakwa, Hiranyabarn, Jasō-

[1] These buildings and images are still standing at the Pātan durbār.

dhara and Datta, had each a separate Nāïkyā, or chief Bauddha-mārgī. The rank of Nāïkyā was conferred on the oldest Bauddha-mārgīs, and they were called Tathāgats.

Three bihārs, namely Wambāhā, Jyōbāhā, and Dhumbāhā, were established in this reign.

The Rājā called the Nāïkyās of all these bihārs before him, and ordered them to establish the custom of Thapātwaya-guthī[1].

The Rājā gave a place called Ngākā-chōk, in the district of Hiranyabarn, to a Tāntrika of that place who had defeated some jugglers.

He called together the men of these fifteen bihārs to make rules for their guidance, and directed that the order of their precedence should be fixed according to the order in which they arrived. The people of Dhumbahāl came first[2], but they were given only the third place. Those of Tangal remained first, and those of Tava second, on account of the antiquity of their bihārs. To the rest precedence was given according to the order in which they presented themselves.

Because Chaubahāl and Kīrtipur were under the jurisdiction of Lalitpur, the bihārs of those places were amalgamated with the fifteen bihārs of Lalitpur.

Another bihār named Sibahāl was not amalgamated with these, because it was built after the rules had been made by the Rājā for their guidance, and guthīs had been assigned to them.

There were several old bihārs standing empty, which had existed before the founding of Lalitpur, having been

[1] A feast at which the Bauddha-mārgīs of the bihārs assemble and choose their Nāïkyās.

[2] Bihār and Bāhāl or Bāhā are names used indifferently for the same thing. A bihar is simply a large square house, built round an open court, and containing a shrine or shrines, as the case may be.

built by nirbānik bānaprastha bhikshus, who, after entering on the grihastha life, had removed to other places. Siddhi-Narsinha gave these to other bhikshus to live in. These new bhikshus did not perform hōm when one of their family died. They began to have families, but still they did not perform this ceremony, although they performed other ceremonies just like grihasthas. Siddhi-Narsinha decided that, as they lived like grihasthas, whose houses remain impure after a death without the hōm ceremony, they must perform this ceremony.

The Yampi Bihār, built by Sunayasrī Misra was nirbānik (*i.e.*, the inhabitants did not marry); and as a grihastha Āchārya is required for performing the hōm, the Rājā decided that one of the people from Dhum Bihār should act as a priest to perform the hōm in this bihār.

The Rājā next found that there were altogether twenty-five nirbānik bihārs in the places under the jurisdiction of Lalitpur (viz., Chaubahāl, Bogmatī and Chāpāgāon); and in order to make rules for their guidance, he summoned all their bhikshus. They did not, however, all come. The bhikshus of only fifteen bihārs came, namely of those lying on the left hand side of the route taken by Machchhīndra-nātha's rath during his rath-jātrā, and those to whom the Rājā had given empty bihārs to live in.

He made a rule that the five oldest among their bhikshus should be Nāīkyās, and should be called the Panch-buddhas, and he assigned a guthī for their maintenance. He made rules for electing their Nāīkyās or headmen, and for performing the ceremonies after a death. He also ruled that the son of the oldest Nāīkyā

Bhikshu should have the charge of the worship of the deities of all the bihārs; and he put a stop to the old custom, by which the worship was performed by the head bhikshu of each bihār. If this worshipper became one of the Panch-buddhas, then his son succeeded him in the performance of the worship.

He also amalgamated these fifteen bihārs with the fifteen mentioned before.

Afterwards he made separate rules for the remaining ten bihārs, which lay to the righthand of the route taken by Machchhīndra-nātha's rath, and appointed headmen for them.

The people of Lalitpur, as they could not worship such a number of bhikshus, worshipped only two, namely, the oldest among the bhikshus of all the bihārs standing at the top of the public road, and the oldest of those standing at the foot of it[1].

The bānaprastha bihārs were called by some *bahī*, *i.e.* outside, because the bānaprastha bhikshus did not live in cities, but in forests.

Bhīma Malla, a kājī of Lakshmi-Narsinha Rājā (of Kāntipur), having established thirty-two shops in Lhāsā, Kuti, etc., and having made a treaty with the ruler of Bhōt, the merchants of Lalitpur also began to go to trade there. Siddhi-Narsinha decided that the ceremony of purification of those who returned from Bhōt should be superintended by the five old Nāïkyās of Tava, Hakwa, Bū, Yam, and Vishnuksha bihārs; but that the fees should go to the Rājā. After undergoing this purification, the travellers were readmitted into

[1] This is very obscure—not to say nonsensical. The Pandit explains it to mean that one of these is the oldest of the bhikshus of the fifteen bihārs first mentioned, and the other the oldest of the bhikshus of the other ten bihārs.

their caste. If one of the five Nāïkyās died during the ceremony, his successor had to give a feast, and undergo the usual ceremony for becoming a Nāïkyā, before he could be admitted as one of them. This is called the Twaya-guthī.

Siddhi-Narsinha made many other rules, and peopled the town, which contained 24,000 houses, but had become depopulated. He made a dhārā and a tank in Bhandārkhāl[1], in N. S. 767 (A.D. 1647). On the 2nd of Jēth Badi in the same year, he put a golden roof on the Dēgutalē, and on that occasion he feasted a number of Brāhmans, and gave them each a mohar. On the 5th of Baisākh Badi in the same year, he consecrated the dhārā within the durbār. On this occasion also he feasted Brāhmans and gave each a mohar. In N. S. 768 (A.D. 1648), on the 8th of Bhādon Badi, a Rānī of Rājā Pratāpa Malla died, and was burned according to custom; but Siddhi-Narsinha did not go into mourning, and celebrated the Dasāīn as usual. On the ninth day of the Dasāīn he went to Hatkō Bahāl to fetch the Kumārīs, but he could not do so, as Māhēswarī was crying[2]. Eight days after this, on the 1st of Āswin Badi, Bhānumatī, the wife of Siddhi-Narsinha, died at midnight on Friday, and on Saturday morning her body was taken on a *palang*[3], as usual, to the burning-ghāt and was burned. No one was allowed to perform the Āragmata-dīpa-dān[4]. The mourning was continued for

[1] A court in the durbār.

[2] Little girls are selected to represent the various Kumārīs at this festival, and are carried in the procession.

[3] A peculiar litter used by the Newārs for carrying the dead bodies of great people. Common people are wrapped in a sheet, tied neck and heels to a pole, and so carried to the ghāt.

[4] A light in a lantern hung upon a tall bamboo and kept burning all night during Kārtik.

three fortnights. The Arāgmata-dīpa-dān was therefore commenced on Sukharātri, or the 1st of Kārtik Sudi, instead of Badi. The Rājā only allowed musical instruments to be sounded, and no worship was performed at Vatyādō-mandal, Balambu, Rātrī-mandal, Thasiwan, Masānadō, Pīthi, Jatlan, Phatasō-mandal, Thanthachhō-māju, and Dhānmunisi. The Dasāin was not celebrated this year.

In N. S. 769 (A.D. 1649) he made a Bhūgōl-mandap[1] in Bhandārkhāl, representing the celestial bodies. In the same year, on the 9th of Pūs Sudi, he gave each Newār Brāhman, and after them each man having the right of entrance to the Panchlinga Bhairava, ninety pāthīs of rice and two kurwās of ghī. To every beggar who came from the hills, Kāntipur, Bhaktapur, and the plains of India, he gave twenty pāthīs of rīce and two pāōs of ghī. The rice thus given in charity amounted to 30,505 pāthīs. On the Makar Sankrānti, which fell on the 10th of Pūs Badi, he gave the eighteen purāns to Jānakīnāth Chakravarti[2], who lived at Bāhālukhā. In N. S. 769 (A.D. 1649) he gave some land to the gardener of Bhandārkhāl.

On the 3rd of Sāwan Sukla, N. S. 769, Srī Jaya Mangalā-dēvī Thakunī of Thanthō-bahāl died.

In this year Gōpī of Ikhāchhē, Dām Bandya of Slakō-bahāl, and Mādhava Chitrakār of Kōthōsātigla, prepared to make a Bānra-jātrā; but, as the Rājā did not allow them to bring the deity, they made no rejoicing, but only gave the alms. The Rājā did not go to the jātrā.

On the 12th of Māgh Krishn, N.S. 772, Siddhi-Narsinha relinquished worldly affairs, and went on a pilgrim-

[1] A temple with carved wooden images placed round the roof.

[2] A Bengālī, not a Nepalese name.

age. On the 6th of Āswin Sudi, in the same year, Srī Srī Jaya Srī Jyōti Narsinha Malla died. His wife Rānī Chhatramatī became a satī, and a slave girl also immolated herself. The roads to Kāntipur and Bhātgāon being closed, on account of enmity, the body was taken to Nikhu Khōlā to be burned[1].

This year the Dasāīn was not publicly celebrated, but the Rājā and priests only performed the ceremonies. The deity was not even brought down, and no buffaloes were sacrificed. The god of Madichhē (a part of the Durbār) was brought down stairs, and the god of Thanchhēmandal had a buffalo sacrificed to him, but the head of the buffalo was not made to dance[2]. No musical instruments were played on, and the Bisarjan, or bidding adieu to the goddess, was done privately. The Prasthāpana was only made to go seven paces, and the deity was not taken outside.

In N. S. 774 (A.D. 1654) the roof of Yappā Pītha was carried away by a storm, and the fire, with which a dead body was being burned at the time, fell on the Pītha, and the (sacred) stone cracked. In N. S. 774, on the 1st of Chait Badi, the painters of Bhātgāon did not come to the Snān-jātrā of Machchhīndra-nātha[3]; the image was taken out by Gangārām of Kōbahāl and two others, and the deity was bathed by two instead of four persons. The jātrā commenced, but the rath stopped after advancing a bowshot. The next day the same thing occurred. On the sixth day the rath reached Gwālti-chōk. The next day the wheels again stuck in

[1] A small stream south of Pātan, falling into the Bāgmati just above Chaubahāl. On this stream the new cannon manufactory and workshops are built.

[2] After sacrificing the buffalo, a man cuts off the head and dances with it before the shrine.

[3] It was their duty to take out the image for bathing.

the ground; and the following day the rath did not reach Ēkaltyāgal, for in Satyāvagāl it jumped and the front broke. The next day it was repaired and dragged to Ēkaltyāgal. This day the rath was moved in the afternoon, and it got as far as Dēvagāl in Ēvalā. On the 1st of Baisākh Sudi it reached Punkhēl. The next day it got to Purchōk-jhangrā, and the jātrā of Gāobahāl was held. The next day the wheels stuck at Mahāpāl, and the rath did not reach Nōgal; therefore the Nōgal-jātrā was held on the next day, the 4th of Baisākh. On the full-moon the Lagan-jātrā did not take place. Next day the rath arrived and stopped at Thanti. After this it reached Jyābal in twelve days, on the 1st of Jēth Sudi. On the 4th of Jēth Sudi the rath moved, but, before reaching Lisōchāk, the right wheel stuck in the earth, and the next day the other broke. The following day the rath was repaired, but the two wheels broke immediately on its being put in motion. The day after it remained at Yēpākulō, and the next day it crossed Nikhu Khōlā, but the right wheel stuck in the earth. The next day the shaft broke, and the next day the rath stopped at Ukālōmani, where it stayed for twelve days without moving. After this the image was taken out of the rath, put into a *khat*[1], and conveyed back to its own place. This year Jidēva Nāyak and Amrit Sinhadēva Nāyak were the priests of Machchhīndra-nātha. This year perspiration was seen constantly on the face of Charpōt Ganēsha for fifteen days, commencing from the 4th of Jēth Sudi. On the 8th a sānti was made by hōm, and animals were sacrificed, to avert the misfortunes which this foreboded.

In N. S. 776 (A.D. 1656) Siddhi-Narsinha assigned

[1] A wooden shrine carried on men's shoulders.

lands to the gardener of the Bhandārkhāl, and he then consecrated a Garuḍ Nārāyana. Formerly, in Hapātal[1], no house was allowed to be built higher than the rath of Machchhīndra-nātha, but Siddhi-Narsinha built a very high temple, which he called Tava-gōl. This Rājā was a great devotee of Srī Krishna. He used to regulate his diet by increasing it daily by one handful of rice until it amounted to one pāthī; and then he decreased it daily by a handful till it came down again to a single handful. He slept on a stone couch, and passed his days in prayer and worship.

In N. S. 776, early in the morning of the 15th of Phāgun Badi, the gajura of the temple of Bug-dēvatā in Tava-bahāl was struck by lightning, and the flag fell down. This year, during the rath-jātrā of Bug-dēvatā, at the time when the rath reached the cross roads at Mahāpāl, a child, whose pāshnī[2] had just taken place, came and sat on the rath, and the dēvatā taking possession of him, he spoke thus, "Come, Rājā Siddhi-Narsinha! I am not at all pleased at thy building this high temple." Siddhi-Narsinha, however, did not come, and the dēvatā disappeared, exclaiming, "I will never come to speak any more."

In N. S. 777 (A.D. 1657) Siddhi-Narsinha became a fakīr and went away.

"Siddhi-Narsinha, the omniscient, the jīvan-mukta (having obtained salvation while still on earth), the chaste, the favourite of Krishna, the master of Yōga, the chief of poets, the relinquisher of the world, the son of Hari-sinha. He who repeats this slōk will be ab-

[1] Part of Pātan, in the vicinity of the durbār.

[2] The ceremony of feeding a child with rice for the first time, which takes place when it is between six and eight months old.

solved from sin." The Brāhmans composed this slōk because he was a jīvan-mukta.

3. Srī-nivāsa Malla succeeded him.

On the 12th of Jēth Sudi, N. S. 777, which was the day on which the rath of Machchhīndra-nātha ought to arrive at Jyābal, great exertions were made to drag it to that place, and it got there late in the evening. The following day the rath moved of itself. Again, on the next day, while the priests were taking their food, the rath moved of itself. Lungsinha Yangwāl saw this. In carrying the rath across the Bāgmatī, the shaft of Mīnanātha's rath sunk so low that it touched the ground. On taking the image of Machchhīndra-nātha back to Bugmati, it was found that the Nāg-mani (jewel) in his coat was missing. In the kundal (ear-ornament) one of the feet of the horse harnessed to the car of the sun was wanting. The Garuḍ in the coat and the parrot had also both lost their bills. Such ill omens had never been heard of before. This happened in the reign of Śrī Srī Jaya Srī-nivāsa Malla Thākur Rājā, when Bimalsinha and Dīpankar were the priests. Nivā-sūrya Bandya of Itilanhē reported to the Rājā that Rūp-sinha Bandya of Ilāyanhē had seen the grandson of Māl-sinha bring the missing jewel to Hāku Bandya, to get it mounted in a ring, and that he had had it in his own hands. The Rājā, however, went to visit Machchhīndra-nātha on the 14th of Jēth Krishna, on which day the priests are relieved by others, who take over charge of the ornaments, etc., and he found that the ruby was lying in one of the folds of the coat. He had it mounted with twelve diamonds round it, and presented it to the deity. He punished Rūp-sinha Bandya by confiscating all his property, and Nivā-sūrya Bandya by confiscating all his property outside of his house, for making a false accusation.

On the 6th of Sāwan, N. S. 778 (A.D. 1658), Bhātgāon and Lalitpur fought against Kāntipur, and the road to Bhātgāon was thrown open. On the next day Srī-nivāsa and Pratāpa Malla took an oath upon the Haribansa, the Kālī-purāna (two sacred books), and a khukrī (knife), and the road between Lalitpur and Kāntipur was thrown open. On the 10th, the troops of Kāntipur and Lalitpur went together to fight with the people of Nālā, and, after eight days, communication with Ināyaka was restored, after which all the roads were thrown open.

On the 14th of Pūs Sudi, N. S. 780 (A.D. 1660), Jagatprakāsa Malla, Rājā of Bhātgāon, set fire to a small military outpost at the foot of Chāngu, beheaded eight men, and carried off twenty-one. Next morning, the daughter of Pratāpa Malla went to Pātan. On the following day, the twenty-one men, who had been carried away, were beheaded as sacrifices to deities. On the 5th or 6th of Āswin, N. S. 780, Pratāpa Malla and Srī-nivāsa conquered Bundēgrām, in the time of Chautarā Pramānbīrjū. After this, they took a military outpost at Champā, on the 4th of Kārtik Sudi, N. S. 781 (A.D. 1661). On the next day they took Chōrpurī, and on the 10th of Aghan Badi they accepted an elephant and money from Bhātgāon.

On the 3rd of Aghan Badi, N. S. 782 (A.D. 1662), Srī-nivāsa Malla went to live at Bōdēgāon. Seven days after, he took Nakdēsgāon, and gave it up to be plundered. On the 10th of Māgh Sudi, he took Thēmī; and on the 11th of the same month Pratāpa Malla and Srī-nivasa returned to their respective capitals.

In N. S. 783 (A.D. 1663) Srī-nivāsa repaired, and

raised to three stories in height, the temple of Dēgutalē in the Pātan durbār. In N. S. 787 (A.D. 1667), he built a three-storied temple at the top of the southern side of the Mūla Chōk, and placed an Āgama dēvatā in it. As he was sitting one night at a window on the eastern side of the durbār, he saw that the Asta-mātrikā-ganas[1] entered the durbār and, after dancing, vanished again. The Rājā was pleased, and calling into his presence the Bauddhāchāryas of Buyā Bihār, Nakbahil Tōl, and Ōnkulī Bihār, he ordered them by turns to worship the Asta-mātrikās in their houses during the Āswin Navarātri, and to bring them to dance at the durbār. The cost was to be defrayed by the durbār. This custom is observed to the present day. He built a three-storied temple of Dēgutalē to the north of the Mūla Chōk, and also a hōm-kuti, or room in which to perform hōm. He also raised the temple of Sarbēswara to five stories in height, and repaired the tank and the kund (well). In this kund a duck was once lost and could not be found; but the owner, happening to go to Gōsāīn Thān, found it there; and so, from that time, it became known that this kund was filled with water from that holy place. On the night of the full-moon of Sāwan people place Sarbēswara in the kund, and those who cannot go to Gōsāīn Thān, bathe in this kund instead, and worship Sarbēswara.

In this reign, in N. S. 793 (A.D. 1673), one Satyarām Bhārō of Tangal Tōl repaired the chaitya and the bathing-place in front of Mīna-nātha.

Srī-nivāsa extended the period of dancing in the month of Kārtik, established by his father Siddhi-Narsinha,

[1] Brāhmanī, Māhēswarī, Vaishnavī, Kaumārī, Vārāhī, Indrānī, Chamundā, and Mahālakshmī.

from fifteen to twenty-five days. His minister Bhāgīrath Bhaiyā, and his brother Bhāgī Bhārō, built the three-storied temple of Mahādēva in front of the durbār; and also the Lāmu Pātī (dharmasālā) called in Newārī Tāhāphalē, in N. S. 798 (1678).

In N. S. 801 (A. D. 1681) the Rājā built the great temple of Bhīmasēna. He repaired the temple of Machchhīndra-nātha in Tau Bahāl, and made some more rules for the rath-jātrā, which he inscribed on a stone, that he caused to be placed in the temple, at the spot whither the deity is brought after he has been concealed for four days. He made his son Yōga-narēndra Malla and Kājī Bhāgīrath Bhaiyā witnesses to this inscription. He also placed his statue, made of gold, on a stone pedestal, to be exhibited in jātrās.

In this reign, in N. S. 821 (A. D. 1701), Uddhava Sinha Bābu, of Nōgalbhōnt, repaired the Sun-dhārā, in the name of his mother Phiku-lakshmī. This is written on a stone placed to the left of the dhārā[1]. This dhārā was built in the following manner. A dhārā was made by a man of Satgal Tōl, but it was much below the level of the ground, and people had a long way to descend to it. When it was finished, the man gave a feast to his friends, and one of the party, when praising the water, said that a person coming to drink from this dhārā would require to bring food with him to give him strength to ascend again! This man then began to worship Phulchōkī Dēvī, who after some time was pleased and gave him a small pebble. He took this home and locked it up in his dhukutī (treasure-

[1] This dhārā appears to have been built before the beginning of the Nepāl Sambat, because the inscription on a stone to the right of the dhārā has been effaced, which must have been done at the time of the introduction of the new era, when all bonds and similar documents were destroyed.

room), and was thinking that he would make by its help a dhārā as high as the top of his house. One day, however, in his absence, his wife entered the room in which the stone was kept, and thinking it was a useless thing, told the servant to throw it away outside of the city. The husband, on his return, discovered what had happened, hastened to the spot where the pebble had been thrown down, and found that a clear fountain had sprung up there. He then constructed a covered water-course, and made the water run to a spot near his house, where he built the Sun-dhārā. The place where the pebble was thrown down is called Nāg-khēl[1].

4. His son Yōga-narēndra Malla succeeded Srī-nivāsa. He extended the period of the Kārtik dance from twenty-five days to a month. He set up an image of Bhīmasēna, representing him in a passion, killing Dus-sāsan, instead of with a pacific aspect. An Āchār of Jhatāpōl, with the sanction of the Rājā, assigned land for the annual rath-jātrā of this Bhīmasēna.

The Rājā built a house, and placed a stone throne in the middle of it, where the astrologers assembled and consulted together to find out an auspicious day for the rath-jātrā of Machchhīndra-nātha. This house was named Mani-mandapa.

He gave a copy of the Kāranda-Byūha, containing the history of Machchhīndra-nātha, written in golden letters, to Dharmarāj Pandit of Ōnkulī Bihār, who recited this Purān in Mani-mandapa. The Pandit gave the following benediction to the Rājā. "O Rājā Yōga-narēndra, may the Lōk-nātha, who has vanquished the wicked and made the people go in the right path, protect thee! O Rājā, the history contained in the book which thou hast

[1] Outside of Patan, on the road to Gōdāvarī.

given to me, has been recited to the people, and shall be recited again and again. For this meritorious act may happiness attend thee, and mayest thou live long with good health, and reign over the people[1]."

He also assigned many guthīs to Machchhīndra-nātha, and lands for the daily worship of Harsiddhi dēvatā. He erected a pillar in front of Dēgutalē, and placed on it his own and his son's statues[2].

The Rājā of Bhātgāon became jealous of him, and built a temple to the south of the durbār in Pātan, with the object of making the Rājā childless. Yōga-narēndra was ignorant of the purpose for which the temple was built. His son Siddhi-Narsinha, the heir apparent, died young, and from grief the Rājā relinquished the world, and went away. He told the minister that as long as the face of his statue remained bright and untarnished, and the bird on its head had not flown away, he would know that the Rājā was alive, and should cherish and respect his memory. For this reason a mattress is still every night laid in a room in the front of the durbār, and the window is left open[3].

5. After him Mahīpatīndra, or Mahīndra Sinha Malla (rājā of Kāntipur), became also rājā of Pātan.

In N. S. 826 Rudramatī, a daughter of Rājā Yōga-narēṇdra, built a three-storied temple to the south of the pillar supporting her father's statue, and placed Hari-sankara in it. On the 11th of Bhādon Badī, N. S. 842 (A. D. 1722)[4], Mahīndra Malla died.

[1] This book is still in the possession of the Pandit, and is recited yearly. I have myself seen it.

[2] This pillar still stands in the square before the durbār.

[3] This is still done, as the face of the statue remains bright.

[4] This date does not correspond with that which is given in the account of the kings of Kāṭhmāṇḍū.

6. Jaya Yōga-prakāsa succeeded him.

In N. S. 843 (A. D. 1723) he performed a kōtyāhuti-yagya. After this Vishnu Malla, a grandson (daughter's son) of Yōga-narēndra, became rājā of Lalitpur.

7. Srī Srī Vishnu Malla Rājā.

This Rājā built a beautiful durbār, south of Bhandār-khāl and north of the road taken by the rath-jātrā, in which he placed a window, having a golden image of Āryāvalōkitēswara producing Brahmā and other gods from his body. This palace he named Lujhyāl-chaukbāth Durbār. In building this durbār, the Rājā set an example to his subjects by mounting an elephant one moonlight night and carrying two or three bricks upon it. The people were thus induced to work. Seven layers of bricks used to be laid one day, and the next day four layers were taken off and seven layers again laid. By doing this the structure was made very strong. On the day of roofing the durbār, Jōthājū of Thaināyakō brought to assist in the work a great crowd of people, whom he had assembled to help in roofing the Jōthā Bihār, which he had built. For this service he received a dress of honour.

There was a drought and famine at this time, and Vishnu Malla sent Sarbānand Pandit of Mahābuddha to Kwāchhē-bāl-kumārī to perform purascharana and nāg-sādhana, after which rain fell.

In order to terrify his enemies, the Rājā offered a large bell to Talēju, in front of the Mūla Chōk, in N. S. 857 (A. D. 1737). He gave birtās to many Brāhmans, and adopted them as sons. He offered a silver jalhari to Pashupati-nātha. He had no sons, and therefore appointed Rājya-prakāsa Malla as his successor, and died shortly afterwards.

8. Rājya-prakāsa Malla.

This Rājā was a pacific man, and worshipped a number of Sāligrāms. The six Pradhāns, taking advantage of his simplicity, deprived him of his eyesight. He did not long survive this, and after his death the Pradhān of the Dhālāchhēkāchha caste brought (9) the Rājā of Bhātgāon, Ranjīt Malla, and made him Rājā of Pātan also. After a year's reign, however, the Pradhāns drove him away, when he had gone to bathe at Sankhamūla.

10. After this the Pradhāns made Jaya-prakāsa, the Rājā of Kāntipur, Rājā of Pātan also, and he ruled over both cities. At this time Sōdhan, gubahāl of Bū-bahāl, which is within Gāda-bahāl, used to visit the temple of Vaishnavī of Yapa Pītha very early in the morning, accompanied by twenty or thirty companions. One morning they saw a Sannyāsī Gōsāīn sitting on the body of a man, whom he had sacrificed, and performing anjan-sādhan. The Sannyāsī, seeing these men enter the temple, ran away before he had completed the sādhan. Sōdhan occupied his seat, completed the ceremony, and gave the anjan to his companions, who through its virtue became fascinated and obeyed Sōdhan implicitly. They returned home and hired a house in Nak-bihār, where they began to live. Sōdhan gave the name of a deity to each of his companions, who assumed the character assigned to him. He told the people not to go to any temple, but to come to his house, where, he said, every god was to be found. He even sent men to fetch to his house the umbrellas, etc., belonging to the gods. The people brought many offerings, and Sōdhan and his companions ate and drank freely. Jaya-prakāsa heard of this, and sent men to arrest them. Many escaped,

but all those who were caught were sacrificed, each to the Pītha dēvatā whom he had personated[1].

Jaya-prakāsa ruled for one or two years; but the Pradhāns were afraid of him, and one day, when he went to Tēkhu-dōbhān to bathe, they expelled him.

11. They then installed as rājā a grandson (daughter's son) of Vishnu Malla, named Viswajīt Malla, who reigned for four years. The six Pradhāns were soon displeased with him, and, in order to get rid of him, they accused him of adultery with one of their wives, and killed him at the door of Talēju. His Rānī was sitting at a window above the Hapyātal, at the south-west corner, and she cried for help to the people, but no one would give aid. She then uttered a curse against the people of the city, to the effect that their voice might fail them in their time of need, and that they might be in terror when their trouble came.

Thus the Rājā died, and the Pradhāns went to Noākōt and brought Dalmardan Sāh, whom they made rājā with the permission of Prithwīnārāyana Sāh.

12. Dalmardan Sāh reigned four years. Being a Gōrkhālī, he did everything without consulting the Pradhāns, who were therefore displeased and expelled him.

13. Then they brought a descendant of Viswajīt, named Tēj-narsinha Malla, and made him rājā. He reigned for three years.

[1] Can this possibly be a reference to some persecution of the Christian colony which existed at this time at Pātan? It is very strange that there is no mention of these Christians in this history; and still more so, that none of the people of Pātan know anything about them, or have any traditions connected with them. One of the priests died, and was buried somewhere at Pātan, and the others were expelled from the country by Prithwīnārāyana; but nothing is known of this by any one at Pātan, though it took place barely a hundred years ago. Their descendants now live at Bettiah.

In his time Prithwīnārāyana came into Nepāl, and Tēj-narsinha fled to Bhātgāon.

Prithwīnārāyana, knowing the six Pradhāns to be traitors, bound and killed them. One only escaped, who went ahead of all the others and could not be seized. The wives of the Pradhāns became satīs.

CHAPTER VIII.

Progress of the Gōrkha invasion under the command of Prithwīnārāyana. Taking of Bhātgāon. Fate of the three kings of Bhātgāon, Kāṭhmāṇḍū and Pātan.

THE Gōrkhālīs fought for six months with the people of Dhulkhēl. After this Prithwīnārāyana Sāh built a fort[1] on the top of the mountain south of Chaukōt, and collected a large number of troops[2]. On consulting with his followers, he was told by the Kājīs that small villages were easily taken, as the people fled when they heard the shouts of the assailants, but that this village, Chaukōt, would require some military skill to take it. After this consultation the troops blockaded Chaukōt. Some of the people fled to Pyuthānā by the way of Bāsdōl, and others to other places. Namsinha Rāī went to Mahīndra Sinha Rāī[3], and said, "We are unable to cope with the Gōrkhālīs, with the help of only fifty houses. The rest of the people have fled, and I am come to tell you. Do not delay, but fly soon." Mahīndra Sinha reproached him and charged him with cowardice, saying, "Do not

[1] There are the remains of such small *garhīs* or forts on all the low ridges round the valley. They consist of circular ditches and mounds, and could hardly have held more than forty or fifty men.

[2] Chaukōt and Dhulkhēl or Dharkhēl lie east of Bhātgāon.

[3] It does not appear who these were; probably district officials.

stay for me, but escape with your lives. As for myself, I will repulse the whole force of the Gōrkhālīs, and having earned great renown, will enjoy my possessions in happiness. If I do not succeed, I shall leave my body on the field of battle, and earn an abode in heaven, by the merit of which my sons and grandsons will obtain happiness." He then called together his faithful followers, who were desirous of securing happiness in the next world, and encouraged them.

On the 6th of Jēth Badi a severe battle was fought, which lasted from evening till 12 gharīs of the night. The Gōrkhālīs, having lost 131 men, retreated. The battle was renewed daily for fifteen days, without the Gōrkhālīs making any impression. Prithwīnārāyana and his Kājīs were much disheartened, and seeing that a small village made such a determined resistance, wondered what was to be expected from large towns. On the 6th of Jēth Sudi a hardly contested battle was fought, which lasted till 14 gharīs of the night. At this time a sipāhī, getting behind Mahīndra Sinha, killed him with a khoḍā and a lance, and wounded Namsinha in the left shoulder with a khukrī, so that he fell senseless to the ground. Seeing this, the Chaukōtiyās fled, and the village was set on fire. In this battle the Gōrkhālīs lost 201 men, which, with the 131 killed on the former day, gives a total of 332 men killed.

Namsinha Rāī, having recovered from his swoon, and seeing no Gōrkhālīs near, raised himself, and binding up his wound with his waistcloth fled to Pyuthānā, through Bāsdōl. He saw Mahīndra Sinha Rāī lying on the ground lifeless, being pierced from behind by a khoḍā and a lance, but he had no time to wait longer.

The next morning Srī Prithwīnārāyana Sāh inspected

the field of battle, and seeing Mahīndra Sinha Rāī's lifeless body pierced with wounds, he praised his bravery, and sent for his family, that they, being the relatives of so brave a man, might have proper protection. They were brought and fed morning and evening from the royal kitchen. After this, having with ease taken five villages, viz., Panāvatī, Banēpā, Nālā, Khadpu, and Sāngā, Prithwīnārāyana returned to Noākōt.

After eight months, Prithwīnārāyana came to attack Bhātgāon, where he had previously gained over the Sātbāhālyās[1] by promising to leave to them the throne and revenue, and to content himself with a nominal sovereignty over the country. According to previous arrangements, therefore, the troops commanded by the Sātbāhālyās fired blank cartridges on the enemy, admitted them within the fortified walls with little opposition, and secretly sent them ammunition. Thus Bhātgāon was taken. The Gōrkhālīs entered the town, but met with great resistance at the durbār, which they surrounded. After some fighting, the golden door of the Mūla Chōk was broken open, and the Gōrkhālī troops entered the durbār. Jaya-prakāsa Malla fought for three or four gharīs, but he was disabled by receiving a bullet in his foot. Every one then yielded. The Bhōtiyā sipāhīs, having been suspected, had been shut up in a building, and on their clamouring to be let out to fight, Ranjīt Malla set the place on fire.

Prithwīnārāyana Sāh now entered the durbār, and found the Rājās of the three towns sitting together, whereat he and his companions began to laugh. Jaya-prakāsa was offended at this, and said, "O Gōrkhālīs, this has come to pass through the treachery of our servants, or

[1] Seven illegitimate sons of Ranjīt Malla.

else you would have had no cause for mirth." The Gōrkhālīs then became silent. Some conversation took place between Prithwīnārāyana and Jaya-prakāsa, in which the latter praised the former, but cautioned him against his own officials, who he said were faithless and not to be trusted. Prithwīnārāyana then paid his respects to Ranjīt Malla, and respectfully asked him to continue to rule as he had hitherto done, although he (Prithwīnārāyana) had conquered the country. Ranjīt Malla replied that Prithwīnārāyana had obtained the sovereignty by the favour of God, and that all that he now asked for was to be sent to Benāres. Prithwīnārāyana entreated him to remain; but the recollection of the treachery of the Sātbāhālyās was fresh in his memory, and he would not consent. Prithwīnārāyana then gave him leave to go, and also provided for his expenses on the road.

When Ranjīt Malla reached the top of the Chandrāgiri pass, he took a last view of Nepāl, and with tears in his eyes exclaimed, "The Sātbāhālyās have killed my son Bīr-Narsinha, and have caused me this sorrow." He then cursed them. "May they look like Chandāls, and live in beggary. May their offspring perish. May their birtās be taken from them; and may no respectable person ever associate with them. May they be reduced to selling windows, houses, clay, and tiles." There are several songs on the subject composed by him. He then bade farewell to Tuljā (Turjā or Talēju), Pashupati, and Guhjēswarī, and went to seek an asylum with Biswēswara-nātha and Gangā.

Prithwīnārāyana Sāh then caused the members of the Sātbāhālyā families to be brought bound before him; and reflecting that they had been traitors to their father, for the sake of obtaining the gaddī, and that they could not be expected to be faithful to others, he caused the noses of some of them to be cut off, and confiscated the whole of their property.

Prithwīnārāyana Sāh then asked Jaya Prakāsa Malla what he intended to do. He replied that, by the favour of God, he had ruled the country for a long time, enjoyed royalty, and built many monuments; that now he had nothing to desire but that he might be conveyed to Āryā Ghāt at Pashupati, where he would obtain salvation (*i.e.*, die).

Prithwīnārāyana was touched by this speech, and consented to his being taken to Pashupati. He moreover gave orders to supply Jaya Prakāsa with anything which he might desire to give away in charity; and for this purpose a sawār was sent to ask what he wanted to give away. Jaya Prakāsa said that he wanted nothing but an umbrella and a pair of shoes. The sawār returned and gave the message to the Gōrkhālī Rājā, who was at once plunged into grief, and remained silent a long time. The request was repeated by the sawār, and the courtiers expressed surprise at the hesitation shown by the Mahārāj in granting such trifles, when he had promised him anything he wanted to give away in charity. Prithwīnārāyana said that they did not understand the meaning of the request, which was that Jaya Prakāsa wanted to be born again as his son, and thus to enjoy the kingdom again, which he was very loath to grant[1]. However, as he had already promised to give him anything he wanted, the Rājā mounted his horse, went to the place where Jaya Prakāsa was, and, presenting to him an umbrella and a pair of shoes, said: "I give you what you want, to be enjoyed by you, not, however, during

[1] The shoe denotes the earth, and the umbrella the crown.

my lifetime, but in that of my grandson." Jaya Prakāsa consented, and took the gift. He then said that the person who should offer a silver jalharī to Pashupati-nātha would be himself returned to the earth. After saying this he died, and was absorbed into the southern or Aghōr face of Pashupati-nātha.

Tēj-Narsinha, the Rājā of Lalitpur, thought that all this evil was brought about by Ranjīt Malla, and that there was no use in speaking to any one. He therefore sat engaged in the worship of God, and would not speak. For this reason he was sent to Lakshmīpur, to be kept in confinement; and there he died.

CHAPTER IX.

The Gōrkha dynasty in Nepāl. Death of Prithwīnārāyana. War with Tibet and China. General Bhīmasēna Thāpā made prime minister. War with the British. Great earthquakes.

1. After this Rājā Prithwīnārāyana returned from Bhātgāon to Kāntipur, and began to rule over the three towns. He built a large dharmasālā, and named it Basantpur. He granted the right of near approach to the royal person to Putwārs, in N. S. 890 (A.D. 1770), in consideration of the services they had rendered in the attack upon Kīrtipur. To the Kasāīs also he assigned lands, and appointed them to perform menial services in the temple of Guhjēswarī. Because Surpratāp Sāh (his brother) had lost one of his eyes in the war with the people of Kīrtipur, Prithwīnārāyana ordered the nose of every male in that town, above twelve years of age, to be cut off. These noses weighed seventeen dhārnīs (about 80 lbs.), and the people thus mutilated were 865 of those who had fought valiantly and kept the Gōrkhālīs out of the town.

In this reign one Rāmkrishna Kavar, with the permission of the Rājā, made a road from Guhjēswarī to Pashupati, and paved it with stone. The Rājā built a bridge across the Rudramatī, where the main road crossed it.

The Rājā sent Kājī Kahar Sinha to subdue the whole country lying between Bijayapur on the east, the Sapta-Gandakī on the west, Kirōn and Kūti on the north, and Makwānpur and the Taryānī (Terai) on the south.

Prithwīnārāyana reigned seven years, and died on the Sankrānti day, N. S. 895 (A.D. 1775), at Mōhan Tīrtha on the Gandakī.

2. His son Sinha Pratāp Sāh reigned three years.

This Rājā, regarding Guhjēswarī as the mistress of Nepāl, vowed to sacrifice to her a lākh and 25,000 animals. He caused the Linga of Noākōt to be brought to the Durbār, and assigned a guthī to maintain the Linga-dhāli-jātrā (known now as the Indra-jātrā). He performed all the ceremonies in the worship of Turjā Dēvī, assisted by Āchārs, and died in N. S. 898 (A.D. 1778).

3. His son Ran Bahādur Sāh reigned 19 years.

He was a powerful monarch. Suspecting the Āchārs of having caused the premature death of his father by *prayōg* (*i.e.*, repeating mantras), he caused many of them to be put to death near the Indrānī Pītha. He also, for some reason, caused the Mantri-nāyak (prime minister) Bansrāj Pāṇḍē to be cut down in the Durbār. He made a silver jalharī and offered it to Pashupati-nātha[1].

In the west he conquered Lamjung and Tanhau, and the country of the Chaubīsī Rājās. His rule extended as far as the Gangā. The British trembled in the south. He sent Sarūp Kājī, who conquered the whole of the Kirātī country, and extended his conquests as far as Sumbēswara in the east. Having learned the particulars of the northern country from Syāmarpā Lāmā, whom he had sent for, he despatched troops to Sikhārjun,

[1] Thus showing that Jaya Prakāsa had returned to the world, as predicted by himself.

who plundered Digarchā, and did not respect the Chinese authority. The Chinese Emperor, being unable to brook this insult, sent a large army, under the command of Kājī Dhurīn and minister Thumthām. This army reached Dhēbun[1], when the Rājā employed one Lākhyā Bāndā of Bhinkshē Bahāl to perform purascharan, while Mantri-nāyak Dāmōdar Pāṇḍē cut the Chinese army to pieces and obtained great glory[2]. Afterwards the Chinese Emperor, thinking it better to live in friendship with the Gōrkhālīs, made peace with them.

Bahādur Sāh (the uncle of the king), being ill-advised, measured the whole land, and on account of this sin of ascertaining the limits of the earth, he was put into prison, and died there.

This Rājā used to give 1000 cows in charity on great days. He caused meritorious acts (dharma) to be repeatedly performed, and fed Brāhmans and Fakīrs in Pachlī-khēl[3]; and every Saturday he caused curds and *chiūrā* to be distributed at Pashupati-nātha.

He impressed all the people in the country, and built the temple of Jagan-nātha on the Tudi-khēl, which had no equal; but it was not completed. He repaired the kavacha (coat) of Pashupati-nātha. He appointed Gujar-ātī music to be performed at the temples of Guhjēswarī, Bajra Joginī, Chāngu Nārāyana, Dakshin Kālī, Talēju, Dēgutalē, and Lomḍī, and assigned guthīs for the maintenance of mahāpūjā and sadābart (daily alms-giving of food, &c., to the poor). He gave many other

1 A hill north of Noākōt.

2 The Nepalese were utterly defeated, and had to conclude an ignominious treaty of peace at Noākōt. This was the time when Colonel Kirkpatrick was sent by the British to intercede with the Chinese, but arrived after the treaty had been concluded.

3 Near Panchlinga Bhairava, close to the junction of the Bāgmatī and Vishnumati.

guthīs, and obtained praise. He put a great bell and a large image of Bhairava in front of the Durbār. The images of the Mātrikā Joginīs were there before.

Some time after this the Rājā made the daughter of a Misra his Rānī[1], and a son was born, who was ascertained to possess illustrious qualities, and was named Gīrbān-juddha Vikram Sāh. The Rājā abdicated in his favour, and, assuming the name of Nirgunānanda Swāmī, went to live in Dēva-pātan, where he laid out three sorts of gardens and dedicated them to Pashupati-nātha. Thirty-two houses were demolished to make room for the gardens, but compensation was given for them. He used to see bulls fight. The monkeys were very troublesome, and many were put to death. Vultures and cats also shared their fate, as they were ill omens[2].

This Swāmī Rājā was very just, and a great proficient in music. After residing for three months at Dēva-pātan he went to live at Lalitpur. He sent his son Gīrbān-juddha to Noākōt, quarrelled with his nobles and officers, made excrement be used as incense for Talēju and other deities, whose images he caused to be destroyed, and put Baids to death[3]. Srī Talējū he caused to be sent to Karbīr Smasān, to be burned like a dead body, after making the Āchārs weep as for a dead person, and causing Kasāī and Kahāl music to be performed.

He then assembled his subjects and enlisted them as sipāhīs, and quarrelled with his son. There was fear

[1] This was a Brāhmanī widow from Tirhūt. Independently of her being a widow, the marriage was illegal, as being between a Rājpūt and a Brāhmanī. Hence the allusion to incest hereafter.

[2] I know a large house, a part of Thāpāthalī, which is not used as a dwelling-house, because a vulture once perched on the roof!

[3] All this was because, on the occasion of the illness of his favourite Rānī, he had performed pūjās, &c., to these deities without avail.

in the three cities; but at this time, in order to purify himself from sin, and through fear of Dāmōdar Kājī, he went to Vārānasī (Benares)[1].

During his absence the Māhila (second) Mahārānī ruled the country. She built the three-storied temple of Nandikēswara and a dharmasālā, constructed a tank, and assigned lands to keep up a sadāvart and the daily worship of Siva. She offered beautiful bells to Gōrakhnātha and other deities. At this time Kājī Kīrtimān made a general paijnī[2] of chautarās (relatives of the royal family), kājīs, sardārs, ministers, grooms, grass-cutters and pauwālīs; and in consequence some ill-disposed persons killed the Kājī in the durbār. The Rānī caused these persons to be put to death.

The Swāmī Rājā, after a residence of four years at Benāres, returned to Nepāl, and put to death Dāmōdar Kājī and others of his enemies. He made new laws and issued many orders, stopped the main roads, confiscated all the birtā lands of the Brāhmans in the country, raised money by reassessing the lands, and from fear of small-pox ordered all the children to be taken out of the city.

He conquered the country of Sansār Chand of Kāngrā.

The distressed Brāhmans, especially the Bhaimālyās, came before the Rājā, and clamoured for redress. They recited the following slōk:

"Oh Mahārāj, poison is not so deadly as the spoiling of the Brāhman; for poison kills one only, but the spoiling of the Brāhman kills sons and grandsons."

The Rājā, however, paid no attention to them. He

1 In reality he was forced to abdicate by the nobles.

2 Annual muster, when all officials in the country may be turned out or confirmed for another year.

was the first Rājā who brought gold ashrafīs into currency. His rule extended to Kāngrā and Garhwāl, but bad ministers curtailed his kingdom in the west.

An ill omen happened at this time. A large jackal entered the city, passed through the bāzār, and left the city by the northern gate. This happened on the night of Saturday, the 7th of Baisākh Sudi, N. S. 917 (A. D. 1807)[1], and was the consequence of the resumption of Brāhmans' lands, the stoppage of the main roads, ill usage of children, the desecration of many deities, and incest. The brother of the Rājā killed him with a sword, through fear that he himself might be killed.

4. His son Gīrbān-juddha Vikram Sāh reigned 20 years.

This Rājā was of a very benevolent, pacific temper, and a worshipper of Vishnu. He caused all the expelled children to be brought back to their homes. He was a great respecter of Brāhmans and of the Shāstras. Having had explained to him the meaning of the Himavat Khanda[2], he fasted the whole day and night of Sivarātri, and dedicated the whole of Dēva-pātan to Pashupati-nātha on the 14th of Phāgun Badi, Vik. S. 1870 (A. D. 1813).

This Rājā appointed Bhīmasēna Thāpā to be prime minister and protector of the whole country. He built the bridge near Tankēswara, and a ghāt, and made a golden dhārā. He also built a bridge over the Bāgmatī, near the Kālmochanī Tīrtha, and placed a lion on a pedestal. He conferred the title of General on Bhīmasēna. He made good roads through every tōl in the city. He built the great kōt in Majā-dēval, and named

[1] The MS. has 927.

[2] A part of the Skanda Purāna, describing the holy places of Nepāl.

it Kampu, in which to assemble the troops and keep their muskets.

In this reign an insane Brāhman came in the shape of Kalanki[1], and sacrificed a Kusalyā (a person of low caste), a horse, and a Brāhmanī, to Guhjēswarī.

The Rājā offered a silver image to Pashupati-nātha, and placed it at the western door of the temple on the silver-plated floor.

On the 10th of Jēth Sudi, N. S. 930 (A. D. 1810)[2], a violent earthquake occurred, and many houses fell down. The great temples, such as Pashupati and Talēju, escaped injury. In Bhātgāon numerous lives were lost.

He built a powder magazine on Thambahil-khēl, and brought into currency dhyāk or double pice.

In his reign a war broke out with the British in the Taryānī (Terai), but depriving them of wisdom, the Rājā saved his country. Then calling the British gentlemen, he made peace with them, and allowed them to live near Thambahil[3].

At this time dogs used to bring human flesh into the city, and as much trouble was caused by this, a great many of them were destroyed[4].

The Sītalā Dēvī (smallpox), having been insulted for twelve years, at last became furious, and entered Nepāl. Innumerable children died, and their dead bodies were not burned, but buried near the Bāgmatī. The effluvia

[1] Or Kalki; the incarnation of Vishnu which is to appear at the end of the Kali Yuga.

[2] Altered into 928 (A. D. 1808).

[3] Such is the native account of what we call the Nepāl war, which ended in their total defeat at Makwānpur, and the loss of a great part of their possessions below the hills. War was declared on the 1st November, 1814, and peace concluded on the 5th March, 1816.

[4] In times of plague the bodies of the poor, instead of being burned, are merely singed with fire and thrown into the beds of the rivers, where dogs and vultures may be seen devouring them.

from the dead bodies spread abroad, the water was poisoned, and vultures and wild beasts, which fed on the corpses, died in numbers. All the Nandis (stone images of bulls) having been brought out, a plentiful rain fell and washed away the corpses. The Rājā being of a pacific nature, Sītalā entered the durbār, and he died of smallpox at Āryā Ghāt, on the 1st of Aghan Sudi, N. S. 938 (A. D. 1818)[1]. At this date Sītalā first appeared in Nepāl.

5. His son Rājēndra Vikram Sāh.

This Rājā repaired the umbrella of Pashupati-nātha. The principal timber in Swayambhū having become rotten, a Lāmā was summoned from Lhāsā, and it was replaced by a new *sāl* beam.

In this reign, in Vik. S. 1877 (A. D. 1820), General Bhīmasēna offered gold and silver doors to the southern side of the temple of Pashupati-nātha. Afterwards, with the permission of the Rājā, he made silver doors for the temple, placing four in the inner apartment and one in each of the four outer sides.

In this reign one month of the year was lost[2], and Dasāīn was celebrated in Kārtik instead of Kuār, Vik. S. 1879 (A. D. 1822). To insure the salvation of the Rānīs of the Swāmī Mahārāj, he built temples near Kālmōchan Tīrtha[3], naming them Tripurēswara and Pūrnēswara. Near the temples he constructed ghāts on the Bāgmatī, and erected an image of Hanumān. He built a cantonment for the troops at Mālthalī.

[1] Read A. D. 1816. By this calculation he reigned 19 years.

[2] The astrologers sometimes increase or decrease the number of months in the year, so as to keep the lunar months, by which the time of the festivals is fixed, at the same periods. Otherwise the months and festivals would fall at various times of the year, as is the case in the Mohammedan calendar.

[3] On the bank of the Bāgmatī between Kāṭhmāṇḍū and Thāpāthalī, where Sir Jung Bahādur has just built a new temple.

Maclure & Macdonald Lith. London.

(Plate XIV) GENERAL BHĪMASENA'S DHĀRĀ, WITH A PĀṬĪ OR DHARMASALĀ (p. 262)

In this reign a thief stole the ornaments of Jaya Bāgēswarī, but after two years he was found out. He restored some of the ornaments, and was made to pay the price of the others, which he had sold and expended. With the money a new Bhandār-sālā (store-house) was built.

In N. S. 944, and Vik. S. 1880 (A.D. 1823—24), through the influence of Saturn and other planets, which secretly came together in one sign of the zodiac, Mahāmāī appeared in Nepāl, and numerous persons died from the effects of her evil eye. Through the influence of the seven planets, a disease called Bisūchi (cholera) appeared in the east, as far away as Dhākā and Buḍhī-Gangā, and then at a place in the east called Bisankhu. Many lives were lost. By the 1st of Māgh it spread over the whole of Nepāl, and extended as far as the Kālī Gandakī; but after two months it disappeared.

In the same year seventeen shocks of earthquake were felt in one day and night. The Rājā performed a sānti (ceremony of purification).

When the Rājā first visited Guhjēswarī and Pashupati-nātha, he made an offering of one rupee daily to each, and this custom is continued to the present time. It was not the custom before this.

In this reign Mahābārunī (a conjunction of certain planets at a certain time) took place, and many meritorious acts were performed. General Bhīmasēna placed a Narbadā Siva on the Tudi-khēl, and named it Bhīmabhaktēswara. The General made golden dhārās, tanks, and gardens. Colonel Māthabar Sinha also built many edifices; and Colonel Ranbīr Sinha constructed a sālā, and established a sadābart. The Rājā offered a golden lion on a pedestal to Guhjēswarī. He also caused the

Mōhan Chōk Durbār to be repainted. He offered an umbrella to each face of Pashupati-nātha. He decided that Brāhmans of all tribes should be exempt from impressment for labour.

On the 11th of Pūs Sudi, N. S. 949 (A.D. 1829), he collected a lākh and 25,000 oranges from all the gardens, and offered them to Pashupati-nātha. The whole temple was filled with them, only the head of Pashupati-nātha being above them. He made frequent offerings of mangoes and āmrātak fruit (guavas) to Guhjēswarī and Pashupati-nātha, being such a wise king.

Again a month was lost in this reign, the year being of eleven months only, and a great many people, as well as beasts, birds, and fishes, died in consequence. On the 5th of Baisākh Badi, Vik. S. 1887 (A.D. 1830), the powder-magazine at Noākōt was struck by lightning, and 62 men were killed. In the same year, on the 14th of Asārh Badi, about 10 p.m., the Thambahīl magazine was struck by lightning and exploded, and 18 men were killed.

On the 9th of Chait Badi, Vik. S. 1888 (A.D. 1831), the senior Mahārānī died. Except the Brāhmans, all castes shaved their heads and beards, as a sign of mourning. The Brāhmans were only four days in mourning, but all officers and other subjects had to observe the full period of mourning (*i.e.*, a whole year). Riding on horseback, military music, travelling in dolīs or palanquins, were all stopped, except in the case of marriages. A bride and bridegroom were allowed to wear red clothes till the ceremonies were finished.

The Rājā was now in his 18th year, and the Sambat was also 88, whence cholera broke out in the country[1];

[1] Any year in which 8 occurs is considered unlucky.

but he caused purascharan to be performed at Bachhalēswarī by Brāhmans, and the disease disappeared. On the day that this Dēvī's jātrā was to take place, the Rānī of the Swāmī Mahārāj died, but the jātrā was celebrated. No other jātrā was allowed to take place.

At about 10 or 11 a.m. on the 4th of Aghan Sudi, Vik. S. 1889 (A.D. 1832), the Mahārāj mounted a female elephant, named Kunjkalī, and Bhīmasēna Thāpā was seated behind him on the same elephant. When they reached Bhunēswara, a male elephant, named Lālbahādur, chased them. General Bhīmasēna fell off at the entrance of the bridge over the Bāgmatī, and the Rājā fell into the river, but no serious injury was received.

In Vik. S. 1890 (A.D. 1833), on the 12th of the second Bhādon Sudi (being a leap year there were two Bhādons), a shock of earthquake was felt towards evening, and another at 12 gharīs of the night. Four shocks were felt in all, and the fourth was so violent that many buildings and temples fell down in Kāṭhmāḍōn, Pātan, Bhātgāon, and the villages.

In Pātan the number of buildings damaged was 824[1]. Of these there were

Houses completely destroyed	213
Roofs damaged	98
Kausīs (open platforms on the roof with a parapet) damaged	22
Houses partly do.	117
Walls do.	374
Temples do.	17
Pātīs do.	14

Two people were injured, of whom one died, and the other was only wounded.

[1] There are errors in several of these numbers.

In Kāṭhmāḍōn 643 buildings were damaged. Of these there were

Houses totally destroyed	365
Roofs do.	10
Two-storied pātīs do.	3
One-storied pātīs do.	5
Doors injured	2
Minarets (dharēras)	2

one of which was thrown down, and the other only injured. The great temple of Jagan-nātha, on the Tudikhēl, also fell down, and 22 persons were buried under the ruins and died, and 30 more were injured. The parapet-walls of the bridge over the Bāgmatī were damaged to the extent of 20 hāths (cubits). The top of the Tripurēswara temple also fell down.

In Bhātgāon 2747 buildings were damaged. Of these there were

Walls injured	311
Roofs do.	204
Half-destroyed	971
Kausīs injured	174
Houses totally destroyed	1186

Out of 16,456 inmates of 270 houses, 177 were killed, and 252 injured[1].

In Sānkhu 236 houses were destroyed, and 21 temples and pātīs. 18 people were killed, and 10 injured.

In Banēpā 269 houses were damaged; and in Sānāgāon 33 houses were injured, and 2 people hurt.

The temples of Pashupati, Guhjēswarī, and Talēju, received no injury.

Such a catastrophe had once before occurred in the

[1] This gives about 60 inmates to each house; but a Nepalese house is a large range of buildings round a central square, and the population is very dense, there being a family in every room or two.

reign of Shyāma Sinha. The present Rājā, being wise, offered a golden crown to Panchlinga Bhairava.

In this reign, on the 6th of Asārh Badi, Vik. S. 1891 (A.D. 1834), the powder-magazine at Thēmī was struck by lightning and exploded. On the 5th of Asārh Sudi, in the same year, a shock of earthquake was felt at night. Several shocks were felt from the 1st to the 2nd of Kārtik Badi in the same year. Much rain also fell, which commenced and ended with the earthquakes. The Bāgmatī overflowed its banks, and washed away 200 stacks of rice. The eastern parapet of the bridge over the Bāgmatī fell, and the image of Ganēsa at the Bhairava Ghāt was washed away. The water rose to the wall of the enclosure of Lakshmēswara Mahādēva.

In this year the Rājā made the elephants Haḍbaḍprasād and Hirāgaj fight. They fought in the bed of the Bāgmatī for a whole day and night. The mahāuts of both elephants received great rewards in dresses of honour, ornaments, and money. Tiger and elephant fights were also exhibited.

In this reign, in Vik. S. 1893 (A.D. 1836), a woman in Pātan gave birth to two children joined to each other. People went to see them, and made offerings of money and rice.

In Vik. S. 1894 (A.D. 1837), in the month of Sāwan, the minister (Bhīmasēna) was imprisoned by the troops, by order of the Rājā, at the instigation of the sons of the former wicked minister, and his whole property was confiscated. The former minister's sons also abused him. This was unendurable by the high-minded minister, who thus received ingratitude for the faithful direction of the affairs of state, through the machinations of those who, as he said, were fed on the leavings of his table. He therefore cut his own throat and died[1]. This Bhīmasēna is said to be the same who, in a former birth, appeared as Bhīma Malla, a minister of the Newār Rājās[2].

The Rānī of this Rājā made a copper roof for the temple of Pashupati-nātha, in Vik. S. 1895 (A. D. 1838). In Vik. S. 1891 (A. D. 1834), Subā Kulānand Jhā made silver doors in three sides of the temple of Pashupati. Hirīlāl Jhā, the son of this Subā, made golden roofs for the temples of Gnātēswarī, Ichāngu Nārāyana, and Ākāsbāni or Bhātbhatyāni.

In this reign the people of the city paved the roads and streets[3].

1 This suicide (or murder) really took place on the 29th of July, 1839.

2 Similarly, the present prime minister, Sir Jung Bahādur, is believed to be an incarnation of the king Ran Bahādur Sāh.

3 This monarch, Rājēndra Vikram Sāh, who was deposed in 1847, is still alive.

CHAPTER X.

Special history of the Gōrkhālī Dynasty.

OBEISANCE to Guru Ganēsa and to Kul-dēvatā.

Formerly Sūryabansī and Chandrabansī Rājās (*i.e.*, kings of the solar and lunar dynasties) ruled over the people, until their kingdoms were taken from them by the Yavanas (Musalmāns), and they were deposed.

Srī Vikramāditya and Sālivāhana were two powerful kings of the solar dynasty, and they sought out the rājās of the two dynasties and allotted to them kingdoms, according to their abilities, wisdom and power, and placed them on the thrones, giving them tīkā (*i.e.*, the mark on the forehead). They installed in this way eight hundred rājās.

Among these was one Rishi-rāj Rānā-jī, of the lunar dynasty, who was made the rājā of Chitaur-garh[1], and received the title of Bhattārak. Sālivāhana died shortly after the installation of Rishi-rāj Bhattārak, and his territories were overrun by Maunās and Yavanas, who established their rule and enforced their orders. Their rule, however, did not extend to Chitaur-garh, the Rājās of which preserved their independence for thirteen genera-

[1] In Rājputāna, in the Mewār district, near Tonk.

tions. The names of the independent rājās of Chitaurgarh were :—

1.	Rishi-rāj Bhattārak.	8.	Nidhi Bhattārak.
2.	Siva „	9.	Bhāskara „
3.	Srīmad „	10.	Nīlā „
4.	Srī-Tilā „	11.	Abhaya „
5.	Syāmā „	12.	Nāgjāl „
6.	Gōvarddha „	13.	Dēva-sarmā „
7.	Hari „		

Dēva-sarmā Bhattārak had a son named Ayutabam Rānā-jī, who had not yet ascended the throne when the Yavanas subjugated Dēva-sarmā's country, and quitted it after they had established their authority over him. Ayutabam, disgusted at the loss of his independence, gave up the name of Bhattārak, and retained only his original caste-surname of Rānā-jī.

The rājās who retained the title of Rānā-jī were :—

14.	Ayutabam Rānā-jī.	16.	Kanakbam Rānā-jī.
15.	Barābubam „	17.	Yasōbam „

The son of the last, named Audumbar Rānā-jī, pleased the Emperor by his address and skill in sword exercise, and had the title of Rāva (Rāo) conferred on him. The rājās who held the tītle of Rāva, in addition to their caste-surname of Rānā-jī, were :—

18.	Audumbar Rānā-jī Rāva.	26.	Hari Rānā-jī Rāva.
19.	Bhattārak „ „	27.	Brahmā „ „
20.	Bīr Vikramājit „ „	28.	Bakhān „ „
21.	Jilla „ „	29.	Manōratha „ „
22.	Ajilla „ „	30.	Jaya „ „
23.	Atal „ „	31.	Jagatra „ „
24.	Tuthā „ „	32.	Bhōj „ „
25.	Bimiki „ „	33.	Bhūpati „ „

This Rājā had three sons:—

Udayabam Rānā-jī Rāva.
Fattē Sinha " "
34. Manmath " "

Fattē Sinha had a daughter named Sadal, who was unrivalled in beauty. The Emperor Akbar (*sic*) having heard of this, called the Rānā-jī, and asked him to give her to him, saying that, as she was the most beautiful lady in the whole kingdom, she ought to be given to him, because everything excellent in the country was the property of the Emperor. The Rānā-jī told him that he would consult his relatives, and returned to Chitaur. He then made this known to his brothers, sons and nephews, and spoke thus: "Every one is great in his own caste. Intermarriage is only honourable in one's own caste. If an enemy attack the Emperor—we are Rājpūts, and we are ready to sacrifice our lives in his defence. If he want wealth--whatever belongs to us, belongs to the Emperor. But we will not put a stain on our caste by giving our daughter to him."

An answer to this effect was sent to the Emperor, who, being enraged, attacked Chitaur, and a bloody battle was fought. Bhūpati Rāva, Fattē Sinha, and a great many Rājpūts were killed, and thirteen hundred Rānīs immolated themselves as satīs. The daughter of Fattē Sinha killed herself by leaping into a pan of boiling oil.

The survivors, under Udayabam Rānā-jī Rāva, founded Udaypur and settled there; and Manmath Rānā-jī Rāva went to Ujjain. He had two sons, Brahmanīka Rānā-jī Rāva and (35) Bhūpāl Rānā-jī Rāva. These two brothers, being on bad terms with each other, separated, the elder remaining there, and the younger going to the northern hills.

The latter arrived at Riḍi. When setting out from Ujjain, he took with him his Ishta-dēvatā (patron deity), who told him to halt and not to go beyond the place where he put him (the dēvatā) upon the ground. In Sākā 1417 (A.D. 1495) he set out from Riḍi and reached Sarghā, where, being much fatigued, he put the dēvatā on the ground, and the dēvatā remained there. Bhūpāl Rānā-jī stayed there for a short time, but, finding that, without some settled mode of life, it was difficult for him to live there, he went to Khilum, a place in Bhirkōt, and brought its waste land into cultivation. In that place two sons were born to him, Khānchā and Michā. Their bratabandha (taking the brahmanical thread) was performed there, and daughters of Raghubansī Rājpūts were brought from the plains for them to marry.

The elder with his rānī went to Ḍhōr, conquered Mangrāt, and reigned over Garhōn, Sathun, Bhirkōt and Ḍhōr.

The younger, Michā Khān, went to Nuwākōt[1] with his rānī, and ruled over it.

The rājās who ruled over Nuwākōt were :—

36. Michā Khān	39. Michā Khān.
37. Jayan „	40. Bichitra „
38. Sūrya „	41. Jagdēva „

Kulmandan, the son of Jagdēva Khān, obtained the sovereignty over Kāskī. He pleased the Emperor in something, and received from him the title of Sāh. He had seven sons. The eldest succeeded him in the government of Kāskī. The second, Kālu Sāh, was asked

[1] Not the Noākōt near Kaṭhmāṇḍū, but another far to the west.

for from his father Kulmandan Sāh by the people of Durā Ḍānḍā in Lamjung, and was made their king.

The Sēkhānt tribe of the people of Lamjung one day took him to the forest to hunt, and stationed him on a high detached rock. They then dispersed themselves in the wood, and under pretence of shooting at deer, they killed him with poisoned arrows.

For sometime after this Lamjung remained without a rājā; but at last the people, unable to manage without one, again went to ask Kulmandan Sāh for another son to become their rājā. He, however, replied that he had no cheap son to give to them, to be shot like a deer, by the wicked Lamjungyās. Upon this they swore with joined hands that the deed was not committed by them, but by the people of the Sēkhānt tribe, who ate cows' flesh, and were not to be trusted. They said they had been deceived by the Sēkhānts, and repeated their petition, declaring that they would never be able to manage their affairs without a rājā; and they swore to be faithful.

Kulmandaṇ Sāh told them that he had still six sons; and that, setting aside the eldest, he would make the others sleep on one mattress, and then they might, without his selection, take the one whom Māhēswarī gave to them. The Rājā then made them swear, though he knew they did not fear sin, that, if they again played the traitors, they would incur the sin of murdering a crore (ten millions) of Brāhmans. According to their instructions, they went with a light into the room where the five sons were sleeping. They saw that the heads of the four elder were just in the places where they had first laid them, but the head of the youngest had moved upwards a long way. They thought therefore that he whose head had moved upwards in his sleep, must be a very fortunate man, and they selected him, and made him their Rājā. His name was Yasōbam Sāh.

42. Kulmandan Sāh, rājā of Kāskī.

43. Yasōbam Sāh, rājā of Lamjung.

Yasōbam Sāh had two sons. The elder, Narhari Sāh, ruled over Lamjung. The younger, Drabya Sāh, went to Gōrkhā, and gained over the subjects of that town, the rājā of which was of a Khadkā tribe of the Khas race.

On Wednesday the 8th of Bhādon Badi, Sākā 1481 (A.D. 1559), Rōhinī Nakshatra (*i.e.*, the moon being in the Rōhinī mansion), being an auspicious day, Drabya Sāh, aided by Bhagīrath Panth, Ganēsa Pāṇḍe, Gangārām Rānā, Busāl Arjyāl, Khanāl Bōhra, and Murlī Khawās of Gōrkhā, concealed himself in a hut. When Ganēsa Pāṇḍē had collected all the people of Gōrkhā who wore the brahmanical thread, such as the Thāpās, Busāls, Rānās, and Māski Rānās of the Magar tribe, they went by the Dāhyā Gauḍā route and attacked the Durbār. Drabya Sāh killed the Khadkā Rājā with his own hand, with a sword, during the battle that ensued. At the same auspicious moment Drabya Sāh took his seat on the gaddī, amidst the clash of music.

44.	SrīDrabya Sāh,	Sākā 1481 (A.D. 1559),	reigned	11 years.
45.	„ Purandar Sāh,	„ 1492	„	35 years.
46.	„ Chhatra Sāh	„ 1527	„	7 months.
47.	„ Rāma Sāh	„ 1528	„	27 years.

Chhatra Sāh having no issue, his brother Rāma Sāh succeeded him. Chhatra Sāh reigned only seven months.

Rāma Sāh introduced the measures mānu, pāthī, and muri, and the use of scales and weights. He also made laws for debtors and creditors, fixing the rate of interest at ten per cent. for money, and one-fourth of the quantity of grain. If the debtor was unable to pay within ten years, the creditor after that time might take twice the principal in money, and three times the amount in grain, but no more. He made many other laws.

48.	Srī Dambar Sāh,	Sākā 1555 (A.D. 1633),	reigned	9 years.
49.	„ Krishna Sāh	„ 1564	„	11 „
50.	„ Rudra Sāh	„ 1575	„	16 „
51.	„ Prithwī-pati Sāh	„ 1591	„	47 „
	His son Bīrbhadra Sāh.			
52.	His grandson Narbhūpāl Sāh,	Sākā 1638	„	26 „ and 8 months.

Of the senior rānī of Prithwī-pati Sāh was born Bīrbhadra Sāh, who was the eldest son. He married the daughter of the Rājā of Tanhun. She was pregnant, but no one knew of her state when she went away to her father's house, being on bad terms with her mother-in-law. Bīrbhadra Sāh alone knew that she was pregnant. He was unwell, and calling his youngest brother, Chandrarūp Sāh, said to him: "Great intimacy has existed between us from our boyhood, and I wish to open my bosom to you alone. My disease seems a serious one, and I have no hope of recovery. My rānī is pregnant and has gone to her father's house. If anything happens to me by God's pleasure, you will make inquiries as to the result of her pregnancy, and give her your support." His brother replied that he would carry out his desires to the utmost of his power, life, and wealth, and assuring him that nothing would go amiss in his household, comforted him, and told him to think no more of it.

After two or three days Bīrbhadra Sāh died. Chandrarūp Sāh privately ascertained that the deceased's rānī had given birth to Narbhūpāl Sāh in Tanhun; but he kept it a secret.

In Gōrkhā, Mahārāj Prithwī-pati, being very old, began to consider as to the selection of a successor. He reflected that his eldest son had been taken away by God, and had left no heir. He could not give the gaddī to his second son, Dal Sāh, as he was excluded by having only one eye. If he gave it to the third, Udyōt Sāh, it would appear unjust to put a younger son on the gaddī to the prejudice of an elder claimant. His council was divided in its choice. Some were in favour of the second, and others of the third son, and they could not determine to whom to give the gaddī. Chandrarūp Sāh now presented himself to the Rājā at a private audience, and said that all the sons of a rājā could not succeed their father; the rules enjoined by the Vēdas, Purānas and Shāstras, and the practice heretofore observed, should still be followed. "The counsellors," said he, "are knaves. An heir of the Sāhib-jī is in existence."

Prithwī-pati hereupon asked him to explain himself, and he then related all the particulars as to the rānī of Bīrbhadra Sāh having been pregnant, and having given birth to Narbhūpāl Sāh. The Rājā was glad to hear this, but was still full of doubt. Chandrarūp Sāh sent a messenger to fetch Narbhūpāl Sāh, but the Rājā of Tanhun, thinking that, by means of this child, the sovereignty of Gōrkhā might fall into his own hands, refused to send him. Chandrarūp Sāh then bribed the nurse and attendants of Narbhūpal Sāh, and by their help he succeeded in having him brought to his own house in Gōrkhā, where he kept him carefully for three years. In the beginning of the fourth year, he one day sent him on the back of a slave into the presence of the Rājā, who inquired who the boy was, but on being told by the slave that it was the Sāhib-jī (heir apparent), he said nothing. One day Narbhūpāl was swimming naked, and his whole body being exposed to the Rājā's view, he exclaimed that he was an incarnation of Bīrbhadra Sāh, and carrying him off to the Durbār, he seated himself on the gaddī with his grandson in his lap.

He then called Chandrarūp Sāh, and praised him for his endeavours to restore his lost descendant. Giving him a slap on the back, he exclaimed: "Syābās! You have done your duty to the utmost. My descendants will henceforth regard yours as their own brothers. Your jāgīrs and birtās will descend to your posterity rent-free."

After the death of Prithwī-pati, Narbhūpāl Sāh became rājā. To him was born Prithwī-nārāyana Sāh. Narbhūpāl was not very fond of governing, but devoted his time to the worship of God. When he died, Prithwī-nārāyana Sāh took his seat on the gaddī, at the age of twelve, in Sākā 1664 (A.D. 1742).

53. Srī Prithwī-nārāyana Sāh, Sākā 1664, reigned 32 years.
54. „ Pratāp Sinha Sāh „ 1696, „ 2 years and 9 months.
55. „ Ran Bahādur Sāh „ 1699, „ 22 years.

Prithwī-nārāyana Sāh, when twelve years old, determined to take Nuwākōt. He failed in his first attempt, but succeeded in his second attack, and then took all the country around Nepāl.

At this time Nawāb Kāsim Alī Khān of Murshidābād, having been defeated by the British, had taken refuge in Nepāl for some time. In return for the hospitality shown him, he sent 60,000 troops to help the Nepalese, by the route of Makwānpur, but they were cut to pieces by only 400 scouts of Prithwī-nārāyana Sāh. After this 5,000 Nāgās were coming to the assistance of the Nepalese, but they shared the same fate on reaching Panāvatī. Again the Rājā defeated the British troops (under Captain Kinloch), who were coming to Sindhulī Garhī. In this manner he took all the country around Nepāl. To the east, his rule extended as far as Bijayapur Sukhim.

At this time Prithwī-nārāyana Sāh died, and Pratāp Sinha Sāh succeeded him. He reigned two years and nine months. In his reign conquest was carried as far as Sumbhēswara.

Pratāp Sinha Sāh was succeeded by Ran Bahādur Sāh, whose mother Rājēndra-Lakshmī-dēvī was regent for nine years, during which time the territories of Tanhun, Lamjung, and Kāskī, were brought under the Gōrkhā rāj.

When the Rānī died, the affairs of state were taken in hand by Bahādur Sāh, the uncle of the Rājā. During his regency, the country of the Chaubīsī and Bāīsī rājās in the west, and all the region as far as Garhwāl, were conquered and brought under the Gōrkhā rāj. In Garhwāl a rājā was installed by the Gōrkhālīs. At this time a Chinese army invaded the country, but it was defeated, and a treaty was concluded between the two states.

Ran Bahādur having now come of age, Bahādur Sāh made over the reins of government to him, and went on a pilgrimage, in which he died.

At this time Gīrbān-juddha Vikram Sāh was born, and the Rājā's councillors told him that his Highness's twenty-fourth year would be very unlucky, and that he would lose either his throne or his life in it. He therefore abdicated in his son's favour, in Sākā 1721 (A. D. 1799).

56. Srī Gīrbān-juddha Vikram Sāh reigned 17 years.

When giving up the gaddī to his son, Ran Bahādur Sāh ordered that no change should be made in the offices of state for the next twelve years, and he appointed Dāmōdar Pāṇḍē, Kīrtimān Sinha Bashnyāt, Tribhuvan, and Narsinha, to be Kājīs. After this he lived the life of one removed from worldly cares.

The Kājīs, however, did not adhere strictly to the instructions of the late Rājā, who, on receiving a defiant reply to some of his angry remarks, thought it best to remove himself to Kāsī (Benāres), for fear of an outbreak on the part of the traitor ministers.

In Benāres Bhīmasēna Thāpā became his confidant, through his talents. He advised him to make some arrangement with the British, and to return to Nepāl, where he would then be able to punish the faithless and ungrateful, as the unlucky days were past.

The Swāmī Mahārāj then returned to Nepāl, after taking a friendly leave of the British. He killed some of the traitors and dismissed others. After putting Bhīmasēna at the head of the government, with the title of Chief Kājī, he began to seek for seditious persons; and Shēr Bahādur, a son of Pratāp Sinha by a Newārī woman, fearing for his own life, one night killed the Rājā.

Gīrbān-juddha came to the gaddī in Sākā 1721 (A. D. 1799). On the death of Ran Bahādur Sāh, his junior rānī, Lalit-Tripur-Sundarī-dēvī became regent, and Bhīmasēna managed the affairs of state under her orders.

The Gōrkhā rūj now extended as far as Kāngrā. As a reward for his services, Gīrbān-juddha conferred the title of General, as well as that of Kājī, on Bhīmasēna.

57. By the will of God Gīrbān-juddha died young, and his son Srī Rājēndra Vikram Sāh, when only two years old, was placed on the gaddī, in Sākā 1738 (A.D. 1816). His step-grandmother Lalit-Tripur-Sundarī-dēvī became regent, and Bhīmasēna continued to manage the affairs of state.

When the Rājā reached his eleventh year, Bhīmāsēna represented to the Regent Rānī that, as the members of the Royal House were decreasing, it would be better to have his Highness married; and with her consent he caused two daughters of legitimate Rājpūt families of Gōrakhpur to be brought and married to the Rājā.

In Sākā 1751 (A.D. 1829), on Sunday the 7th of Āswin Sudi, the Sāhib-jyū (heir apparent) Srī Surēndra Vikram Sāh was born[1].

[1] Surēndra Vikram Sāh is the present king of Nepāl, his father, who is still alive, having been deposed in A.D. 1847. The heir apparent, Trilōk (Trailōkya) Bīr Vikram Sāh, was born on 1st December, 1847; and his son was born on 8th August, 1875.

End of the History of Nepāl, as contained in the original manuscript.

Maclure & Macdonald Lith^rs London

SRĪ SURĒNDRA VIKRAM SĀH,
THE REIGNING KING OF NEPĀL

(Plate XV) (p. 284.)

CHAPTER XI.

Genealogy of Swasti Srīmad Ati-prachand Bhujdandētyādi Srī Srī Srī Mahārāj Jang Bahādur Rānā, G.C.B. and G.C.S.I., Thong-lin-pim-mā-kō-kāng-vāng-syān, Prime Minister and Commander-in-Chief of Nepāl[1].

Tattā Rānā was rājā of Chitaur-garh. His nephew Fakht Sinha Rānā had a son named Rāma Sinha Rānā, who, when Chitaur was taken, came to the hills with four of his followers, and entered, and remained for some time in, the service of a hill rājā. The hill rājā treated him with much kindness, and regarded him in the light of a brother. He built a house for him to live in, near his durbār, made him his tutor, and began to learn fencing from him.

The hill rājā, having associated with Rāma Sinha Rānā for ten or twelve months, with a view to keep him in the country, told him that, if he came to the hills, he must marry. He could not refuse the Rājā's request, and the rājā asked for the daughter of the rājā of Bīnātī, a Bagālē Kshētrī, and married her to Rāma Sinha Rānā, who in ten or twelve years had six sons.

One of these six sons showed much bravery in a battle which was fought between the hill rājā and the rājā of Satān Kōt, for which he had the title of Kunwār Khadkā conferred on him, by which title his descendants are known to the present day.

[1] This genealogy is not contained in the History of Nepāl, but derived from another source.

At this time the younger brother of Rāma Sinha Rānā set out from his home in search of him, and, having found him, they passed three or four days in the enjoyment of each other's company; after which the younger brother said that it was ten or twelve years since Rāma Sinha had left his home; that the members of his family, whom he had left at home, were weeping and longing to see him, and that he ought to pay them a visit once at any rate, and then return, if he chose to do so.

Rāma Sinha complied with this request, and, having taken leave of the rājā, set out for Chitaur-garh, after making arrangements for his rānī and sons. Rāma Sinha died shortly after reaching his home.

The hill rājā made Rāut Kunwār, a son of Rāma Sinha, a nobleman (sardār) and commandant of troops, in which post he rendered the services required of him.

A son named Ahirāma Kunwār was born to Rāut Kunwār. He was invited by the rājā of Kaskēlī, who made him a nobleman, and gave him a village named Dhuāgē Sāghū as a birtā or jāgīr. He had a daughter of great beauty, who was sought by the rājā, who wished to marry her only by kalas-pūjā[1]. Ahiramā replied, that he would give his daughter only in lawful marriage, and in no other way. The rājā then wanted to take her by force, and brought his troops to the village; but Ahirāma was assisted by the people of the village, of the Parājuli Thāpā caste, and an affray took place, in which persons on both sides were wounded. The same day Ahirāma took his family, amongst whom were his two sons, Rāma Krishna Kunwār, and Jaya Krishna Kunwār, aged twelve and ten years, and went

[1] This ceremony does not admit to the full standing of a lawfully married wife.

to Gōrkhā, to take service under Srī (5)[1] Mahārāj Prithwī-nārāyana, who gave him the village of Kunwār khōlā to live in, and made him a nobleman. He died in the rājā's service at the age of 56.

His son Rāma Krishna Kunwār became a nobleman at the age of fourteen, and having given proof of his bravery in one or two battles, which he fought and gained against hill rājās, he raised confidence in the minds of every one.

At that time kājī was the title corresponding to mukhtār at the present day; and sardār was equivalent to commander-in-chief of the army.

Rāma Krishna Kunwār was made a sardār, and selected to subjugate Nepāl. He built a fortress on the hill above Bālājī, and carried on the war. After some time it was arranged to attack the country simultaneously from different sides with troops under different sardārs, and Rāma Krishna Kunwār entered the durbār by the Sinha-dhōkā gate and took it.

After taking Pātan and Bhātgāon, Mahārāj Prithwī-nārāyana sent him towards the east, along with three or four other sardārs, and after some fighting he conquered the country as far as Mēchi. After his return he was sent to Pyuthānā, and established a magazine there. He died there at the age of 59.

His son Ranjit Kunwār, when 21 years old, obtained the post of Sūbah of the whole of Jumla. The country had been only recently conquered, and authority had not been established. The Jumliyās fled to Hōmlā, whence they brought troops to retake the country, but were repulsed by Ranjīt Kunwār, and order was well established by him. To show his appreciation of his services,

[1] Srī (5) means that the word is to be repeated five times.

the Mahārāj made him one of the four principal kājīs. Ranjīt was then ordered to conquer Kāngrā, and, having captured Jhapabēsar in Kumāon, he attacked and took it by storm, after a severe encounter with Sansār Sinha.

During the attack, as Ranjīt was scaling the wall by a bamboo ladder, he received a bullet in the right breast and fell down. After some time he died from the effects of this wound, at the age of 58.

His son Bāl-narsinha Kunwār was then 22 years old, and was made the principal among the four kājīs. He was one day present, engaged in some work, when Mahārāj Ran Bahādur Sāh was struck with a sword by his step-brother Shēr Bahādur. The Mahārāj called for help, and Bāl-narsinha, turning round, saw what had happened and killed Shēr Bahādur.

Kājī Bāl-narsinha died a natural death at the age of 59.

His eldest son is Srī (3) Mahārāj Jang Bahādur Rānā, G. C. B., G. C. S. I., and Thong-lin-pim-mā-kō-kāng-vāng-syān. The meaning of this Chinese title (conferred by the Emperor of China in 1871), as given by a person who knows a little Chinese, is: "Leader of the army, the most brave in every enterprise, perfect in every thing, master of the army, Mahārāj."

Maclure & Macdonald, Lith. London

XVI.) MAJOR GENERAL JAGAT JUNG BAHĀDUR, ELDEST SON OF SIR JUNG BAHĀDUR, AND A NEPALESE GENTLEMAN (p. 288)

CHAPTER XII.

A brief Genealogy of Srī(5)man Mahārājādhirāj Surēndra Vikram Sāh Bahādur Shamshēr-jang Dēva, king of Nepāl[1].

Srī (5) Mahārājādhirāj Surēndra Vikram Sāh Bahādur Shamshēr-jang is of the Rājpūt caste, and 46 years of age.

In his reign a war has been waged against Bhōt (Tibet), and a victory gained, in consequence of which the duty levied by the Tibetan government on Nepalese merchants has been remitted, and Tibet pays an annual tribute of 10,000 rupees to Nepāl.

Through the friendship of the British government, a territory of 200 miles in length, which had formerly been lost, has been restored to Nepāl.

In Sambat 1907 (A.D. 1850) the true Bansāvalī, or history of the reigning dynasty, was destroyed by fire, with other papers. The following narrative has, therefore, been compiled from other sources.

Srī (5) Mahārāj Drabya Sāh sat on the gaddī of the Gōrkhā rāj in S. 1616 (A.D. 1559). He enacted many laws and regulations, and made settlements which are still extant, and are well known as the "Band-o-bast of

[1] This narrative, too, is not contained in the History of Nepāl, but has been derived from another source.

Drabya Sāh." He reigned 11 years, and died in S. 1627 (A.D. 1570).

His son Srī (5) Mahārāj Purandar Sāh reigned 35 years, and died in S. 1662 (A.D. 1605).

His son Srī (5) Mahārāj Chhatra Sāh reigned only seven months. He had no son, and therefore

His brother Srī (5) Mahārāj Rāma Sāh succeeded him. He reigned 27 years, and died in S. 1690 (A.D. 1633).

His son Srī (5) Dambar Sāh reigned 9 years, and died in S. 1699 (A.D. 1642).

His son Srī (5) Mahārāj Krishna Sāh reigned 16 years, and died in S. 1715 (A.D. 1658).

His son Srī (5) Mahārāj Rudra Sāh reigned 11 years, and died in S. 1726 (A.D. 1669).

His son Srī (5) Mahārāj Prithwī-pati reigned 47 years, and died in S. 1773 (A.D. 1716).

His son Srī Bīrbhadra Sāh died in the lifetime of his father, and

His son Srī (5) Narbhūpāl Sāh succeeded to the throne, and reigned 26 years and 8 months. He died in S. 1799 (A.D. 1742).

His son Srī (5) Mahārāj Prithwī-nārāyana Sāh succeeded him. Being very brave and enterprising, he won by his wisdom and sword the throne of Nepāl on Sunday the 14th of Bhādon Sudi, S. 1825 (A.D. 1768). He conquered Makwānpur and the territories of the east, as far as Mēchi. He reigned 32 years, and died in S. 1831 (A.D. 1774).

His son Srī (5) Mahārāj Sinha Pratāp Sāh reigned only 2 years and 9 months, and died in S. 1834 (A.D. 1777).

His son Srī (5) Mahārāj Ran Bahādur Sāh was a wise and brave monarch, and very fond of war. He conquered the Bāīsī and Chaubīsī rājās in the west, and his victorious arms reached as far as Kāngrā in the east. After reigning 22 years, he abdicated in favour of his son, in S. 1856 (A.D. 1799), and led the life of a Swāmī or monk.

Srī (5) Mahārāj Gīrbān-yuddha Vikram Sāh reigned 17 years, and died in S. 1873 (A.D. 1816).

His son Srī (5) Mahārāj Rājēndra Vikram Sāh reigned 30 years and 5 months. In S. 1904 (A.D. 1847) he resigned the throne to

His son Srī (5) Mahārāj Surēndra Vikram Sāh Bahādur Shamshēr-jang, who has sat on the gaddī for 28 years.

All the rājās who reigned in Gōrkhā and Nepāl are fifteen generations, and so long the state has been independent.

The reigning king is the father of a son, the heir-apparent, who is also the father of a son.

APPENDIX.

APPENDIX.

I. MUSICAL INSTRUMENTS.

Dhyāmaya. A sort of drum played on one side with a cane, twisted into a coil at one end; on the other side with the bare hand. It is peculiar to the Jyāpu caste.

Bhūsyā. A pair of cymbals, played in company with the above.

Tāīnāī. A small plate of bellmetal, struck with a stick. A companion of the previous two.

Kōnchā-khin. A hollow earthen or wooden cylinder, one end of which is covered with leather, the other remaining open. The left hand is thrust through the uncovered end, while the other end is played on with the right hand. It is peculiar to the Jyāpu caste.

Khwālīmīlī. A pair of small cymbals, played along with the previous instrument.

Baya. A kind of flute, made of bamboo.

Nāya-khin. It is like the Dhyāmaya, and played in the same way, but a straight stick is used instead of the twisted cane. It is called Kasāī bājā, or Kasāī's music.

Chhūsyā. A pair of cymbals, played with the previous instrument. This and the Nāya-khin are used in making proclamations.

Kahāl. A long, straight, copper trumpet. This is used, together with the Nāya-khin and Chhūsyā, when dead bodies are taken to be burnt, and also in worship.

Mādal. A sort of tāmtām or drum, played with both hands. It is peculiar to the Magar caste.

Manjurī. A pair of small cymbals, played with the Mādal.

Kartāl. A pair of castanets.

Damrū. A small wooden or clay instrument, in the shape of an hourglass, covered at both ends with leather, having a ball attached to its middle by a string, so that, when the Damrū is turned quickly with the hand, the ball strikes the ends alternately, and produces a sound like a small drum.

Dhōlak. Like the Mādal, played with both hands.

Mōhālī. A kind of pipe or flageolet, peculiar to the Khusliyā caste.

Tamrā. A small kettledrum.

Khanjan. A tambourine.

Dangō-khin. A sort of Dhōlak, played in the same way.

Bāmtāl. A small tambourine, used to beat time.

Dhōṇdhōṇ. A sort of drum, peculiar to the Bhōtiyas.

Karnāl. A trumpet, made of copper or brass.

Narsinghā. Another kind of trumpet, used in marriage processions.

Hōng. Another brass trumpet.

Panchtāl-khin. A sort of Mridang. Both ends are covered with leather, and a small kettledrum is fixed in the middle. The kettledrum and the ends of the cylinder are played on alternately with both hands.

Pōnga. A copper trumpet, shaped like a Kahāl.

Dhāk. A sort of Dhōlak, but played on with a stick at one end, and the hand at the other.

Ngēkū. A buffalo-horn.

Mridang or Pakhāuj. A large drum, like a Dhōlak, played on with both hands.

Khin. A sort of Mridang.

Babhū. A pair of small cymbals, of thin metal.

Bānsrī. A flute.

Bīnā or Bīn. A sort of double cithern or guitar, having a gourd at each end. It is played with both hands.

Sitār. It is like the Bīn, but with only one gourd, played with the hand.

Sārangī. A sort of fiddle.

II. AGRICULTURAL IMPLEMENTS.

English.	Parbatiyā.	Newārī.
Digging hoe	Kōdālī	Kū
Large weeding hoe	Kūtō	Kūkichā
Small weeding hoe	Tīkhō Kūtō	Tōkū
Spud	Khurpī	Khurpī
Wooden pulveriser	Dallāthōk	Khattāmūgal
Hatchet	Bancharō	Pā
Sickle	Hasiā	Īṇ
Basket	Kharpan	Khumū
Bānghī pole	Nōl	Nō

III. NEPALESE COINAGE.

Gold.		Silver.		Copper.	
Nepalese Names.	Value in Anglo-Indian Coin.	Nepalese Names.	Value in Anglo-Indian Coin.	Nepalese Names.	Value in Anglo-Indian Coin.
	R. A. P.		R. A. P.		R. A. P.
Ashrafī	20 0 0	Rūpī	0 13 4		
Pātlē	8 5 0	Mōhar	0 6 8		
Sūkā	4 2 8	Sūkā	0 3 4		
Sūkī	2 1 4	Sūkī	0 1 8		
Ānā	1 0 8	Ānā	0 0 10	Paisā	0 0 2
Dām	0 4 2	Dām	0 0 5	Dām	0 0 ½

IV. WEIGHTS AND MEASURES.

Weights used in weighing gold.

10 rattīs or lāls = 1 māsā.
10 māsās = 1 tōlā.

Weights used in weighing silver.

8 rattīs or lāls = 1 māsā.
12 māsās = 1 tōlā.

Weights used in weighing metal utensils.

$4\frac{1}{2}$ tōlās = 1 kanwā.
4 kanwās = 1 tuknī or pāo.
4 tuknīs = 1 sēr.
3 sērs = 1 dhārnī = 5 pounds avoirdupois.

Dry Measure.

2 manās = 1 kurwā.
4 kurwās = 1 pāthī = 8 pounds avoirdupois.
20 pāthīs = 1 murī.

Liquid Measure.

4 dīyās = 1 chauthāī.
2 chauthāīs = 1 ādh tuknī.
2 ādh tuknīs = 1 tuknī.
4 tuknīs = 1 kurwā = 1 sēr.
4 kurwās = 1 pāthī.

V. MEASUREMENT OF TIME.

60 bipalās = 1 palā.
60 palās = 1 gharī = 24 minutes.
60 gharīs = 1 day of 24 hours.

The day begins when the tiles on the roof of a house can be counted, or when the hair on the back of a man's hand can be discerned against the sky.

A copper vessel with a small hole in the bottom is so constructed that, when put on the surface of water in a tub, it fills sixty times a day; and each time it fills and sinks, the gharī is struck.

The gharī, which is a flat metal plate or gong, is struck regularly in progressive numbers from morning to noon; one, two, three, &c. If the day is twenty-four gharīs in length, the striking of the gharī will give the number of gharīs from morning till noon; after that, the first gharī struck will indicate the number of gharīs which remain of the day till sunset. The same holds good for the night. That is to say from sunset to midnight the gharīs are struck, one, two, three, &c., and from midnight the striking indicates the number of gharīs still to elapse before dawn.

VI. VOCABULARY.

English.	*Parbatiyā.*	*Newārī.*
Man	Mānis	Manukh
Woman	Swāsnī	Mīsā
Child	Bālak	Machā
Boy	Kētā	Kāya machā
Girl	Kētī	Mhyāya machā
Father	Bābā	Bubā
Mother	Āmā	Māṇ
Brother, elder	Dājyū	Dājū
Brother, younger	Bhāī	Kijā
Sister, elder	Dīdī	Tatā
Sister, younger	Bahinī	Kēhēṇ
Uncle :—		
Father's brother, elder	Jēthā bābū	Abājū
Father's brother, younger	Kānchhā bābū	Kakājū
Mother's brother	Māmā	Pājū
Father's sister's husband	Phūpājū	Jīlachapājū
Aunt :—		
Father's sister	Phūpū	Nini
Mother's sister, elder	Jēthī āmā	Dhōm mā
Mother's sister, younger	Sānī āmā	Chamājū
Father's brother's wife, elder	Jēthī āmā	Dhōmā mā
Father's brother's wife, younger	Kānchhā āmā	Māmajū
Grandfather	Bājyā	Ajājū
Head	Tāukō	Chhyōṇ
Body	Āng	Mha
Forehead	Lilā	Kapā
Eye	Ānkhā	Mīkhā
Nose	Nāk	Nhāsa
Cheek	Gālā	Nētāl
Lip	Oṭh	Mhutusī
Teeth	Dāṇt	Wā
Tongue	Jibhrō	Mē

English.		*Parbatiyā.*	*Newārī.*
Chin		Chimdō	Mana
Neck		Ghichrō	Galapat
Chest		Chhātī	Nūgala
Rib		Karang	Bapī
Belly		Pēt	Pwātha
Back		Pītheoṇ	Jandhū
Shoulder		Kum	Bōha
Arm		Pākhurā	Lappā
Elbow		Kōhnū	Chulyā
Hand		Hāth	Lāhāta
Finger		Angulā	Pachiṇ
Nail		Nang	Lusī
Thigh		Tigrā	Khampā
Leg		Pēndulā	Twānāl
Knee		Ghundā	Pulī
Ankle		Guli gāṇṭhā	Gauchā
Foot		Godā	Pālī
Toes		Godā kō angulā	Tuti pachiṇ
Hair		Rauṇ	Saṇ
Elephant		Hāthī	Kīsī
Buffalo	bull	Rāngā	Thumē
	cow	Bhaisī	Mē
Cow		Gāī	Sā
Bull		Sāṇḍhē	Dōha
Calf	male	Bāchhā	Dōhcha
	female	Bāchhī	Sacha
Horse, pony		Ghōḍā	Sala
Sheep	ram	Bhēḍā	Bhyā
	ewe	Bhēḍī	Phai
Goat	he	Bākhrā	Chōlaya
	she	Bākhrī	Chōlaychā
Pig		Sūngar	Phā
Dog		Kūkur	Khīcha
Cat	male	Birālō	Bhau
	female	Birālī	Bhauchā
Rat		Musā	Chhuṇ
Goose		Rāj hāns	Ba haiṇ
Duck		Hāns	Haiṇ
Hen		Kukhurā	Mākhā

English.	*Parbatiyā.*	*Newārī.*
Cock	Kukhurō	Gōngal
Chicken	Challā	Khāchā
Crow	Kāg	Kō
Partridge	Tītrā	Tita
Pheasant	Dāphiā, Muhnāl, Kālij	Gūṇkhā
Hare	Chaugaḍa	Kharahā
Quail	Batai	Batai
Wild duck	Pānī hāṇs	Khukucha
Snipe	Lamchōchiā	Khōyaṇ mōcha
House	Ghar	Chhēṇ
Wall	Gārō	Angōl
Room	Kōṭhā	Kōṭhā
Window	Jhyāl	Jhyā
Door	Dhōkā	Lukhā
Bed	Khāṭ	Khātā
Chair	Mēj	Khatchā
Table	Takhtā	Tasi
Temple	Dēval	Dēva
Roof	Chhānā	Pōla
Pillar	Khāmā, thām	Thāṇ
Bell	Ghant	Gaṇ
Umbrella	Chhatā	Kusā
Coat	Bakhū	Ankhalaṇ
Drawers	Sarwāl	Sarwā
Stockings	Mōjā	Mōjā
Shoes	Jutā	Lākāṇ
Gloves	Panjā	Panjā
Turban	Pagrī	Bētālī
Cap	Tōpī	Tuplī
Rice	Chāṇwal	Jākī
Wheat	Gahūṇ	Chhō
Barley	Jau	Tachhō
Buckwheat	Phāpar	Phāpar
Ginger	Aduā	Pālū
Turmeric	Bēsār	Halū
Garlic	Lasuṇ	Lābhā

English.	*Parbatiyā.*	*Newārī.*
Onion	Piāj	Piā
Chillies	Khursāni	Malibhatā
Potatoes	Ālū	Ālū
Maize	Makai	Kanī
Flour	Pīṭho	Chūṇ
Pepper	Marich	Malaya
Salt	Nūn	Chi
Milk	Dūdh	Durū
Flesh	Maṇsū	Lā
Oil	Tēl	Chikaṇ
Tobacco	Tamākhū	Bajhaṇ
Ghee	Ghiu	Gheo
Water	Pānī	La
Wood	Kāṭh	Siṇ
Stone	Dhōngā	Lōhaṇ
Lime	Chūn	Sakhwa
Brick	Īnt	Apā
Mortar	Bajralēp	Bajralēp
Straw	Parāl	Lū
Bamboo	Bāns	Paṇ
String	Dōrī	Khipa
Rope	Thulō dōrī	Tapū khipa
Saw	Karaunti	Kati
Hammer	Ghan	Namuga
Hatchet	Bancharō	Pā
Adze	Bansulā	Khulū
Chisel	Chhīnā	Haṇ
Knife	Karda	Kardachā
Scissors	Kainchī	Kainchī
River	Khōlā	Khusi
Hill	Dāndō	Taṇ
Lake	Tāl	Dahaṇ
Tree	Rukh	Simāṇ
Bush	Hāngā	Kaṇchā
Garden	Bagīcha	Kebā
Field	Khēt	Buṇ
Watercourse	Kulō	Dha
Tank	Kund	Pukhū
Road	Bātō	Laṇ

English.	*Parbatiyā.*	*Newārī.*
Bridge	Sāngū	Tā
Boat	Dungā	Dungā
Sword	Tarwār	Tarwā
Gun	Bandūk	Tupa
Shot	Chharra	
Gunpowder	Bārūt	Bārū
Cannon	Tōp	Tōṇ
Bayonet	Sangīn	Sangīn
Spear	Bhālā	Bachhā
Bow	Dhanu	Dhanukh
Arrow	Kānd	Balathū
Medicine	Ōkhdī	Wāsa
Disease	Rōg	Lōgī
Wound	Ghāu	Ghā
Ulcer	Khatira kō ghāu	Pōyagū ghā
Pimple	Bimirā	Bhusākai
Fever	Jarō	Jō
Diarrhœa	Chhērauti	Khimhula
Cough	Khōkī	Khasō
Cholera	Chhērauti	Thaṇ kwawaṇ lōya
Old	purāna	pulāṇ
Young	tannērī	lyāmha
Good	nīkō	bhiṇ
Bad	nanīkō	mabhiṇ
High	algō	tājāva
Low	hōchō	patijāva
Rich	dhanī	tadhaṇ
Poor	nirdhō, kangāl	majū-mha
Hot	tātō	kwāka
Cold	chīsō	khwāūṇ
Sour	amīlō	pāūṇ
Sweet	gulīō	chākū
Hard	sārhō	chhāk
Soft	narm	nāyū
Long	lāmbō	tahāka
Short	chhōtō	chikdhīka, chikhāk
Broad	gaj	byā

English.	*Parbatiyā.*	*Newārī.*
Pretty	rāmrō	bānlā
Ugly	narāmrō	bānmalā
Ripe	pākēkō	pākaējūgū
Unripe	kāchō	kachigū
Black	kālō	hākū
White	sētō	tūyū
Red	rātō	hyāyūṇ
Green	hariō	wāūṇ
Yellow	pahēlō	mhāsū
Blue	nīlō	wachū
Brown	kailō	sīyū
Come	āū	wā
Go	jāū	hūṇ
Bring	lyāū	hakī
Take away	lē jāū	yankī
Run	dagūra	bwāhūṇ
Walk	hīnda	uyāla
Sing	gāū	mē-hā
Strike	kūta	dā
Cut	kāta	pā
Eat	khāū	na
Drink	pīē	tōṇ
Wash	dhōū	sīū
Cook	pakāū	thū
Now	ailē	āva-naktini
Today	āj	thaūn
Tomorrow	bhōlī	kanhasa
Yesterday	hījō	mhīga
Month	mahīnā	lā
Year	barkh	daṇ
Date	mītī	tithī
Quickly	chādaī	yākana
Slowly	bistār	buluhūṇ

VII. NEWĀRĪ SONGS,

WRITTEN DOWN AND TRANSLATED BY MUNSHĪ SHEW SHUNKER SINGH.

I.

Yasodharā matē duhkha tāya
O Yasodhāra do not be cast down.
Bipatisa dhairya sahāya
In misfortune fortitude is the best friend (or helper).
Siya buya jyātha juya
To be born, to die, and to be old,
Rogayā harana yāya
to be sick, I shall get rid of,
Bhāla pāwa wanē gyāna lāya
when I shall be an ascetic. Take this precept.
Māra gana dakō khyāya
I shall drive out the sensual pleasure enticers,
Ahankāra chhamha syāya
Pride I shall kill,
Sansārayā duhkha nāsayāya
This world's miseries I will destroy.
Avasara sa jīvaya
In time I will come,
Kāya pani bhikshū yāya
Sons I will make bhikshūs,
Dharma kathā ana lhāya
Moral precepts there I will impart.
Pāpa yā lapu tīya
Sin's way I will stop.
Dharma yā lasa chhōya
Virtue's way I will show.
Mōksha purasa ānanda yāya
In the city of salvation I will be happy.

Nepāla yā barkha siya
Nepal sambat you must know,
Mīkhā balā pwāla dhāya
Eye (2), bow (5), hole (9), I say. (N. S. 952 = A. D. 1832.)
Lhāka mhayā dona kshamā yāya
The author's defects you must overlook.

II.

Sakhī prabhu juna gana jilu manī
O friend! My husband never thinks of me.
Sākya kula yā mani, tribhuvana yā dhani
Sākya dynasty's jewel, master of the three worlds,
Sansāra sa madu vati gyānī
In the world there is none equal to him in enlightenment.
Wasayā juyāva rānī duhkhī jī garbhinī
Being his rānī I unhappy am pregnant.
Jī pāpī yā gana prāna lēnī
My life, sinful as I am, will never last.
Wasayā rūpa khanī soso kiki mana wanī
His shape will charm the heavenly beauties,
Apsarā gana nāpa chonī
Who will be happy in his society.
Lhāka mha agyānī na sala kisi ranga muna
I the ignorant author having put together horse (7), elephant (8), and colour (5),
Barkha sa thugulī kha ka na
In this year this song made known (N. S. 587 = A. D. 1467.)

III.

Hē maitri bhāva mana tiva
O, friendship in your mind keep.
Mahābōdhī gyāna mārga khawa
Mahābōdhī knowledge's path is this,
Prānī dakō thawa bhāla pāwa
Every living creature regard as yourself.
Triratna yā sewā yāya swa wa jana
Triratna to serve seek, O man.

Karuna na kārya yāwa
With tenderness act.
Kārana karma yā thugū khawa
The cause of good luck is this.
Kāma krodha lobha tola tāwa
Sensual pleasure, anger, covetousness leave,
Harkha na punya yāwa
Cheerfully meritorious acts perform.
Bhawa bhaya harana jūyī wa
Worldly fears will be taken away.
Chhokha phasa kha phāya tōla tāwa
Backbiting, lying, causing emnity between two, leaving off,
Dāna yāyē rasa yāwa
Charity try to practise.
Dīna duhkha pāpa mada yi wa
Poverty, misery, sin will not approach.
Mōha drōha mabhīm maswa yāwa
Illusion, enmity, vice, avoiding,
Sugata bachana sa chara lappya swa wa jana
Follow the directions of Sugata, O man,
Nischa yē na bodhigyāna lā yī wa
Doubtless you will get the happy region.

IV.

Chandikā jaya jaya chhi guna hāya masa yānī
Glory, glory to Chandikā. Your qualities I cannot describe.
Māī chandra sūrya yā kōtī tēja utī
O mother, the light of ten millions of moons and suns
Hinguli khwālayā jwālā na rē
Is in your bright vermillion-like face.
Munda māla sa dē tana swāna māla
A garland of heads adorned with wreaths of flowers,
Sira sa tata kiki swāna rē
On your head rests a kētki (pandanus) flower,
Nhasa sa kundala hera yā mandala
Your ears have beautiful diamond ear-rings,
Jōlala mi chō wasa māna rē
Bright you are as the flame of fire,
Ratana pāyala luyā ghaglāna nhyānā wa
Jewelled ankle-ornaments with gold bells you wear,

Jhananam jhananam nyā wa rē
Jhanana jhanana they sound.
Sinha bāhīnī swa guli bhubana sa barana gathi nya bakhāna rē
Mounted on a lion, mistress of the three worlds, how can one describe you?
Bhūta pari jana rasana harkhana daitya yā hī dako twa nya wa rē
The families of devils merrily drink the blood of giants,
Bājana jantara mridanga dabū dabū tāla dēvana thanyāwa rē
Musical instruments are played by gods and they sound dabū dabū,
Apsarā gana rasana chhī charita hālāwa pyākhuna hūyā wa rē
The apsarās (heavenly musicians) merrily sing your praises.
Māī Chandikē thūlē sahasra jivi mati nya hunya karunā tayā wa rē
O mother Chandikā, hear my thousand prayers with tenderness.
Lhāka mha bālakha anārī nāyaka jūyā jī chhī pāliyā āsā rē
The boy author acknowledges that he walks with the support of the hope of your feet.

V.

Karni mabhim misā wa yī—nhyāthen sanā jū yī wa
When a bad woman comes—she goes her own way.
Khawa katham sanī makhū—makhū katham sanī
She will not go the right path—but will go the wrong way.
Gasu malā misā wa yī—lāthya sanā jū yī
A woman of bad character comes—she will misbehave,
Ghara sāra phunā wanī—pochī thawam jū yī
Wealth will be destroyed—the man himself will be naked.
Nyanya mālī mākha būkha—kothā bākham lhāyi wa
He will have to hear malicious words—in the bedchamber she will relate many stories,
Chalam mabhīm katham sanā—phukī bākāya phā yī
Misbehaving herself—she will cause separation between brothers;
Chhabhī nibhim wanām magāk—hitū hilā jū yī wa
One or two husbands will be insufficient for her—she will roam about,
Jalā khalāya kē sisitayā—toha mālā jū yī
She will keep her things at her neighbours'—and will seek to quarrel.
Jhakariyā misā wa yī—dhukū tūna jū yī wa
A quarrelsome woman comes—she will seek to look into (her husband's) private storeroom,

Yako bastū lagaya lākā—thawa kusa nālī
Every stored up thing she will take—and lay claim to,
Tawa dhanchī dhanjātī madhā—sukham chonē so yī wa
She will not trouble herself about high or low caste—but will live with any one with comfort.
Dara madū misā wa yī—machā wānā jū yī wa
A fearless woman comes—she will go away leaving her children.
Dhari dharma madhā misā—thawa yawa thya jū yī
A woman without virtue—will go her own way,
Nakā tīkā punkā talasā—bhālta matyē nā dhāī
She will love the husband who will feed—clothe and give her ornaments.
Tamam bhatī bhāla tankē nwāsa—misā pham pham jū yī
If her husband is angry—she will be in a rage.
Thakim thākim misā wa yī—luchi phuchim jū yī wa
An idle woman comes—she will misbehave,
Thawa katham malā talyē—nyāsya pyasyam jū yī
Until her wishes are fulfilled—she will flirt,
Dako bastū lona nayā—bhalata tosam dhāī
She will eat all sorts of things—and call her husband poor,
Dhana drabya bisya tayā nam—chonē machonē ya yī wa.
If all the wealth be given to her—she will even then remain unsettled,
Nayā lapatyē sukhū machi wam—pāchu kala haī
The dinner plate will be still wet—when she will leave her husband.
Pahalana gyanā chonī—tisā wasa dhāī wa
She will feign anger—to get clothes and ornaments.
Phako jiko sālā kayā—bhāla tawa lisyam wa yī
Getting as much as she can—she will live with her husband
Baha bhāltō malā talē—mhichā pūī kā so yī wa
Until she gets a young husband—she seeks another with an open bag.
Bhasalai jyāmadhā mīsām—thawa yawa thya jū yī
An immodest woman—will go her own way,
Madu khasa lwāpū thayā—mīsām ajaya bīyī wa
She will quarrel on a false pretext—and cause scandal to spread,
Yasa dhari tayā nakā—bhālta basya kā yī
She will give her husband something to eat in curds—which will bring him under her influence.
Raga thugā kalā kāya—damā nhyata dhā yī
If you get a woman from the street—she will want your money,

Lasa thuyā misā tasyam—kākō pachaya yāyī
Women obtained from the street—will take away everything.
Wasa tisā bōya yāta—upāsana chonī wa
To show off her clothes and ornaments—she will fast,
Sanja bhajū bhāgī yānā—bhālta danda yā kī
She will bow to her paramour—and cause her husband to be fined.
Kha nāyū misā waī—nyā khwaya chhunā jū yī wa
A sweet speaking woman comes—she will fish about for husbands,
Saha madū janma bhasaṇ—mijam kyēna kākā yī
She puts an unbearable noose—on her husband's neck.
Hathhyā hārī misā wa yī—bhālta boya kala ya nī
A murdering woman comes—she will entice away her husband,
Chhasa chōkō dako phuta kā—tivā miuka bwāyī nhāṇ
After destroying everything in the house—she will run away.
Lhakō artha būjhaya yāwa—thawata hita jū yī wa.
Understand the meaning of what has been said—it will benefit you.

VIII. LIST OF THE RĀJĀS OF NEPĀL FROM THE TIME OF NE MUNI, EXTRACTED FROM THE HISTORY.

This list has been carefully revised and collated with the original MS., and gives the most correct forms of the royal names. The reader should compare it with the list in Thomas's edition of Prinsep's *Essays on Indian Antiquities*, Vol. II., pp. 268—271.

D. W.

A. Gupta Dynasty.

1. Bhuktamānagata (*sic*).
2. Jaya Gupta.
3. Parama Gupta.
4. Bhīma Gupta.
5. Bhīma Gupta.
6. Maṇi Gupta.
7. Vishṇu Gupta.
8. Yaksha Gupta.

B. Ahīr Dynasty.

1. Vara Sinha.
2. Jayamati Sinha.
3. Bhuvana Sinha.

C. Kirātī Dynasty.

1. Yalambara.
2. Pavi.
3. Skandharā (*sic*).
4. Valamba.
5. Hriti.
6. Humati.
7. Jitēdāsti.
8. Gali.
9. Pushka.
10. Suyarma.
11. Parva.
12. Bunka.
13. Swananda.
14. Sthunkō.
15. Gighri.
16. Nanē.
17. Luk.
18. Thōra.
19. Thōkō.
20. Varma.
21. Guja.
22. Pushkarā (*sic*).
23. Kēsu.
24. Suga.
25. Sansa.
26. Gunan.
27. Shimbu.
28. Paṭuka.
29. Gasti.

D. Sōmavanshī Dynasty.

1. Nimisha.
2. Matāksha.
3. Kāka-varmā.
4. Pashuprēsha-dēva.
5. Bhāskara-varmā.

E. Sūryavanshī Dynasty.

1. Bhūmi-varmā.
2. Chandra-varmā.
3. Chandra-varmā.
4. Varsha-varmā.
5. Sarva-varmā.
6. Prithwī-varmā.
7. Jyēshṭha-varmā.
8. Hari-varmā.
9. Kuvēra-varmā.
10. Siddhi-varmā.
11. Haridatta-varmā.
12. Vasudatta-varmā.
13. Pati-varmā.
14. Shivavriddhi-varmā.
15. Vasanta-varmā.
16. Shiva-varmā.
17. Rudradēva-varmā.
18. Vrikshadēva-varmā.
19. Shankaradēva.
20. Dharmadēva.
21. Mānadēva.
22. Mahādeva.
23. Vasantadēva-varmā.
24. Udayadēva-varmā.
25. Mānadēva-varmā.
26. Guṇakāmadēva-varmā.
27. Shivadēva-varmā.
28. Narēndradēva-varma.
29. Bhīmadēva-varmā.
30. Vishṇudēva-varmā.
31. Vishwadēva-varmā.

F. Ṭhākurī or Rājpūt Dynasty.

1. Anshu-varmā.
2. Krita-varmā.
3. Bhīmārjuna-dēva.
4. Nanda-dēva.
5. Vīra-dēva.
6. Chandrakētu-dēva.
7. Narēndra-dēva.
8. Vara-devā.
9. Shankara-dēva.
10. Vardhamāna-dēva.
11. Bali-dēva.
12. Jaya-dēva.
13. Bālārjuna-dēva.
14. Vikrama-dēva.
15. Gunakāma-dēva.
16. Bhōja-dēva.
17. Lakshmīkāma-dēva.
18. Jayakāma-dēva.

G. Vaishya-Ṭhākurī Dynasty, from Nuwākōṭ.

1. Bhāskara-dēva.
2. Bala-dēva.
3. Padma-dēva.
4. Nāgārjuna-dēva.
5. Shankara-dēva.

H. Second Rājpūt Dynasty.

1. Vāma-dēva.
2. Harsha-dēva.
3. Sadāshiva-dēva.
4. Māna-dēva.
5. Narasinha-dēva.
6. Nanda-dēva.
7. Rudra-dēva.
8. Mitra-dēva.
9. Ari-dēva.
10. Abhaya Malla [Nepāl era introduced, beginning in Oct., A.D. 880].
11. Jayadēva Malla. }
12. Ānanda Malla. }

I. Karnāṭakī Dynasty.

1. Nānya-dēva.
2. Gangā-dēva.
3. Narasinha-dēva.
4. Shakti-dēva.
5. Rāmasinha-dēva.
6. Hari-dēva.

J. Mukunda-sēna invades and conquers the country.

K. After his expulsion, various Vaishya-Ṭhākurī dynasties for 225 years.

L. Ayōdhyā Dynasty.

1. Harisinha-dēva, from Simraungaṛh, A.D. 1324.
2. Matisinha-dēva.
3. Shaktisinha-dēva.
4. Shyāmasinha-dēva.

M. The Malla Rājās, descendants of Abhaya Malla.

1. Jayabhadra Malla.
2. Nāga Malla.
3. Jayajagat Malla.
4. Nāgēndra Malla.
5. Ugra Malla.
6. Ashōka Malla.
7. Jayasthiti Malla.
8. Yaksha Malla [division of the kingdom].

a. Rājās of Bhaktapur or Bhātgāoṇ.

9. Rāya Malla, eldest son of Yaksha Malla.
10. Suvarṇa Malla.
11. Prāṇa Malla.
12. Vishwa Malla.
13. Trailōkya Malla.
14. Jagajjyōti(r) Malla.
15. Narēndra Malla.
16. Jagatprakāsha Malla.
17. Jitāmitra Malla.
18. Bhūpatīndra Malla.
19. Raṇajit Malla.

b. Rājā of Banēpā.

9. Raṇa Malla, second son of Yaksha Malla.

c. Rājās of Kāntipur or Kāṭhmāṇḍū.

9. Ratna Malla, youngest son of Yaksha Malla.
10. Amara Malla.
11. Sūrya Malla.
12. Narēndra Malla.
13. Mahīndra Malla.
14. Sadāshiva Malla.
15. Shivasinha Malla.
16. Lakshmī-narasinha Malla.
17. Pratāpa Malla.
18. Mahīndra (Bhūpālēndra) Malla.
19. Shrī-Bhāskara Malla.
20. Jagajjaya Malla.
21. Jaya-prakāsha Malla.

d. Rājās of Lalitāpur or Pātan.

1. Harihara-sinha Malla, younger son of Shivasinha Malla (15) of Kāṭhmāṇḍū.
2. Siddhi-Narasinha Malla.
3. Shrī-Nivāsa Malla.
4. Yōga-Narēndra Malla.
5. Mahīndra (Mahīpatīndra) Sinha Malla, of Kāṭhmāṇḍū.
6. Jaya-Yoga-prakāsha Malla.
7. Shrī-shrī-Vishṇu Malla.
8. Rājya-prakāsha Malla.
9. Raṇajit Malla, of Bhātgāoṇ.
10. Jaya-prakāsha Malla, of Kāṭhmāṇḍū.
11. Vishwajit Malla.
12. Dalmardan Sāh (a Gōrkhālī).
13. Tēja-Narasinha Malla.

N. Gōrkhālī Rājās of Nepāl.

1. Prithwī-Nārāyaṇa Sāh.
2. Pratāpa-sinha Sāh.
3. Raṇa Bahādur Sāh.
4. Gīrvān-yuddha Vikrama Sāh.
5. Rājēndra Vikrama Sāh.
6. Surēndra Vikrama Sāh, now reigning.

IX. LIST OF MY COLLECTION OF SANSKRIT MANUSCRIPTS.

The following rough list of the manuscripts procured by me in Nepāl for the University Library of Cambridge[1] has been drawn up from the notes furnished, at the time of purchase, by the Mīr Munshī and Paṇḍit attached to the Residency, with occasional corrections by Professor Cowell. The manuscripts were mostly bought through the said Paṇḍit and other Paṇḍits residing at Bhātgāoṇ and Kāṭhmāṇḍū.

The material on which they are written, is, for the older manuscripts, palm-leaf (*tāla-pattra*, vulgarly *tāl-pattar*, whence the name of the "talipot" palm); for the younger, paper. The bark of the birch (*bhūrja*, vulgarly *bhōj*) is used in Nepāl only for charms and amulets, of which I brought home one specimen (Add. MS. 1578). At least I never saw or heard of a book of this material. The paper on which the later manuscripts are written is sometimes dyed black, in which case the writing is either yellow or white, according as a mixture of gold or silver is employed.

Many of these manuscripts, particularly the older palm-leaves, contain pictures, brilliantly coloured and occasionally gilt. Among those of later date Add. MS. 864 is especially noteworthy. The wooden covers are also sometimes lacquered and painted with figures. One has fine carved brass covers (Add. MS. 1556). Some of the boards exhibit marks of worship on certain occasions, as they are covered with small hard cakes or lumps of rice, sandalwood dust, and red and yellow pigments, used by the natives in "doing *pūjā*." The sacred threads, which were also attached to them, have been removed.

Some of these Nepalese books are, I believe, among the oldest, if not the very oldest, Sanskrit manuscripts in Europe. The dates depend, for the present, upon the authority of the native paṇḍits, but will, of course, be carefully investigated by Professor Cowell in the catalogue which he is now preparing. In form, size and appearance, many are

[1] Other MSS. purchased by me in Nepāl are in the collections of the British Museum, the German Oriental Society at Halle, the University Library of Berlin, the University Library of St Petersburg, and the Library of the Imperial Academy of St Petersburg. The whole number of these is, however, comparatively small.

identical with the oldest manuscripts of Mr Hodgson's collection, in the possession of the Royal Asiatic Society of London, of which a catalogue has been lately published by Professors Cowell and Eggeling. Of the four manuscripts of which photographs are given in their work, no. 1 is dated N. S. 286 = A.D. 1166; no. 3, N. S. 218 = A.D. 1095; and no. 4, N. S. 484 = A.D. 1364; while no. 2 was written in the fourth year of king Gōvinda-pālā, whose name, however, does not occur either in my lists or in those of Prinsep and Thomas. Perhaps he may only have been one of the numerous rājās of petty villages. I may add that the dates are expressed in several ways. Sometimes they are written out in full; at other times they are indicated by words, to which a peculiar numerical sense is attached (as in the Newārī songs, nos. I. and II., p. 307); and lastly they are noted either by letter-numerals or by arithmetical figures (for which see Professors Cowell and Eggeling's *Catalogue of the Hodgson Collection*, p. 52).

Regarding the names and contents of the Tibetan manuscripts I have no information. Some of them appear to be of considerable age. Add. MS. 1666 is a huge book of great beauty, with several large pictures; and Add. MS. 1667 is also deserving of special mention. I bought the former from the son of a merchant, who had brought it many years ago from Lhāsā, and carefully preserved it as a charm till his death.

D. W.

ADD. MS.

864. Book of pictures.
865. Divyāvadāna.
866. Ashṭasāhasrikā-prajñā-pāramitā, palmleaf, N.S. 128 (A.D. 1008).
867. Dasha-bhūmīshwara.
868. Saptashatakā-prajñā-pāramitā.
869. Bōdhicharyāvatāra.
870. Swayambhū-purāṇa-panjikā.
871. Swayambhū-chaitya-bhaṭṭārakōddēsha.
872. Avalōkitēshwara-guṇa-kāraṇḍa-vyūha.
873. Himavat-khaṇḍa.
874. Maṇī-chūḍāvadāna.
875. Suvarṇa-prabhā.

ADD. MS.

899. Naipālīya-dēvatā-stuti-kalyāna-panchavinshatikā; Bhadracharī-mahā-praṇidhānarāja; Ārya-vritta; Saptabuddha-stōtra.
900. Ashṭamī-vrata-vidhāna-kathā.
901. Tathāgata-guhyaka.
912. List of books, said to be a Catalogue of the Library in the Palace at Kāṭhmāṇḍū.
913. Bōdhisattwāvadāna-kalpalatā.
914. Copy of an inscription from an old temple on the hill of Swayambhū.

ADD. MS.

915. Saddharma-lankāvatāra.
916. Samādhi-rāja.
917. Gaṇḍa-vyūha.
918. Lalita-vistara.
1032. Saddharma-puṇḍarīka.
1039. Nepalese astrological paper.
1040. Aphorisms of Chāṇakya.
1041. Abhidharma-kōsha-vyākhyā.
1042. Two specimen pages of the Divyāvadāna, and three of the Lankāvatāra.
1049. Pāramēshwara-tantra, palmleaf.
1050. Tibetan MS.
1104. Nāma-sangīti and Sragdharā-stōtra of Ārya-tārā.
1105. White Yajur-vēda, one palmleaf, with accents.
1106. Amaru-shataka, one leaf.
1107. Part of a hymn to Vishṇu, one leaf.
1108. Nāma-sangīti-ṭippanī, or Amrita-kaṇikā, A.D. 1392.
1156. Hitōpadēsha, one palmleaf.
1160. Nepalese History (Hindū redaction).
1161. Shishya-lēkha-kāvya, palmleaf, N.S. 204 (A.D. 1084).
1162. Dhātu-pāṭha, palmleaf, N.S. 476 (A.D. 1356).
1163. Ashṭasāhasrikā-prajñā-pāramitā, palmleaf.
1164. Pancha-rakshā.
1267. Kāraṇḍa-vyūha, prose, palmleaf.
1268. Bāla-bōdha, etc., 153 years old.
1269. Shīghra-bōdha.
1270. Avalōkitēshwara-guṇa-kāraṇḍa-vyūha, poetical version, 105 years old.
1271. Vāgīshwara-pūjā.

ADD. MS.

1272. Sragdharā-stuti, with Newārī commentary, N.S. 904 (A.D. 1784).
1273. Sugatāvadāna.
1274. Dwāvinshatyavadāna-kathā.
1275. Kāraṇḍa-vyūha, prose.
1276. Pāpa parimōchana.
1277. Aparimitāyu-nāma-dhāraṇī-mahāyāna-sūtra.
1278. Ādi-yōga-samādhi.
1279. Nishpanna-yōgāmbalī, or Nishpanna-yogāmbarā-tantra.
1280-1304. Tibetan MSS.
1305. Piṇḍapātrāvadāna.
1306. Bōdhisattwāvadāna-kalpalatā, palmleaf, N.S. 422 (A.D. 1302).
1307—14. Tibetan MSS.
1315. Saptavāra, N.S. 921 (A.D. 1802).
1316. Pūjā-paddhati.
1317. Prayers and mantras.
1318. Ārya-tārā-bhaṭṭārikāyā-nāmāshṭōttara-shataka.
1319. Chaṇḍa-mahā-rōshaṇa-tantra (Ēkaravīra-tantra), N.S. 944 (A.D. 1824).
1320. Ādi-yōga-samādhi, A.D. 1838.
1321. Kāraṇḍa-vyūha, prose, N.S. 931 (A.D. 1811).
1322. Avalōkitēshwara-guṇa-kāraṇḍa-vyūha, poetry.
1323. Nāma-sangīti, with Newārī translation, N.S. 979 (A.D. 1859).
1324. Saddharma-puṇḍarīka.
1325. Pancha-rakshā, N.S. 939 (A.D. 1819).
1326. Dhāraṇī-sangraha, N.S. 839 (A.D. 1719).
1327. Dwāvinshatyavadāna-kathā.

ADD. MS.

1328. Jātaka-mālā.
1329. Tathāgata-guhyaka (Guhya-samāja).
1330. Kāraṇḍa-vyūha, prose, N.S. 761 (A.D. 1641).
1331. Amara-kōsha, part 1.
1332. Nāma-sangīti.
1333. Stōtras of Machchhīndra and songs of Buddha, A.D. 1823.
1334. Pūjā and stōtra of Machchhīndra (Bhīmasēna-pūjā).
1335. Prayer to Shākya Muni, Mahāyāna-sūtra.
1336. Dhāraṇīs to Ushṇīsha-vijaya and Parṇa-shavarī.
1337. Mantra of the Ashṭa-mātrikā.
1338. Ashṭa-mātrikā.
1339. Mahāvastu.
1340. Hē-vajra-tantra, N.S. 962 (A.D. 1842).
1341. Suvarṇa-varṇāvadāna.
1343. Suvarṇa-prabhāsā.
1343. Dhāraṇī-sangraha.
1344. Amara-kōsha.
1345. Kāpīsāvadāna.
1346. Buddhi-chāṇakya, with Newārī translation, N.S. 965 (A.D. 1845).
1347. Lokēshwara-pārājikā.
1348. Pratyangirā, N.S. 937 (A.D. 1817).
1349. Navagraha-stōtra, N.S. 962 (A.D. 1832).
1350. Chhandō-manjarī.
1351. Astrology, N.S. 982 (A.D. 1862).
1352. Mahākāla-tantra, N.S. 985 (A.D. 1865).
1353. Nāma-sangīti, with Newārī translation.

ADD. MS.

1354. Dhananjaya-nighaṇṭa, palm-leaf, N.S. 572 (A.D. 1452).
1355. Vasundharā-kalpa, palmleaf, N.S. 696 (A.D. 1576).
1356. Saptavāra, N.S. 860 (A.D. 1740).
1357. Ashwaghōsha-nandimukhāvadana, N.S. 973 (A.D. 1853).
1358. Pratyangirā.
1359. Bhīmasēna-kā patha.
1360. Pārthiva-pūjā, V.S. 1869 (A.D. 1812).
1361. Dāna-vākya, N.S. 977 (A.D. 1857).
1362. Sragdharā-stōtra, with Newārī notes, N.S. 966 (A.D. 1846)
1363. Sāraswata, N.S. 802 (A.D. 1682).
1364. Kālachakra-tantra, palm-leaf, V.S. 1503 (A.D. 1446).
1365. Tathāgata-guhyaka, N.S. 986 (A.D. 1866).
1366. Ashṭamī-vrata-māhātmya.
1367. Karuṇa-puṇḍarīka.
1368. Sukhāvatī-vyūha.
1369. Chhandō-'mrita-latā, N.S. 963 (A.D. 1843).
1370. Lalita-vistara, N.S. 967 (A.D. 1847).
1371. Kāsī-khanda, part of the Skanda-purāṇa.
1372. Nāma-sangīti.
1373. Hitōpadēsha, N.S. 809 (A.D. 1689).
1374. Kāraṇḍa-vyūha, prose, N.S. 993 (A.D. 1873).
1375. Maṇi-chūḍāvadāna.
1376. Durgati-parishōdhana.
1377. Sugatāvadāna.

ADD. MS.
1378. Durgati-parishōdhana.
1379. Stōtras.
1380. Snātāvadāna.
1381. Kaushigha - vīryōtsāhanāvadāna.
1382. Shaṭpanchāsikā, Sanskrit, Newārī and Parbatiyā.
1383. Yōgāmbara - samādhi - pūjāpaddhati, N.S. 964 (A.D. 1844).
1384. Durgati-parishōdhana.
1385. Aparimitāyur - nāma - mahāyāna-sūtra, N.S. 779 (A.D. 1659).
1386. Avadāna-shataka.
1387. Buddha - charitra - kāvya, N. S. 950 (A.D. 1830).
1388. Gīta - gōvinda - shataka, N.S. 738 (A.D. 1618).
1389. Gōpīchandra-nāṭaka.
1390. Naishadha-kāvya-ṭīkā, N.S. 850 (A.D. 1730).
1391. Mantra-muktāvalī.
1392. Shrāddha - paddhati, Shāka 1725 (A.D. 1803).
1393. Krishṇa-pūjā-paddhati, V.S. 1830 (A.D. 1773).
1394. Champū-rāmāyaṇa.
1395. Pancha - rakshā, palmleaf, N.S. 508 (A.D. 1380).
1396. Raghuvansha-ṭīkā.
1397. Rudra-chintāmaṇi.
1398. Maṇi-chūḍāvadāna.
1399. Nalōdaya-ṭikā.
1400. Vasundharā - vrata - kathā, N.S. 888 (A.D. 1768).
1401. Nandimukhāshwa - ghōsha, N.S. 224 (A.D. 1804).
1402. Dhātu-pāṭha, Shāka 1741 (A.D. 1819).
1403. Tīrtha-prabhā.
1404. Vajra-sūchī, V.S. 1838 (A.D. 1781).

ADD. MS.
1405. Chaitya-pungala (ra), N.S. 734 (A.D. 1614).
1406. Kriyā - kāṇḍa - kramāvalī, palmleaf, N.S. 10 (A.D. 890).
1407. Hitōpadēsha, palmleaf.
1408. do. , in Newārī.
1409. Rāma - nāṭaka, palmleaf, N.S. 480 (A.D. 1360).
1410. Chikitsā-nibandha.
1411. Bhadrakalpāvadāna, N.S. 952 (A.D. 1832).
1412. Pūjā-kāṇḍa, N.S. 398 (A.D. 1278).
1413. Vidwān - mōda - taranginī, N.S. 948 (A.D. 1828).
1414. Shringabhērī.
1415. Jātaka-mālā, N.S. 757 (A.D. 1637).
1416. Durgati-parishōdhana.
1417. Nāga-pūjā.
1418. Kathināvadāna.
1419. Lōkēshwara-shataka.
1420. Lōkēshwara-pārājikā.
1421. Vajrasūchī.
1422. Saptābhidhānōttara.
1423. Amōghapāsha - lōkēshwara - pūjā.
1424. Manju-ghōsha-pūjā.
1425—43. Tibetan MSS.
1444. Various prayers.
1445. Newārī songs.
1446. Pūjā.
1447. Dhāraṇī (Shīrshavijaya).
1448. Mantras.
1449. do.
1450. Pūjā with mantras.
1451. Mantras.
1452. do.
1453. Ēka-jaṭā dhāraṇī.
1454. Mantras.
1455. do.
1456. One leaf from a tantra.
1457—59. Tibetan MSS.

ADD. MS.
1460. Pancha-rakshā.
1461. Prayer-cylinder.
1462. Gīta-gōvinda, N.S. 892 (A.D. 1772).
1463. Sabhā-taranginī.
1464. Ashṭasāhasrikā-prajñā-pāramitā, palmleaf, N.S. 5 (A.D. 885).
1465. do. do., palmleaf, N.S. 3 (A.D. 883).
1466. Shushma-jātaka, palmleaf.
1467. Gaṇḍa-vyūha.
1468. Swayambhū-purāṇa.
1469. do. Sanskrit and Newārī.
1470. Karavīra-tantra, N.S. 932 (A.D. 1812).
1471. Bhadracharī.
1472. Vrishṭi-chintāmaṇi.
1473. Shasha-jātakāvadāna.
1474. Vaidya-jīvana.
1475. Pancha-rakshā, N.S. 802 (A.D. 1682).
1476. Pancha-rakshā, Abhayankarī-dhāraṇī, Tārā-shatanāma, Mahākāla-tantra, N.S. 911 (A.D. 1791).
1477. Parā-tantra, N.S. 940 (A.D. 1820).
1478. Shikshā-samuchchaya.
1479. Brihaj-jātaka, palmleaf, N.S. 666 (A.D. 1546).
1480. Mahāyāna-sūtra.
1481. Samādhi-rāja, N.S. 915 (A.D. 1795).
1482. Ashōkāvadāna, N.S. 895 (A.D. 1775).
1483. Vinaya-sūtra, N.S. 901 (A.D. 1781).
1484. Vritta-ratnakāra.
1485. Dhāraṇi-sangraha, N.S. 797 (A.D. 1677).

ADD. MS.
1486. Vasundharā-kalpa, N.S. 841 (A.D. 1721).
1487. Ashṭamī - vrata - vidhāna, N.S. 928 (A.D. 1808).
1488. Amara-kosha, palmleaf, N.S. 500 (A.D. 1380).
1533. Ashwaghōsha-nandimukhāvadāna.
1534. Nāga-pūjā, N.S. 811 (A.D. 1691).
1535. Piṇḍa-pātrāvadāna.
1536. Swayambhū - purāṇa, N.S. 803 (A.D. 1683).
1537. Kāpīsāvadāna.
1538. Vīrakushāvadāna, N.S. 964 (A.D. 1844).
1539. Buddhi-chāṇakya, Sanskrit and Parbatiyā, V.S. 1929 (A.D. 1851).
1540. Udyōga - parva, N.S. 787 (A.D. 1667).
1541. Raghuvansha-kāvya, N.S. 827 (A.D. 1707).
1542. Virāṭa-parva.
1543. Prajñā-pāramitā (2500 shlōkas), palmleaf.
1544. do. do., a larger work, with a note of *recitation*, N.S. 499 (A.D. 1379), palmleaf.
1545. Sheet of Tibetan writing.
1546. Mahā-samvara-hridaya.
1547. Nāma-stōtra.
1548. Nāma-sangīti.
1549. Nāmāshṭōttara-shataka.
1550. Pancha-mahā-rakshā-sūtra.
1551. Mahā-rōshaṇa-tantra.
1552. Dhāraṇīs.
1553. do.
1554. do.
1555. do.
1556. Sapta-shati, N.S. 703 (A.D.

ADD. MS.

1583), with beautiful brass covers.

1557. Shaṭpanchāshikā.

1576. Tibetan MS.

1577. A charm of seven letters.

1578. A charm, written on birch-bark.

1579. Tamil MS., palmleaf.

1580. Shambūkāvadāna, palmleaf, N.S. 543 (A.D. 1423).

1581. Dharma-lakshmī-samvāda.

1585. Sumāgadhāvadāna.

1586. Rāshṭrapālāvadāna, N.S. 781 (A.D. 1661).

1587. Shivārchana-chandrikā.

1588. Dēvī-māhātmya, N.S. 789 (A.D. 1669).

1589. Vichitra-karṇikāvadāna, N.S. 994 (A.D. 1874).

1590. Kalpa-drumāvadāna.

1591. Hitōpadēsha, book 1, N.S. 858 (A.D. 1738).

1592. Ratna-mālāvadāna.

1593. Sādhana-mālā, N.S. 939 (A.D. 1819).

1594. Tantrākhyāna, N.S. 949 (A.D. 1829).

1595. Vaidyānga, medical, N.S. 832 (A.D. 1712).

1596. Ratnaguṇa-sanchaya, N.S. 950 (A.D. 1830).

1597. Bhagavad-gīta and stōtras, N.S. 694 (A.D. 1574).

1598. Avadāna-sangraha.

1599. Shiva-purāṇa, Shāka 1504 (A.D. 1582).

1600. Mudrā-rākshasa.

1601. do. in Parbatiyā.

1602. Siddhānta-dīpikā.

1603. Vasishṭhāvadāna, N.S. 919 (A.D. 1799).

ADD. MS.

1604. Buddhi-chāṇakya, N.S. 862 (A.D. 1742).

1605. Kāma-shāstra.

1606. Naishadha-kāvya, N.S. 777 (A.D. 1657).

1607. Lankāvatāra, N.S. 902 (A.D. 1782).

1608. Nēpāla-māhātmya.

1609. Bali-pūjā.

1610. Upōshadhāvadāna.

1611. Avadāna-shataka, N.S. 765 (A.D. 1645).

1612. Muhūrta-chintāmaṇi.

1613. Mantra-chāṇakya, N.S. 862 (A.D. 1742).

1614. Stōtra-sangraha.

1615. Avadāna-mālā, N.S. 923 (A.D. 1803).

1616. Kriyā-yōga-sāra, N.S. 807 (A.D. 1687).

1617. Guhya-samāja, N.S. 924 (A.D. 1804).

1618. Dashabhūmīshwara, N.S. 916 (A.D. 1796).

1619. Bētāl-pachīsī, Sanskrit and Newārī, N.S. 795 (A.D. 1675).

1620. Ratna-mālāvadāna.

1621. Himavat-khanda.

1622. Aparimitāyu.

1623. Sarva-durgati-parishōdhana, N.S. 820 (A.D. 1700).

1624. Drōṇa-parva.

1625. Ashṭasāhasrikā-prajñā-pāramitā, N.S. 948 (A.D. 1828).

1626. Prajñā-pāramitā, part 1.

1627. do. do., part 3.

1628. do. do., part 5.

1629. do. do., part 1.

1630. do. do., part 2.

1631. do. do., part 3.

ADD. MS.

1632. Prajñā-pāramitā, part 4, N.S. 923 (A.D. 1803).
1633. Prajñā-pāramitā, part 5.
1634. Kīrti-patāka, N.S. 772 (A.D. 1652).
1635. Vasundharā-vrata, N.S. 805 (A.D. 1685).
1636. Ratnamālā.
1637. Bhāgavata-purāṇa, N.S. 884 (A.D. 1764).
1638. Vrihach-chāṇakya, N.S. 802 (A.D. 1682).
1639. Amara-kosha, N.S. 802 (A.D. 1682).
1640. Siddhānta-sāra.
1641. Sangīta-talōdaya, N.S. 783 (A.D. 1663).
1642. Shuddha-dīpikā.
1643. Ashṭasāhasrikā-prajñā-pāramitā, palmleaf, N.S. 135 (A.D. 1015).
1644. Pancha-mahā-rakshā-sūtra.
1645. Shivadharma-tantra, palmleaf, N.S. 259 (A.D. 1139).
1646. Kuladatta-panjikā-kriyā-sangraha, palmleaf.
1647. Pancha-rakshā, palmleaf.
1648. Sādaua-mālā, palmleaf, N.S. 226 (A.D. 1106).
1649. Siddhi-sāra, palmleaf, N.S. 532 (A.D. 1412).

ADD. MS.

1650. Amara-kōsha, palmleaf.
1651. Amara-kōsha, palmleaf.
1652. Vaidyānga, medical, palmleaf.
1653. Tattwa-sangraha, palmleaf.
1654. Saraswatī, palmleaf.
1655. Bētāl-pachīsī, palmleaf and paper.
1656. Pancha - rakshā, palmleaf, N.S. 518 (A.D. 1398).
1657. Chāndra-vyākaraṇa, palmleaf.
1658. Nishka-nāṭaka, palmleaf.
1659. Rājā-nītisāra, palmleaf, N.S. 621 (A.D. 1501).
1660. Jyōtisha, Vyākaraṇa, etc., palmleaf.
1661. Amara-kōsha, palmleaf.
1662. Sāhasrapramardana - mahāyānasūtra, Mahā-shitavatī, Mahā-māyūrī-vidyā, palmleaf.
1663. Sāra-sangraha, palmleaf, N.S. 549 (A.D. 1429).
1664. Treatise on religious customs, palmleaf, N.S. 520 (A.D. 1400).
1665. Jyōtisha, palmleaf, N.S. 577 (A.D. 1457).
1666—1678. Tibetan MSS.

STILL UNNUMBERED.

a. Unsorted fragments of Naishadha-charita and other MSS.; palmleaf.

b. Unsorted fragments of Bhadracharī-praṇidhāna, Chaitya-pungala, and other MSS.; palmleaf.

c. Leaves containing alphabets and lists of numerals, in the handwriting of Paṇḍit Guṇānand.

The following MSS. are also not yet numbered and placed.

1. Saddharma-puṇḍarīka, palmleaf, N.S. 159 (A.D. 1039).

ADD. MS.

2. Saddharma-puṇḍarīka, palmleaf.
3. do. do., palmleaf, N.S. 185 (A.D. 1065).
4. Amara-kōsha, palmleaf, N.S. 500 (A.D. 1380).
5. Sādhana-mālā, palmleaf.
6. Kāraṇḍa-vyūha, N.S. 754 (A.D. 1634).
7. Pancha-rakshā, palmleaf, N.S. 19 (A.D. 899).
8. Mēgha-sūtra, palmleaf, N.S. 494 (A.D. 1374).
9. Vasundharā-kalpa, palmleaf, N.S. 212 (A.D. 1092).
10. Hiranya-saptaka, N.S. 235 (A.D. 1115).
Kurukullā-kalpa, N.S. 299 (A.D. 1179).
Abhishēka-vidhi, N.S. 560 (A.D. 1440).
Vyākaraṇa (two small MSS.).
Chāndra-vyākaraṇa, N.S. 532 (A.D. 1412). Palmleaf.
11. Yuddha-jayārnava, N.S. 566 (A.D. 1446).
Anga-vidyā-jyōtisha.
Varāhamihira-krita-jyōtisha. Palmleaf.
12. Ashṭasāhasrikā-prajñā-pāramitā, palmleaf, N.S. 285 (A.D. 1165).
13. Shiva-dharma; Shiva-dharma-sangraha; Vrisha-sāra-sangraha; Dharma-putrikā-tantra. Palmleaf.

ADD. MS.

14. Haragaurī-nāṭaka, Sanskrit and Parbatiyā, by Rājā Jagajjyōti(r) Malla, N.S. 749 (A.D. 1629).
15. Jyōtisha, palmleaf.
16. Kuladatta-panjikā-kriyā-sangraha; Yōginī-pūjā-vidhi; Stōtra; Ḍākinī-jāla-samvara-tantra; Jyōtisha; Bali-mālā. Palmleaf, N.S. 583 (A.D. 1463).
17. Amara-kōsha, with Parbatiyā translation, palmleaf, N.S. 506 (A.D. 1386).
18. Panchakāra; Guhyāvalī-vritti; Yōga-ratna-mālā. Palmleaf, N.S. 37—39 (A.D. 917—919).
19. Nāma-sangīti-ṭīkā, palmleaf, N.S. 570 (A.D. 1450).
20. Pancha-rakshā, palmleaf, N.S. 509 (A.D. 1389).
21. Bōdhisattwa-yōgasthāna, palmleaf.
22. Vajrāvalī-tantra, palmleaf, N.S. 549 (A.D. 1429).
23. Guhya-pīṭha-tantra, palmleaf.
24. Vyākaraṇa-ṭīkā, palmleaf.
25. Dēva-lakshaṇa, N.S. 399 (A.D. 1279); Pratimā-lakshaṇa; Khaḍga-pūjā, N.S. 391 (A.D. 1271). Palmleaf.
26. Vaidyānga, medical, palmleaf, N.S. 396 (A.D. 1276).